We Are Not Babysitters

WE ARE NOT BABYSITTERS

Family Child Care Providers Redefine Work and Care

MARY C.
TUOMINEN

RUTGERS UNIVERSITY PRESS
New Brunswick, New Jersey, and London

Library of Congress Cataloging-in-Publication Data

Tuominen, Mary C., 1952–
  We are not babysitters : family child care providers redefine work and care /
Mary C. Tuominen.
     p.   cm.
Includes bibliographical references and index.
  ISBN 0-8135-3282-5 (hc) — ISBN 0-8135-3283-3 (pbk.)
1. Family day care.   2. Child care workers.   I. Title.
  HQ778.5 .T86 2003
  362.71'2—dc21

                                                              2002015876

British Cataloging-in-Publication information is available from the British Library.

Manufactured in the United States of America

Contents

Acknowledgments

This book reflects the efforts of many people who have been generous in sharing their time, insights, stories, and skills. First, I am indebted to the family child care providers who opened their homes to me and shared the stories of their lives and their work. It is my goal, through this book, to increase the public visibility of these women and thus inform policy debates that have failed to recognize the social and economic value of family child care work and the women who perform this work.

I thank my friends and colleagues Sandy Runzo, Sylvia Brown, Lynet Uttal, Suzanne Ashworth, and Cameron MacDonald for the support and skill they shared as I conceptualized, wrote, and rewrote. Their critiques and conversations proved invaluable in helping me determine what was most important to say and how best to say it. My thanks to Margaret Nelson and Heather Fitz Gibbon for their assessment of early drafts of selected chapters; to an anonymous reviewer for substantive and constructive comments on the initial manuscript; to Barrie Thorne for introducing me to David Myers, my acquiring editor at Rutgers University Press; and to David for his clarity and consistency in supporting this project.

Many people played essential roles in introducing me to the family child care providers whose stories are told in this book.

These include Margaret Casey, Paula Shelton, Ray Kennedy, Arlene Buchanan, and the staff of King County Child Care Resource and Referral.

I thank Paula Shelton and Betty Hauser for their skill as translators; Mary Prophet and Susan Scott for help in finding government documents and data; and Dang Vadysirisack, Rachel Haught, Siira Gunderson, and Emma Draves for their assistance in transcribing interviews. The R. C. Good Faculty Fellowship awarded by Denison University provided the research support that enabled me to complete this project. Adrianne Frech's organizational skills and her assistance in compiling the final manuscript were nothing short of remarkable. I am grateful to Carol Goland and Lisbeth Lipari for the personal and professional support they provided in the final months of this project's completion. And finally, I want to thank the person who has taught me, on the most personal level, the importance and value of care work in families: my mother, Louise Tuominen.

We Are Not Babysitters

"SOME PEOPLE DON'T CONSIDER IT WORK"
Investigating the Work of Family Child Care

On a gray and cloudy morning, I head north on Interstate 5 toward Seattle. I take the Yesler Way exit and drive east toward the central district. The street passes rental units, housing projects, and storefront businesses. Men gather in clusters of three and four near the storefronts—some just opened for business, some clearly closed permanently. I approach a major intersection, turn left, and pull up to the curb at my destination—the home of Sharon Fleming. The house, like others on the block, is a large two-story and looks like it was built in the 1930s or 1940s. The yard, like those of the houses that line the street, is tiny. What distinguishes this house from the others nearby is the sandwich-board sign in the front yard. It reads, "Small Friends Family Child Care."

How did I, a woman in my late forties with no children of my own end up on the front porch of a family child care home? My journey to Sharon Fleming's family child care home actually began a decade earlier, when I served as a policy analyst for the Washington State Legislature's Comparable Worth Committee. The committee explored issues of gender discrimination in employment, particularly the lower wages assigned to sex-segregated jobs such as those held by secretaries, nursing assistants, and child care providers. As the committee completed its assigned task of making policy recommendations to address gender-based wage discrimination, I began to think about the next big issue on the horizon: child care. If women were to participate fully and equitably in paid employment, quality child care that was both affordable and accessible was essential. But, I asked myself, as middle-class mothers of young children increasingly work outside the home and the demand for child care increases, who will provide the child care previously offered by mothers? A bit of quick research provided the answer: other women, frequently women of color, who are often themselves the mothers of young children, constitute the emerging paid child care work force. Yet beyond the question of *who* was doing the work, the really interesting question was *why*. Given the low wages, lack of employment benefits, and lack of status associated with child care employment, why would a woman willingly choose to enter the work of paid child care?

These questions led me to the doorstep of Sharon Fleming's family child care home. As I peered through the windows of the glassed-in front porch, I saw the walls lined with hooks topped by children's jackets, coats, backpacks, and hats. Large plastic bins filled with toys were stacked in the areas not filled with jackets and coats. As I considered what I saw, I began to wonder if I had misunderstood. All the signs indicated that this was a child care center rather than a family child care setting in which a woman provided paid group child care in her own home. Perhaps when I spoke with Sharon on the phone I had misunderstood. "Well," I thought as I knocked on the door, "I'll soon find out."

Sharon, a tall, slender, African American woman, came to the front door with an infant in her arms. She welcomed me quietly and invited me into the front room. Upon my entry into the living room, my questions were answered. Yes, this was a family child care home, not a center. While sparsely furnished, the living room contained two large comfortable couches, an overstuffed chair, more toys, and five small children sleeping on mats lining the floor. Sharon invited me to join her on the couch while she calmly rocked and patted the baby in her arms. We began our conversation with Sharon telling me about her family. "I have Little Malcolm, who is four. Tamara will be three on Monday, Lord willing. I have a daughter, Aliah, that's one. And my husband, Big Malcolm, is twenty-seven. And I'm twenty-four." As our conversation continued, I asked Sharon to describe how she began working as a licensed family child care provider nearly four years ago. Early in their marriage, Sharon and Malcolm had lived with Sharon's mother. At that time, Sharon was providing unlicensed child care for pay in her mother's home. "I had four children to care for already at my mother's house," Sharon reported (her own young son and three other children). "[My husband and I] were living with my mother. And we had the downstairs area. And there was a living room down there and a bedroom. And so we were just living there. And Mark [my brother-in-law] came down one day and said, 'Hey Sharon. How would you like it if I got this house? You come in and do day care and you don't have to pay rent.'"

Although they both worked for wages, Sharon and her husband wanted to increase their family income enough to live on their own. In considering employment options, they faced the question encountered by all parents of small children: who will care for their child while they work for pay? Expanding her home-based child care, receiving training in early childhood education, and becoming a licensed family child care provider seemed like a viable way for Sharon to support her family economically while providing care for her own child. "So I said to my husband, 'Let's pray about it.'" In both Sharon's family and her African American community, her church, Talbot Temple, plays a central role.[1] Moving to their own residence and opening a licensed family child care home were big steps requiring thought and prayer. "And then we said, 'Yes.' . . . So we looked at a house, and about two weeks later we were moving in!"

As in Sharon and Malcolm's case, child care is key to families' attempts to achieve economic independence. In order to work for pay outside the home, mothers must find sources of care to substitute for their own because, like Sharon, employed mothers continue to assume primary responsibility for child care within their own families (Crittenden 2001, Ferree 1991, Harrington 2001). Policy debates during the past several years acknowledge the centrality of child care to families' economic self-sufficiency and to the ability of mothers to support their families through paid work. Nonetheless, while the importance of child care to women's and families' economic self-sufficiency is recognized, little attention is paid to the economic needs and job demands of working mothers such as Sharon: family child care workers who provide paid care for children when other mothers work outside the home. In facing the challenge shared by all working mothers of young children—finding affordable, accessible child care—Sharon presents us with an interesting twist. Sharon's paid work is that of a licensed family child care provider. Thus, while Sharon is a child care consumer (as a mother), she is also a child care provider (as a paid worker). As such, family child care providers like Sharon offer us a unique and more fully faceted perspective as we seek to understand the social organization and provision of paid child care work.

ASKING THE QUESTIONS

In this book, the story of how and why women enter paid child care work is told through the eyes and experiences of women such as Sharon Fleming—twenty family child care providers of diverse racial ethnic identities. In sharing their stories, these women help us learn more about why women join the child care work force. More specifically, as mothers of young children increasingly enter paid employment outside the home, what are the social processes by which other women (also frequently the mothers of young children) come forward to meet the need for child care? As family child care providers tell their stories, they expose the social forces as well as the personal responsibilities that draw women and their child care labor into the market economy. When we analyze paid child care work through their eyes, we are able to move beyond commonly held assumptions about why women enter the work of family child care. We are better able to understand the actual processes through which child care enters the market economy as well as the folk wisdom and public perceptions that offer incomplete explanations about why women choose to provide paid child care in their own homes.

Why Do Women Enter the Work of Family Child Care?

Sharon, like other young mothers, entered the paid labor force in order to support her family. But why do women enter family child care when other employment options are available? Common public perception as well as many previous research studies hold that women enter family child care work to live out the ideal of the full-time, at-home mother. At first glance, Sharon appears to be no exception. When I asked her why she chose to become a licensed family child care provider, she recounted emphatically, "My goal was to have my own place and to raise my children at home. And if this [family child care] is how I need to do it, this is how I'm going to do it."

Sharon's response suggests that the folk wisdom regarding women's entry into family child care may be accurate: that women seek to enter the work because of a commitment to a particular ideology of motherhood. But a deeper analysis of Sharon's answer enables us to understand the myriad ways in which ideological and structural forces as well as individual choices and responsibilities influence the employment options available to women and the choices they make regarding paid work.

When child care becomes paid work, members of the emerging child care labor force are largely, like Sharon, women. Gender is a primary force that influences who becomes a paid care worker (Cancian and Oliker 2000), and child care is no exception. While women comprise 42 percent of the paid work force, they comprise more than double that proportion (96 percent) of paid child care workers. Viewing this data in greater detail only confirms the central role that gender plays in influencing who becomes a paid child care worker. Women comprise more than 95 percent of child care center teachers and assistants, more than 97 percent of child care providers in private households, and more than 98 percent of family child care providers (U.S. Department of Labor Women's Bureau 1997). Clearly, gender is a primary force that organizes child care work and needs to be explored in depth to understand women's decisions to enter paid child care work.

Like Sharon, who is twenty-four and the mother of young children, the majority of women working in paid child care are of child-bearing age (Bellm et al. 1997), and nearly half have dependent children (Whitebook et al. 1998). Why do many women who are mothers themselves become paid child care providers—in particular, family child care providers? What might the choice have to do with women's identity as women? What might the choice have to do with women's identity as mothers? Is it true that women enter child care because of a "natural" ability and desire to care for children, including their own children? Perhaps. But when we look beneath the surface, we discover the ways in which ideologies and practices of gender (including motherhood), social class, and race ethnicity entwine to shape women's employment options and thus their decisions to provide paid child care within their own homes.

In contrast to popular opinion, child care providers themselves report a variety of reasons for doing this work. These range from the need to support oneself and one's family, to the desire to care for children, the desire to care for one's own children, the high cost of child care for one's own children, and the desire to be of assistance to mothers working outside the home (Galinsky et al. 1994, Whitebook and Phillips 1999). Frequently, as we will see in subsequent chapters, these forces are not segmented and autonomous. Instead, these social forces (including personal identity, social policies, and labor markets) influence one another and subsequently affect women's decisions to enter child care employment.

What Role Does Race Ethnicity Play in Family Child Care Work?

While gender is a primary force influencing the organization and provision of paid child care, race ethnicity plays an equally central role in organizing the work.[2] As a woman of color, Sharon Fleming is more likely to enter paid child care work than are her Euro-American counterparts. While women of color represent 13 percent of paid workers in the United States (U.S. Department of Labor, Bureau of Labor Statistics 1999a), women of color make up one-third of all paid child care workers (Bellm et al. 1997). Viewed in another way, the representation of women of color is more than 250 percent higher in the child care work force than it is in the work force at large. In addition, women who are members of specific racial ethnic groups are more likely to be concentrated in certain forms of paid child care work. Black women are overrepresented as early childhood teacher's assistants and child care workers. Specifically, both of these positions have less formal responsibility and earn lower wages than those of child care teacher and preschool teacher.[3] And Hispanic women undertake child care work in private households as nannies and au pairs at a rate 150 percent in excess of their representation in the overall work force (U.S. Department of Commerce, Bureau of the Census 2000).

This organization of paid child care work by race ethnicity as well as gender is reflected in the organization of other forms of historically unpaid women's work that have moved from households to the market economy. In particular, the ways in which paid domestic work is structured by race ethnicity are well documented (Dill 1994; Glenn 1986; Hondagneu-Sotelo 2001; Palmer 1989; Parrenas 2001; Romero 1999, 1992). Feminists acknowledge that freeing some women from domestic responsibilities (house cleaning and child care, to name two) transfers this labor to others who are also women and most often members of historically subordinated racial ethnic groups. While such a transfer does take place in child care, the dynamic is more complex than it may appear at first glance. In fact, as we will see in later chapters, family child care providers often demonstrate their agency in making specific decisions about the racial ethnic identity of the children and families for whom they provide care as a means of addressing larger social forces outside their immediate control.

So while gender is a primary force organizing the provision of family child care, other forces are operating as well. Gender ideologies and practices operate in the context of racial ethnic, cultural, and social class ideologies and practices so that women's experiences of gender and motherhood vary widely. As a result, while motherhood may be one factor influencing women's decisions to enter family child care, the stories of family child care providers of diverse racial ethnic identities and economic statuses enable us to understand the varied ways in which gender operates in the lives of women and influences their decisions (consciously or otherwise) to enter family child care work.

Why Do Women Enter Family Child Care Work When It Is Devalued and Poorly Compensated?

One of the primary themes of this book is that a disparity exists between the public need for child care and the public resources devoted to child care. This disparity results in a "care penalty" (England and Folbre 1999, 2002), a term increasingly used by child care providers, advocates, and researchers to describe the low wages, lack of benefits, and reduction in future earnings experienced by care workers. Literally, it is the penalty paid by people (in particular, women) who provide care. Like other forms of paid care work, family child care work is notorious for its low wages and lack of basic employment benefits such as health care insurance.

Despite nearly four years of licensed child care experience, a high school diploma, nearly a year of college, additional training in early childhood education, and full-time employment, Sharon Fleming earned $16,120 as a family child care provider in 1999. These earnings are more than 20 percent below the poverty threshold for a family the size of hers. In fact, Sharon makes so little money as a full-time family child care provider, and her husband makes so little in his full-time employment at a factory making window blinds, that they can not afford to purchase health insurance. "So you don't have any health insurance?" I ask. Sharon confirms with a nod.

"Does your husband get any health insurance?" I continue.

"He doesn't, . . ." she says. "I know I have some resources—the Country Doctor [a public community clinic]. But [my husband] is afraid for me to go to small clinics. . . . But we need to get something. I had medical coupons while I was pregnant. Now we have them for the children, but not for me."

Sharon's poverty-level earnings and her family's subsequent qualification for state-subsidized health care are particularly ironic because her sole source of income is through provision of child care to state-subsidized families in need. By providing government-subsidized child care to low-income families, Sharon, as a de facto government employee, earns so little that she herself qualifies for government-subsidized child care and her children qualify for government-subsidized health care (see chapter 5).

Sharon's low wages and lack of health care coverage are common among paid family child care providers. Because providers are self-employed, they fail to receive the types of benefits that most often are paid by employers. While self-employed workers theoretically pay for their own benefits, the earnings of family child care providers are so low as to eliminate this possibility for the vast majority of them. National as well as regional studies of family child care providers confirm that providers are not covered under even the most basic medical insurance; are unable to invest in pension or retirement savings; and do not charge for paid holidays, vacation time, or sick days (Galinsky et al. 1994, Modigliani 1993, Nelson 1990).

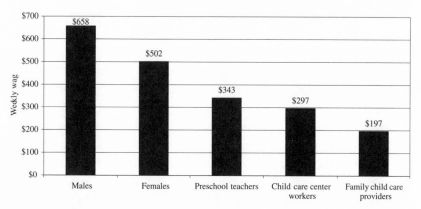

FIGURE 1. Median Weekly Wages, 2000
Sources: U.S. Department of Labor, Bureau of Labor Statistics, 2000, "2000 National Occupational Employment and Wage Estimates: Childcare Workers, Preschool Teachers, Teacher Assistants" and "1999 National Occupational Employment and Wage Estimates: Family Childcare Providers" (www.bls.gov/oes/2000; www.bls.gov/oes/1999); U.S. Department of Labor, Bureau of Labor Statistics, 2001, "Usual Weekly Earnings of Wage and Salary Workers: Fourth Quarter 2001" (www.bls.gov/cps).

Inability to purchase health insurance or to contribute to retirement savings attests to the fact that during the past decade wages of child care workers have remained at near-poverty levels. Child care has the highest concentration of poverty-wage workers of any industry (Kasarda 1996). In 1998 service station attendants and food servers were among those workers making higher wages than child care providers (Center for the Child Care Workforce 2000), even though the work week of family child care providers is 30 percent longer than that of these other occupations (fifty-five hours as compared to forty hours). Figure 1 provides a visual image of the subsistence-level wages earned by members of the child care work force in contrast with the earnings of other paid workers. In 2000, wages in the female-dominated child care work force totaled significantly less than the weekly median wage of both male and female workers, with family child care weighing in as the most poorly paid child care employment. At $197 a week in 2000, family child care providers earned 30 percent of the median male wage and 39 percent of the median female wage. Like Sharon, more than one-half of family child care providers earn incomes below the federally established poverty level (Haack 1998).

It is disconcerting, but not entirely surprising, that as a family child care provider of color, Sharon's wages are among the lowest in an already low-waged child care work force. Just as race ethnicity and gender organize wages in the work force at large, so do race ethnicity and gender organize wages earned by child care providers. While earnings of all child care providers remain extremely low, it is essential to look beyond the average wage picture to gain an accurate understanding of the ways in which race ethnicity as well as gender influence wages in child care and other forms of paid work. Figure 2 demonstrates that in the U.S. labor force the wages of Euro-American women, African American women, and Latinas, respectively, represent an increasingly small proportion of Euro-American male wages. While Euro-American women earn 76 percent of the Euro-American male wage, African American women earn 64 percent and Hispanic women 54 percent. The gender hierarchy of wages is clearly a racial ethnic hierarchy as well.

This racial ethnic hierarchy is also reflected in the wages of child care workers. Poor women and women of color are disproportionately found in entry-level and more poorly paid child care jobs (National Black Child Development Institute 1993). In child care centers, black women are more likely to work in lower-wage jobs with lower levels of responsibility. Hispanic women provide paid child care in the homes of parents (that is, as nannies) at a level vastly disproportionate to their participation in the overall labor force (U.S. Department of Commerce, Bureau of the Census 2000). This racial ethnic hierarchy of child care wages is seen in family child care as well, where the income of Hispanic family child care providers is two-thirds that of white providers and the earnings of black providers are one-half those of white providers (Fosburg 1981, 43). Clearly, a racial ethnic hierarchy of wages exists not only among women workers in the labor force at large but also among child care teachers and providers.

These low wages and lack of benefits have clear consequences for the continuity and stability of care (or lack thereof) for children. Given their extremely low pay, their lack of health care and retirement benefits, and the contribution of these factors to their long-term economic vulnerability, it is no surprise that child care workers often leave the child care work force. A number of studies

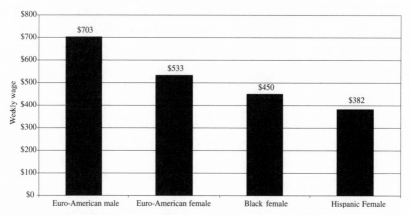

FIGURE 2. Wages by Race and Gender, 2001
Source: U.S. Department of Labor, Bureau of Labor Statistics, 2001, "Usual Weekly Earnings of Wage and Salary Workers: Fourth Quarter 2001" (www.bls.gov/cps).

of family child care indicate that turnover rates among family child care are similar to those of employees in child care centers. Nearly one-third of the child care work force leaves child care employment each year (Kontos 1992), a phenomenally high turnover rate for any occupation.

Sharon Fleming is no exception to those women who consider leaving the child care work force. When I asked her if she has ever thought about leaving child care, she responded immediately: "Do I ever think about it? [laughter]. I think about it a *lot!*" When I talked with Sharon about her desire to leave family child care employment, I learned that her motivation is not entirely governed by low wages. She reflected on the challenges of being a working mother. She spoke of the problems that occur when her home is also the location of her paid work. She spoke of her desire to do her paid work well and the need for more education in order to do so. And threaded throughout this discussion was her commitment to care for her family. She explained:

> [Providing family child care] is a lot for me because I'm a mother of my own young children. It's not like I just have a day care [center] and then it's over with. Maybe if I just worked at a day care center it would be different. But I'm the one that has to talk to the parents when there's a problem. I'm the one that has to collect the money. I'm the one who has to make sure the menus are planned and the groceries are here. There's activities going

on. I'm the one that has to do a lot. I go to school. And I think that's what really wore me down because I was going to school. When I got relicensed, the city required me to take an early childhood education class. So I'm raising my children, going to school, and doing this day care at the same time. That is a lot.

Despite these demands, Sharon continues to remain in family child care. Like her, a number of family child care providers also remain committed to family child care work. National data tell us that a large proportion of providers see their family child care work as their chosen profession (Kontos 1992), and the National Day Care Home Study confirmed that 75 percent of licensed family child care providers see their family child care work as permanent employment (Fosburg 1981).

Despite providers' need to support themselves and their families, family child care work is rarely a living wage job; and child care providers such as Sharon often fail to achieve economic self-sufficiency for themselves and their families through child care employment. Why, then, do women continue to enter the work? And why do many demonstrate a long-term commitment to family child care? Listening to the stories of family child care providers helps us to understand the ways in which individual decisions are made within a larger social context. Women's choices to enter and remain in family child care work are shaped by structural as well as ideological forces. These social forces and ideologies influence the employment options available to women as well as the decisions they make regarding how to best support themselves and their families through paid employment.

THE CHANGING RELATIONSHIP OF WORK, FAMILY, AND CARE

As an employed mother, Sharon asks the same question that other employed parents do: how do I find affordable, accessible child care so that I can work for pay to support my family? When Sharon talked with me about her needs as a working parent she spoke, as do other mothers, of the importance of child care. "Day cares are so much in demand. I mean, what if we didn't have any day cares? Then parents couldn't work. . . . Just to keep up with the cost of living, parents have to go to work. So we need day care." Like other employed mothers, Sharon understands the importance of child care to her family's economic stability. In her case, however, the worlds of work and family are merged in ways that are not common to the vast majority of working mothers. Hence, a paradox emerges in family child care work. Nearly all mothers must be released from the work of child care in home and family in order to enter the world of paid work. In contrast, for family child care providers such as Sharon, home is the site of paid work and child care is the paid work in which she engages. In the "private" world of her home, Sharon provides the work of care that enables other mothers to enter the "public" world of paid employment in the market economy. The work of women like Sharon is essential to parents and to the businesses that seek to employ them. Yet family child care is often viewed as inferior to other forms of care, and family child care providers report that they feel invisible and unaccounted for in child care policy discussions (Haack 1999). As one provider, Martha Buxton, observed, "Some people don't consider [family child care] to be work."

Although paid child care involves three constituencies (children, children's parents, and child care providers), policymakers and academics focus on just two of these constituencies. The primary focus of research and policy initiatives is the need for child care as a service to parents (primarily mothers) to help them work outside the home. A secondary issue is child care as a service for children, expressed most often as a concern regarding the quality of care they receive. But scant attention has been paid to the needs of paid child care providers, the majority of whom are themselves working mothers in need of quality care for their own children as well as a living wage to support themselves and their families.

Despite its lack of visibility among policymakers, government regulators, and researchers, parents are quite familiar with family child care. For the past twenty years, family child care has existed as a large and stable source of child care for employed parents (U.S. Department of Commerce, Bureau of the Census 2002). In fact, currently one-quarter of paid child care for children under the age of five is provided in family child care settings (see figure 3). Employed parents use family child care more commonly than they use au pairs, nannies, or relatives (Galinsky et al. 1994). In particular, parents show a preference for family child care for infants and toddlers (Fosburg 1981, Galinsky et al. 1994, Kontos 1992). Family

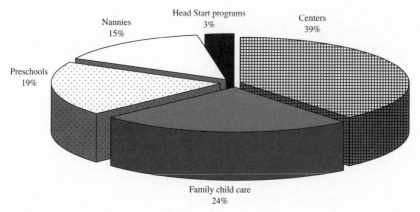

FIGURE 3. Paid Child Care Used by Employed Parents for Children under Age Five, 1997
Source: U.S. Department of Commerce, Bureau of the Census, 2002, "Who's Minding the Kids: Child Care Arrangements: Spring 1997," Current Population Reports, Household Economic Studies, Series P-70, No. 86 (Washington, DC: Government Printing Office, July), table 1.
Note: Because of multiple arrangements, children may appear in more than one arrangement type.

child care serves as an essential source of child care for employed parents—and has done so in a rapidly changing child care market over the past twenty years. Yet despite parents' reliance on family child care and the public need for good care (Folbre 2001), the social and economic value of family child care work remains extremely low. This disparity results in a "care deficit"—a gap between the public need for and the public resources allocated to care. Child care providers largely fill this gap, subsidizing the true cost of child care through their low wages. One of the goals of this book is to provide insights into why this problem exists and continues to grow.

As more and more parents seek child care outside of their own homes, child care is transformed from unpaid caregiving in the private sphere of families and households to paid work in the public sphere of the market economy. Work believed to be performed for love is increasingly performed for money. Thus, child care as paid work emerges as a synthesis of two worlds that have historically been viewed as dualistic and exclusionary: the private world of caring in families and the public world of financial and personal success achieved through participating in the market economy. By providing paid child care but doing so in their own homes, family child care workers synthesize the supposed private world of caring in families with the supposed public world of paid work. They work on the ideological boundary that has historically divided family life from the market economy. Among the women who provide family child care, households and families emerge as a new institutional site for paid child care, one that combines ideologies and practices of the market economy with ideologies and practices of family life. As a result, what do the experiences of family child care providers teach us about the changing nature of gendered and racialized ideologies that seek to delineate family life as something separate from the market economy? What might they teach us about the changing nature of paid work? What might they tell us about how mothers negotiate the demands of the market and the responsibilities of family life? And what might we learn about the discrepancy between the high demand for child care and the low social and economic value ascribed to child care providers and their work? The stories of the twenty women in this book allow us to begin answering these questions and to rethink commonly held assumptions regarding the work of paid child care and the women who do this work.

FAMILY CHILD CARE AS AN UNDERSTUDIED FORM OF CARE

Despite family child care's prominence as a primary form of paid child care, parents' preference of family child care for their very young children, and family child care's existence as a source of employment for a large number of women, it remains the least researched of all child care settings. To date, four major studies form our primary source of knowledge about family child care (Fosburg 1981, Galinsky et al. 1994, Hofferth and Kisker 1991, Nelson 1990). These studies address important aspects of family child care, including its prevalence as a source of care, demographic characteristics of family child care providers, the structure of the family child care market, and the quality of care provided in family child care settings. Only one, Margaret Nelson's, analyzes the daily lives and work of family child care providers as experienced by the women themselves—an ethnographic analysis. In *Negotiated Care* (1990), Nelson goes beyond the description and demographic analysis of family child care to develop the first and only major analysis of the meaning of family child care as told from the perspective of family child care providers. Nelson elucidates the dilemmas faced by family child care workers in their relationships with children, parents, and the state regulatory system, offering an analysis of family child care providers' daily lives and work.

While Nelson's ground-breaking analysis of family child care work reveals that family child care providers have to negotiate an ambiguous mix of market and social principles, her analysis does not explore how the structural context of race ethnicity, gender, country of origin, and social class entwine to shape this dynamic process. In my work, I seek to explore how these historical ideologies and practices regarding the work of white women and women of color complicate the social organization and provision of family child care work.

My interest in family child care and, as a result, my approach to the research differs from Nelson's in two important ways. First, the subjects of her research were native-born, white, rural family child care providers with incomes much higher than those of family child care workers nationwide (a sample that accurately represents the population of providers in Vermont, the location of Nelson's study). Analyzing the work of white family child care providers and their experiences with white parents enabled Nelson to "focus on issues that arise from the nature of the work itself, without the complications of ethnic and racial factors" (228). While her interest was in extracting race ethnicity from an analysis of the daily work of child care, I am interested in race ethnicity as a central force in the organization of paid child care work and its transformation into the market economy. While women make up the vast majority of paid child care workers, women of color are disproportionately represented in the child care work force; and the wages of child care workers of color are generally lower than those of their white counterparts. Thus, I want to explicitly incorporate workers of diverse racial ethnic identity, cultural identity, and immigrant status into my analysis of family child care and explore the ways in which these social forces might be integral to women's choice to enter family child care employment.

A second difference between Nelson's research interests and my own emerges in our chosen focus when exploring family child care. While, like Nelson, I base my analysis in the daily lives of the women who care for our children, my intent has not been to develop a detailed analysis of the day-to-day negotiation and performance of family child care work. Rather, I am interested in the processes by which child care moves from unpaid work in families to paid work in the market—an analysis of the ideologies, social structures, and personal decisions that lead women to enter the work of family child care. When we analyze paid child care work through the eyes and experiences of diverse family child care providers, we are better able to understand the actual processes by which women enter the work of paid child care.

APPROACHING THE RESEARCH

My approach to the study of family child care work is informed by my understanding of standpoint feminism and its links to diversity feminism. Political theorist Nancy Hartsock (1983), one of the first feminist scholars to explore the concept of standpoint, asserts, "A standpoint . . . carries with it the contention that there are some perspectives on society from which, however well-intentioned one may be, the real relations of humans with each other and with the natural world are not visible" (159). Hartsock builds on phenomenology, the philosophy that asserts that what we know emerges from our social location and experience. She argues that the experiential reality (that is, the standpoint) of women as those who give birth to, care for, and socialize children has been historically invisible in the production of knowledge. This understanding of the invisibility of women and their work has become, over the past fifteen years, a well-recognized precept in feminist critiques of knowledge production (Harding 1993).

In particular, our best-known and accepted political and economic theories are rooted in a belief in the centrality of the market economy and its inherent values of independence and individual achievement through paid work. These theories fail to acknowledge that women's unpaid and slave labor in families and households has played a central historical role in creating and sustaining social and economic life. Some individuals (historically, men) are able to engage in paid work outside the home because other individuals (historically, women and particularly women of subordinate racial ethnic groups) are available to provide the social, emotional, and physical work of care for men and their dependents.

Sociologist Dorothy Smith (1987) confirms the centrality of women's work to social and economic life and makes clear that women's work—in particular, the care work of mothers—is historically invisible: "what mothers do . . . does not appear as work. . . . Mothers appear in a peculiar way as necessary links in a causal process, but without agency. Their thinking, the effort and time they have put in, and the varying material conditions under which their work is done do not appear" (164). Consequently, Smith, Hartsock, and other feminist theorists assert that women's experiences and perspectives must be central to our research and that our understanding of the social and political world will be different when women's standpoints become the perspectives from which knowledge is produced.

Building on standpoint feminism, diversity feminism (also called multicultural or multiracial feminism) recognizes that gender is entwined with race ethnicity and social class. Diversity feminists assert that "race is a power system that interacts with other structured inequalities to shape genders. Within the U.S. context, race and the system of meanings and ideologies, which accompany it, is a fundamental organizing principle of social relationships. Race affects all women and men, although in different ways. Even cultural and group differences among women are produced through interaction within a racially stratified social order" (Zinn and Dill 1996, 324).

Thus, while asserting the importance of individual differences and individual agency, diversity feminists and standpoint feminists recognize the importance of group identity and the social relations of power that shape group identity. As a result, women, particularly women of historically subordinated racial ethnic groups, can offer perspectives and insights to the social order that come from the margins—perspectives that emerge from being "outsiders within" (hooks 1984). Making these perspectives visible, then, contributes to more thorough and accurate accounts of the social world and hence to better social science. (See, for example, Haraway 1988, Harding 1998).

Committed to the principles of standpoint feminism and diversity feminism and seeking to understand the social world from varied locations, I have found Smith's (1987) notion of "the every-

day world as problematic" to be invaluable. The research methodology first developed by Smith as "institutional ethnography" has
since been adopted by a number of researchers who, like me, seek
to root their analysis of social processes in daily life and work (see,
for example, DeVault 1991, Diamond 1992, Naples 1998b, G. Smith
1990). Institutional ethnographers draw on elements of the conventional practices of ethnography in which experience and
knowledge gained in the daily lives of people are recognized, valued, and made the foundation of the research. With this ethnographic component, institutional ethnography affirms the
precepts of standpoint feminism and diversity feminism. Daily life
is the starting point of research; and by viewing daily life from the
perspective of women and their work, we see the social world in
new ways and come to new understandings about it.

Nevertheless, while daily life is the starting point of institutional ethnography, it is not the end point. The goal of institutional
ethnography is to understand daily life as it is lived in and influenced by larger social forces. Therefore, institutional ethnography
expands on the conventional research practice of ethnography to
include analysis of the institutional and social processes that influence our daily lives. By *institution*, institutional ethnographers are
not referring to a particular type of organization or an unchanging
structure. Instead, the concept is viewed more dynamically. Institution is construed as the larger social processes and relationships
(such as political, economic, and cultural) that influence our daily
lives and the choices we make (Smith 1987, 1999). For example,
when institutional ethnographers think of family as an institution,
we think of the ways in which family (in both its ideal and real
forms) is created through a variety of actions in a variety of settings—in the roles and responsibilities assumed by mothers, fathers, and children within their homes but also in the ways in
which those roles and responsibilities are encouraged and facilitated in schools, workplaces, legal systems, and public policy.

In addition to making visible the larger social forces that shape
our daily lives, institutional ethnographers seek to clarify the ways
in which our daily lives both contribute to and alter these forces.
Women are active participants in these larger social forces, not just
objects of them. The processes by which daily life is created and
sustained are dynamic ones that are, however, not always fully visible to us as we go about our daily lives and work. According to

Smith (1987), "the social organization [of the everyday world] is only partially discoverable within its scope and the scope of individual's daily lives. Its local organization is determined by the social relations of an immensely complex division of labor knitting local lives and local settings to national and international social, economic, and political processes. Here, then, is where the sociologist enters" (154).

What most appeals to me about institutional ethnography is the sociologist's point of entry into the local setting and the ways in which that entry facilitates an understanding of the larger social context of women's work. I find myself committed to understanding the ways in which social relations and social forces, as well as individual choice and action, shape our daily lives as women. While our lives are embedded in political and economic institutions and processes, we also act in ways that both contribute to and challenge these larger processes. In the dynamic synthesis of social institutions and individual actions, we create, maintain, and transform our social world. As Smith says, "What we [as researchers] are trying to make visible . . . is an ongoing production. The social process is always in the making; it is also always coming into being as a condition of its own activity" (126).

It is this social process—the organization and provision of family child care work—that I explore in this book. When child care becomes paid work but continues to be performed in the home, how does it reproduce as well as challenge existing ideologies of the market and the family? When analyzing this question from the perspective of family child care providers, we come to appreciate the ways in which providing paid care within family settings both conflicts with and reinforces gendered and racial ethnic ideologies that structure both the market and family life. And we come to appreciate the need to rethink the power of these ideologies as well as the social and economic value of care work and the women who care for our children.

FRAMING THE RESEARCH

As I began to explore family child care work and speak with family child care providers, I became increasingly intrigued by the power of family as an institution integral to social processes in the contemporary United States. Specifically, I grew to appreciate the ways in which our understanding and practices of family exist in opposition to those of the market economy and how both shape the organization and provision of family child care. Unlike other forms of paid work, most of which are organized and provided in the context of the formal market economy, family child care is organized and provided in the context of families. For the majority of paid workers, the workplace is separate from home and family; but this is not the case for family child care providers. The paid work of child care takes place in both the physical location and ideological context of families. For family child care providers, no geographic distinction exists between the location of work and the location of family. As such, families as both an ideal and a practice contribute to the organization of the work of family child care in significant ways.

To understand the centrality of the ideology of the family and its gendered and racial ethnic facets in the organization and provision of family child care, it is essential to understand that ideologies are integrally linked to institutions and play a central role in shaping both our actions and the choices available to us. Conventionally, an ideology is recognized as a system of beliefs or values that serve to rationalize social structures, particularly as they relate to power and privilege. Of particular importance here is to understand that ideologies are not just systems of thought and belief but systems of belief that are linked to social relationships and action. Ideology's power as a belief system lies in actually reproducing the social organization that it endorses. An ideology shapes the way in which members of a group or society view the world, their own place, and the place of others within that world. In addition to guiding the beliefs and actions of individuals and groups, dominant ideologies rationalize a society's structure of power and privilege, not only explaining a society's organization and structures but also justifying those structures (Marger 1999). "Dominant ideologies function to comfort those whom the system rewards and to justify the system to those who fail" (Huber and Form 1973, 79). So while ideologies serve as a guide for daily life, they also reflect and reinforce the power relations within a society.

What role does ideology play in our understanding of families and subsequently of family child care? Historically, scholars have recognized families as residential units in which members share resources, consumption, and housework. Increasingly, this definition is applied instead to the term *households*, while families are recognized as much more complex (Rapp 1992). In accordance with emerging feminist theories regarding families, I recognize families as social groups that exist within a set of larger belief systems and social relations that, in turn, organize our daily experiences both in households and broader social networks. While the daily activities of mothers, fathers, and children create and sustain families, these actions of individual people in individual households are shaped by social forces and belief systems that exist both inside and outside of immediate households. Central among these forces and belief systems is that of the institutional ideology of the family—the ways in which belief systems about family life are linked to social practices (for example, work, education, and public policy) and the ways in which those social practices reinforce our belief systems about families.

Family child care work is provided within the location of households and, more broadly, within the (albeit changing) institutional ideology of the family. In my conversations with family child care providers, the power of this gendered and racialized ideology became increasingly clear. As a result, I have chosen to explicitly acknowledge the centrality of this ideology in organizing family child care work and to use the family as an institutional framework for analyzing the work of family child care. In using the family as a framework, I draw on Roxanna Ng's term *ideological framing*. Ng (1995) confirms that an ideology is not just a mental construction but a form of social organization shaped around particular beliefs and values. Ideological framing identifies ideologies as "processes that are produced and constructed through human activities" (36). It draws our attention to social processes and encourages us to explore what actually happens to produce, reinforce, and challenge specific values and practices, especially as they relate to organizing work and work processes in the context of various institutions (such as the family). As Ng explains, "Once an ideological frame is in place, it renders the very work process that produced it invisible and the idea that it references as 'common sense'" (36). Thus, Ng concurs with institutional ethnographer Dorothy Smith. Institutional processes are mediated ideologically.

Historically, ideologies obscure the actual organization and provision of certain forms of work, in particular the work of women (Smith 1987). This is, by now, a well-founded feminist critique of the ideological institution of the family: it facilitates the invisibility of the unpaid work that women have historically performed within households and families.

When child care becomes paid family child care, it remains located within families, a site that historically promotes the invisibility of women and their care work. And this new institutional work site with its attendant ideology of the family continues to obscure the, now paid, care work of women and to influence public perceptions and valuing of the work. This is why it is essential for us to begin our investigation of family child care within the context of women's lived experience. While the ideology of the family is a powerful force that both enables and constrains our daily lives, we must look critically at this ideology to determine whether it is an accurate depiction of our lives as we live them on a daily basis. Locating my analysis in the actual experience of family child care providers, I have sought to bring a fresh perspective to the organization and provision of family child care, which, because it is derived from the lived experience of the women who actually do the work of caring, might differ from commonly held assumptions and historical ideologies about family child care and family child care providers.

DOING THE RESEARCH

With the goal of analyzing the social organization and provision of family child care work, I needed a research design that would enable me to explore the myriad forces that influence women's decisions to engage in the paid work of family child care. In addition, given my commitment to the theories of standpoint feminism and diversity feminism as well as to institutional ethnography, I knew that my analysis had to include women with varied experiences and perspectives on family child care work. As Marjorie DeVault (1999) confirms, "The world 'out there' looks quite different from different locations" (50). Analyzing family child care work from a variety of standpoints would clearly contribute to a stronger and more accurate analysis of the work and the women whose experiences I sought to understand.

While institutional ethnographers are committed to drawing on the experiences of people in different social locations, we do not generalize about a particular population. Our goal is "to find and describe social processes that have generalizing effects" (De-Vault and McCoy 2002, 753). How might people living in different circumstances be influenced by a common set of social and organizational processes? Selecting research participants is done, then, not in accordance with traditional research sampling in which individuals are selected based on categorical descriptions (such as race or income) but in terms of their diversity of experience. What I have sought to create is dimension and depth in our understanding of family child care work. Who does the work? Why do they enter the work? And what do their experiences tell us about how we understand and value (or fail to value) women's care work?

Given these commitments, I needed a research site that provided access to family child care providers with diverse perspectives and experiences of the work. I also needed access to information regarding the larger political and economic context in which family child care work occurs. As a result, I located my study of family child care providers in Washington State, which proved a viable research site for many reasons. While Washington requires some form of licensing or regulation of family child care homes, as do forty-three other states (Children's Foundation 2001), a large portion of family child care is provided by unlicensed providers in what is frequently know as the informal, or underground, economy. As in other states, Washington's educational and training requirements for licensed family child care providers are minimal (that is, CPR training). Moreover, Washington is a state with geographic as well as racial ethnic diversity providing access to both urban and rural family child care workers.

My work as a founding member of the Child Care Action Council in my community as well as my employment in the governor's budget office as an analyst responsible for children's and family services supplied me with contacts in both Washington State and local governments and with state and local child care advocates. While these research participants provided access to information regarding the political and economic context of family child care, the experiences of the family child care providers formed the foundation for my analysis. My first real challenge arose in finding family child care providers to participate in the study. The majority of family child care work is unregulated and unlicensed care that occurs in the informal economy (Galinsky et al. 1994, Tuominen 1994). Because work in the underground economy is unregulated by government agencies and therefore not reflected in public records, locating unlicensed family child care providers to participate in research studies of family child care was a challenge. In addition, given the paucity of ethnographic research incorporating the experiences of family child care providers of racial ethnic and cultural diversity, incorporating the experiences of women of color and immigrant women was central to the depth of analysis I sought to develop.

Through the statewide Child Care Information and Referral network, I contacted local child care organizations and providers in various communities and regions of the state. Staff at the King County Child Care Resource and Referral agency as well as members of the Seattle Worthy Wages Task Force contacted several licensed providers to assess their willingness to participate in the study. From the list of providers willing to participate, I selected women residing and working in both urban and suburban areas of the county. The Catholic Family Services agency of rural eastern Washington identified Mexicanas who provided licensed care and were willing to participate in interviews. And through the Child Care Resource and Referral agency in Olympia, I located small-town providers, primarily licensed Euro-American women, willing to take part in the study.

Locating unlicensed providers proved to be more difficult. Given the illegal nature of the care they give (family child care providers are required by Washington state law to be licensed) as well as their lack of visibility, personal contacts were essential. Initially, I asked the licensed care workers I interviewed to supply names of unlicensed family child care providers, but this method proved ineffective. Having worked to achieve licensed status and advocating the professional status derived from licensing, these providers sought to divorce themselves from unlicensed providers who, they believed, offered poor quality and unprofessional care. When my attempts to go this route proved useless, I located unlicensed providers through contacts in local churches and acquaintances.

My analysis of family child care work is grounded in interviews with twenty family child care providers, women whose experiences of family child care are shaped by their racial ethnic identity and group membership; their experiences as immigrant or native-born women; and their residence in urban, suburban, small towns, or rural communities. While the women experience different racial ethnic group membership, the majority of providers I interviewed are women of color. Of the twenty women, eight are African American, four Mexicanas, one Asian, and seven Euro-American. (See table 1 for a summary of descriptive information regarding the women I interviewed.)

English is not the native language of the Vietnamese provider nor of the four Mexicana providers who participated in this study. In addition, the providers I interviewed range in age from twenty-four to fifty-four, with a mean age of 35.5 and a median age of 36.5. Thus, the care workers I interviewed are uniformly within the average (thirty-four to thirty-seven years old) reported in other family child care studies (Kontos 1992, Galinsky et al. 1994, Fosburg 1981). Six of the twenty care workers I interviewed live and work in densely populated urban areas, three in suburban neighborhoods, six in small towns, and five in rural communities.

Four of the family child care providers in this study provide unlicensed, underground child care, and three of the providers had previously worked as unlicensed providers before becoming licensed. Thus, while seven of the twenty women I interviewed enabled me to incorporate the experiences of unlicensed providers into my analysis, a disproportionate number of the workers I interviewed are licensed (as compared with national estimates that up to 81 percent of family child care providers are illegally unregulated) (Galinsky et al. 1994).

Two of the five immigrant women for whom English was not their native language had completed the equivalent of a high school diploma in their country of origin. As will be seen in chapter 4, however, employers rarely viewed their high school equivalency as relevant when the women applied for employment in the United States. Among the fifteen native-English speaking women, two had completed a G.E.D., two held high school diplomas, six had completed some college course work in addition to their high school degrees, two held an A.A. diploma, and three held B.A.

Table 1. Family Child Care Providers Interviewed, Personal and Demographic Information

NAME	AGE	MARITAL STATUS	RACE/ ETHNICITY	YEARS PROVIDING PAID CARE	MAXIMUM NUMBER OF CHILDREN CARED FOR AT ONE TIME	LICENSED STATUS
Sondra Ames	38	Married	African American	3	12	Licensed
Brenda Beall	49	Married	Euro-American	9	10	Licensed
Annette Bradley	27	Partner*	African American	1	3	Unlicensed
Martha Buxton	48	Married	Euro-American	8	4	Unlicensed
Segunda Cortez	35	Married	Mexicana	8	10	Licensed
Jennie Davis	51	Divorced	African American	3	9	Licensed
Julia Deavers	37	Married	Euro-American	4	12	Licensed
Sharon Fleming	24	Married	African American	3	11	Both**
Valerie Holton	35	Married	African American	15	12	Both**
Isabel Inofuentes	42	Married	Mexicana	8	10	Licensed
Patricia James	33	Married	African American	8	9	Licensed
Cora Jenkins	41	Married	African American	19	5	Licensed
Laura Mayfield	41	Married	Euro-American	11	10	Both**
Allie McGinnis	29	Partner*	Euro-American	3	3	Unlicensed
Elena Molinero	34	Married	Mexicana	8	9	Licensed
Janice Newman	38	Married	Euro-American	12	12	Licensed
Kim Phan	25	Married	Asian	5	3	Unlicensed
Justine Reeves	46	Married	African American	4	8	Licensed
Kay Schilling	36	Married	Euro-American	11	8	Licensed
Gloria Zuñiga	28	Married	Mexicana	4	9	Licensed

Note: Names of all providers are pseudonyms.

*While not married, these women were living with male partners in long-term relationships.

**While licensed at the time of the interview, these providers previously provided unlicensed care.

degrees (all in education). This range in years of formal education and the distribution in levels of education are in keeping with educational levels of family child care providers reported in nationwide studies (Galinsky et al. 1994, Hofferth and Kisker 1991).

I most often met family child care providers for interviews in the homes where they both lived and worked. Nap time is frequently the only time family child care providers are available for interviews because their paid work day is sandwiched between a morning and an evening of unwaged care for their own families. Even during nap time, however, care work is required. As a result, interviews within the providers' homes enabled me to observe (and often participate in) family child care—primarily rocking and holding small children or bottle-feeding infants during interviews.

Even though I met providers in their homes, I observed limited aspects of their care work; and interviews served as my primary source of information and analysis regarding their experiences. I designed my interview guide using questions that arose from my analysis of other studies of paid child care work as well as from my knowledge of child care derived from previous research, my relationships and conversations with family child care providers and child care advocates, and my own child care policy and advocacy work. The questions that served as a basis for the semistructured interviews enabled providers to explore the hours, wages, and working conditions of their family child care labor; their daily routine of both paid and unpaid care work in their homes; their employment history in both family child care and other types of work; their educational and family background; what they liked most and least about family child care work; and why they chose to stay in the work or anticipated leaving. Questions were open-ended and encouraged providers to reflect on and offer insights about their personal history as well as their family child care work. In both interviews and analysis, I listened for the worker's interpretation of her own life, decisions, and options as well as for the broader social relationships that shaped the choices available to her.

Each interview began with my request to tape-record the interview and an opportunity for providers to read and sign the consent form. The interview guide provided a framework for the interview itself. As I taped each interview, I took minimal notes, directing my attention to the participants and their responses to interview questions, probing for additional information, and seeking clarification. Interviews ranged between one and four hours in length and often involved follow-up conversations to clarify providers' experiences and analyses.

I am aware that qualitative research studies such as this one are susceptible to criticism. Whenever participants are selected for a study in a way other than a strict random sample, this question arises: how representative is the sample, and hence how representative are the findings? In responding to this question, one must remember the goals of institutional ethnography. Conventional sociology often tries to understand people's experiences by organizing them into various categories (such as race, gender, or sexuality) and seeking to understand the categories as representatives of the whole. In contrast, the goal of institutional ethnography is to understand how people in different circumstances are drawn into common organizational processes (DeVault and McCoy 2002, 26).

My goal in undertaking this analysis of family child care work is not to create a grand theory regarding who becomes family child care providers and why. Rather, my goal is to make visible the daily lives of the women who care for our children. Through their experiences and stories, I seek to expand our understanding of family child care. Why is it women, and disproportionately women of color, who become paid child care providers? What are the processes by which women (frequently themselves the mothers of young children) come forward to provide paid care and thereby enable the mothers of other young children to engage in paid work outside of the home? Why do women enter and remain in family child care work given its poor compensation and social devaluation? Why is the social and economic value ascribed to family child care so low when the public need for and the public benefits derived from family child care are so great? And how might the stories of these women enable us to understand the changing relationship of work, family, and care?

MAPPING THE TRANSFORMATION OF
CHILD CARE FROM UNPAID TO PAID WORK

As I listened to the stories and experiences of family child care providers, I became increasingly convinced of the inaccuracy of both the folk wisdom and the previous research that explains women's sole or even primary motivation to enter family child care as their attempt to act out the idealized family role of a full-time, at-home mother. Through my conversations with providers it became clear that motherhood and family are central forces influencing women's decisions to become family child care providers. But it also became apparent that the decision to enter family child care work is informed by multiple social forces as well as individual choices and responsibilities. As a result, in their decisions to undertake paid care work for children (but to do so within their own homes), family child care providers are influenced by, but also challenge, our conventional understandings of family, work, and care.

The dualistic ideologies of work versus family and rationality versus care fail to reflect accurately why women choose to provide family child care, clouding rather than elucidating our understanding of the work. The very existence of family child care in which women provide paid care in their own homes challenges the bifurcated ideal that unpaid care occurs within the family while paid work occurs within the market. When child care becomes paid work, caring for children, perceived to occur in the private sphere of families and households, enters the market economy and becomes public work. Work often believed to be motivated by love is increasingly performed for pay. As such, family child care enables—and requires—us to move beyond our current perceptions of the work and to ground our understanding of family child care in the daily lives of the women who perform the work.

Through interviews with family child care providers, I came to appreciate the complex processes by which child care becomes paid work. If we are to understand the social organization and provision of family child care, we need to learn more about these women and their work. In chapter 2 readers begin to learn what is required of family child care providers in their daily work of caring for children. We see not only the tasks and skills but also the relationships that make up the largely invisible work of family child care. We see little difference between providers in the responsibilities they assume in the performance of their daily work. In fact, regardless of racial ethnic identity, cultural identity, and social class, family child care providers all struggle with the ways in which idealized notions of work versus care and market versus family shape their work. While providers report that their relationships with children prove rewarding and encourage them to remain in the work, the relational aspects of care work also complicate the sale of child care services. In addition, providers report the frustration they experience because of the devaluation and lack of respect accorded to their work. Because their work is a synthesis of the ideologically bifurcated worlds of the family and the market economy, family child care providers experience both personal and structural conflicts as they seek to integrate their rights as paid workers with their responsibilities as empathetic providers of care.

Viewing family child care through the eyes and experiences of family child care providers reveals that commonly held assumptions about why women enter family child care work are not always accurate. In chapters 3 and 4, I begin to explore the explicit motives as well as the structural opportunities that influence women's decisions to make family child care their paid work. In chapter 3, I address the common belief that women choose to provide paid care in their homes out of a commitment to the ideology of full-time, at-home mothering. The vast majority of the family child care providers I interviewed did not hold dualistic perceptions of gendered parenthood in which mothers are responsible for unpaid emotional and physical care of family members while fathers are to provide financially for the family. While the responsibilities of caring for their own children proved to be an important factor in women's choices to enter family child care, the responsibilities and opportunities of motherhood varied greatly among the workers I interviewed and were informed by their racial ethnic identity, country of origin, cultural identity, and social class. Among the family child care providers I interviewed, supporting one's family financially was viewed as integral to their responsibilities as mothers and not in any way anathema to their understanding of motherhood or their responsibilities of care. This understanding of motherhood was shaped by experiences derived from and negotiated within interdependent forces of race ethnicity, cultural identity, and social class.

In chapter 4, I examine how economic forces blend with ideologies and practices of gender and race ethnicity to influence women's choices to make family child care their paid work. Among the women I interviewed, entry into family child care proved to be a means of providing economically for their families when accessible and affordable child care was not available for their own children. Family child care supplied these employed mothers with a stable source of income when the cost of child care exceeded the take-home wages available to them in low-waged jobs in sex- and race-segregated occupations. Despite the fact that the women I interviewed made the common choice to enter family child care work, the women experienced their choices to enter family child care work quite differently: as stable and permanent employment, as a source of professional identity and continued professional mobility, or as alternative professional employment. Thus, women from quite different circumstances are drawn into a common occupation from which they derive different employment identities and meaning.

In chapter 5, providers teach us the central role that social networks play in the provision of family child care. Because of both social networks and local markets for care, providers market their child care to families who very often share their own social class, country of origin, racial ethnic identity, and cultural identity. As a result, providers in lower-income communities often serve families in need who qualify for government-subsidized child care, while providers in middle-income communities limit or refuse to provide care for state-subsidized families. While providers in lower- and middle-income communities come to opposite decisions regarding offering their services to state-subsidized families, in both cases providers share a common motivation—the desire to ensure the most stable source of income for themselves and their own families.

In chapter 6, I explore the ways in which community and community membership are relational and political. As a result of their community membership, African American providers often experience family child care work as community care work. The African American providers I interviewed were motivated to provide family child care by a spiritual call to serve families in need as well as by a commitment to racial safety and cultural pride. For these providers, family child care work is work that they undertake in order to enable both community survival and community betterment. By providing community care work, family child care providers play a central and valued role in the social life and development of the community.

In chapter 7, family child care providers challenge the gendered and racialized ideologies that devalue their work. While their provision of family child care is partially motivated by ideals of public service and a commitment to the social value of their work, workers also actively seek higher wages, improved working conditions, and increased public status as professionals. Family child care workers thus bring the care work and caring values historically identified with the world of families and households into the market economy as paid work. In so doing, their experiences require us to reconceptualize our definitions of work and care and to rethink the social and economic value of family child care and the women who care for our children.

2

"I KNOW HOW IT FEELS TO GIVE YOUR KIDS TO SOMEBODY ELSE"

Synthesizing the Family and the Market in the Work of Family Child Care

The lives and work of family child care providers offer insights into the tensions as well as the powerful but false duality of ideologies that distinguish the family from the market and care from work.[1] The family setting in which family child care occurs creates particular challenges for providers. First and foremost, the location of the work within the family contributes to its invisibility. Child care is historically assumed to be an activity motivated by love and altruism that women undertake in their homes. This perception of family-based care as motivated by benevolence obscures the work itself: its skill, demands, and value (Abel and Nelson 1990; Gordon, Benner, and Noddings 1996; Himmelweit 2000). This historical invisibility was continually affirmed in my conversations with family child care providers. Again and again they expressed real frustration and anger that their work was not perceived as "real work."

What are the responsibilities, demands, and challenges of family child care work? How do providers negotiate the competing demands of providing both paid and unpaid child care in their homes? And how do they mediate between their commitment to care (located in an ideology of the family) with their rights as paid workers (located in an ideology of the market)? My conversations with providers revealed that, regardless of racial ethnic identity, cultural identity, country of origin, and social class, the responsibilities that providers assume in the daily performance of their work are very similar. In addition, family child care providers, regardless of their social location, struggle with the ways in which idealized notions of work versus care and market versus family shape their work. These ideological constructions and their practical implications create both personal and structural conflicts for providers as they do their daily work of care. My goal is to make visible this daily work of family child care and, in so doing, enable us to move beyond conventional ideologies and understandings of work as an activity distinct from care and the family as a site distinct from the market.

THE WORK DAY

On a warm fall afternoon, I drive through Janice Newman's suburban neighborhood. Ranch-style homes and the large yards surrounding them are well maintained. Janice and I met two years earlier, when we served together on a statewide committee to review child care policies. Today she greets me warmly, and we walk up the stairs of her split-level home and through the living room, where the children's cots are set up. The children themselves have just finished eating lunch and are washing up and lying down for naps. Debbie, Janice's full-time assistant, takes care of their needs while Janice and I proceed to the kitchen for the interview. Her kitchen carries out the early-American decor evident throughout her home. And like the rest of her house, the kitchen is spotless. We settle down at the table and begin to talk.

Janice cares for fifteen children, twelve at any given time; they, like her, are Euro-American. The youngest child is Dena, eight months old. The oldest is Katie, nine years old. Janice watches Katie after school and has cared for her since she was an infant. Because Janice is a licensed provider and cares for more than six children at a time, she is required by state law to have an assistant. Debbie began working as Janice's assistant three years ago and hopes eventually to offer family child care in her own home. Before entering family child care fifteen years ago, Janice worked as a public school teacher for six years. She shares her home with her husband, who teaches and coaches in the public schools, and with their three children, ages seventeen, fourteen, and eleven.

Janice begins our interview by describing a typical work day. As I consider her morning, I am struck by the way in which the location of her home—her paid and unpaid workplace—shapes her daily work. Every day Janice rises and immediately begins the work of caring for her own children: helping them get ready for school, bathe, eat breakfast, and prepare their lunches. At the same time she prepares for the arrival of family child care children, getting their food ready. Her paid-care work day is interwoven with her unpaid care work for her own family members. Impressed by the similarity of the work tasks she engages in, I also become aware of her mental preparation, the anticipation and planning required before her formal work day of providing direct care for children begins. Janice describes her mornings:

> I get up at quarter to six. When I first get up in the morning, it's like going around and making sure my [own] kids are squared away. That they're getting ready for school. So we've already started that routine. And sorted out who's supposed to have a shower first. You know, make sure everybody's got their lunch packed. Pack them if they haven't. In the back of your mind, even though you haven't opened yet, you're already checking your menu to see what it was that you decided to have for breakfast that day. Organizing at what point you're going to need to start mixing up muffins [for the family child care children] or whether it's an easy day because you decided on cold cereal. You already probably have fielded one phone call prior to opening. That's a given. Because [parents] are giving you some details on what's going to happen for the day. Maybe Dad's going to bring them, and Mom normally does and wants to make sure I get the message. [You] change the sign-in sheet so that you've got a fresh page. That's pretty typical. You're already cooking and preparing.

Janice opens for business at 7:30 each weekday morning; as she reports, she opens later than most providers. Of the women I interviewed, most begin caring for children at 6:00 or 6:30 A.M. By adapting her hours to families' needs, Janice reflects a number of the qualities I found common among providers in their daily family child care work. First, providers appreciate and enjoy the flexibility and autonomy of establishing their own work hours and work practices. They contrast both the flexibility and autonomy they experience with the rigid schedules and routines of more institutional work settings. Second, even in the scheduling of the work day, providers respond to the needs of the families for whom they care in establishing and modifying the conditions of their paid work, including their hours. Third, family child care work requires a nearly invisible task: the work of listening, anticipating, and attending to the needs of others, both parents and children. As Janice says, "I do an awful lot of visiting with parents," "personal catching up," "sharing the news." Fourth, the most visible and most recognized components of child care work are caring for the material and physical needs of children.

> I open at 7:30. That's a luxury that I've taken upon myself this last year. I normally opened at 7:00. Many, many providers open at 6:30 or 7:00. The way my group worked out this year it wasn't necessary for anybody to be here before 7:30. . . . Kids start to arrive. I do an awful lot of visiting with parents about what's going to happen during the day. They'll tell me if the kids had a bad evening. They'll tell me if something happened. They'll tell me if the kids have learned something that they're anticipating doing in the future. But especially on Monday morning, there's a whole lot of personal catching up I need to do with the kids. . . . Typically by about quarter to eight I've got a good handle on who's called in and said they're not coming for breakfast. That kind of thing. And so I'm already well into cooking what I need to cook. And also in between cooking you might need to peel a child away from their parents because it's been a weekend and the child wanted to hang out one more day at home. [You] share the news. That kind of thing. At 8:00 Debbie is here, and breakfast is on the table. And everybody's washed up and eating.

People who have not provided or observed the work of caring for a group of small children have little reason to appreciate the organizational skills involved in the daily planning, preparation, and coordination of activities for twelve children. Janice describes one of her primary responsibilities as being a "facilitator all day"; we see that she facilitates not only activities but also reflection and decision making on the part of the children for whom she cares. Providers report that the time following breakfast is most often an activity time, and Janice discusses projects and activities she has planned (and anticipates) for the children.

[After breakfast] it's a matter of figuring out what direction we're going to go. Somebody might immediately say that they want to be at the table and do a game or a puzzle or something. And then some of them might want to do something more active. I just sort of facilitate where they're going to go and where they're going to be. And if we've got something planned to do, those that want to participate. They come up to the table. We've got some black cats that we're going to make tomorrow [for Halloween]. I've got a lot of little boys this year. And they might just rather do their motorcycles or something else. If you have a bunch of little girls that are three or four years old, they're a lot more likely to want to do that kind of [craft] stuff. There is a really broad spectrum [of activity]. If we're going outside, we tend to all go outside. I can't have three activities going at once. Two at once, we can handle that. But not three. . . . I find my role is, really, it's [being] a facilitator all day. It's like you might find a child sitting on the couch just doing nothing; and if they want to do nothing, that's fine. But sometimes it's a matter of they haven't thought about what their other options are.

Food preparation and feeding occurs again at mid-morning snack time. As Janice says, "You've got these little ones that can't make it [until noon]." Supervising children, suggesting activities, facilitating communication—all continue throughout the morning.

We usually start picking up, tidying up, simmering down around eleven or so. And we'll either have a book or a video or do music around then. And then Debbie can send [children] one at a time to wash up for lunch. That's the goal. And I'm typically in the kitchen cooking. . . . Lunch is at 11:30, quarter to twelve in day care homes. Some of the kids that I've set up at 11:30, they leave the table before noon. It's usually a pretty free play time [after lunch]. I try to put out things that are a little more relaxing, though. That are small motor. That are calmer. Maybe one of our finger plays. Maybe a book. Something quieter, though [because] at one o'clock it's nap time.

Although nap time is a quiet, restful time for the children, it is not relaxing for family child care providers. Again, while direct care for the physical and material needs of children is commonly recognized as the primary component of family child care, record keeping, meal planning, billing, and food preparation are also integral to family child care; and providers often do this work during nap time or in the evenings after their day of direct care for children is over.

> [Nap time] is not exactly down time. That's when we clean up the kitchen. Make sure kids have been signed in. Plan ahead on menus. Do my book work as far as payments. Make out bills as far as invoices to the parents. All of us [family child care providers] do that kind of stuff at nap time. We have to get all that paperwork kind of stuff done. And nap time is usually when you do it. Plus, you prepare snacks. That's a good time to get the cookies baked or the brownies or whatever it is you're going to do. So typically it's busy. . . . Kids start waking up about 2:30 or so. We wake the kids up by three unless they're infants. And then the kids usually get up and go to the bathroom. Wash up. And if there's any school kids, those kids come in around 3:30. And then we have snacks for everybody.

While Janice is clear about the skills and responsibilities that make up her family child care work (listening, facilitating, planning, preparing food), she also expresses an appreciation that "the whole is more than the sum of the parts." She views her work as contributing to the social fabric and quality of life. She speaks about why these daily tasks are important to her and how they form the social value of her work:

> [I appreciate] the opportunity to have some sort of impact on the kids as far as what they're going to be as people when they grow up. You can see when a child comes in and they're a year and a half, two years old, you can already see, sort of, the direction they're going. And sometimes you can put the skids on. Like, if they're turning into a real aggressive kid or they're turning into an uncaring kid because nobody's ever stopped and said, "I'm sorry. Did that hurt?" And you can see that you do make a difference. I think kids in family day care, with the mixed-age settings, learn what it's like to be a caring person—as they see you care. When we say to the kids, "That looks like a really fun game, but I'm afraid that you're going to get so excited and forget that Dena [an infant] is right there on the blanket, and you could just go flop and she'd be a pancake. And she'd be crying, and we'd all be sad." And maybe nobody's ever said anything about caring or watching out for a baby because they're the youngest. We've seen that we make a difference with a lot of these kids. That's the biggest thing. That you feel like you've made a difference to a child.

"Making a difference to a child" requires that the responsibilities of family child care include not only the child but also the child's family. While the "family" in "family child care" refers to the context of care, it is also an apt description of the recipients of care. As in the morning, at the end of the day providers spend significant time speaking with and listening to parents and their concerns regarding their children.

> About 4:30 is usually about the soonest [that parents arrive]. That's when you do a lot of talking to parents. Discussing some of the things you've been observing with the kids—behavior-wise, emotionally. What kind of a day [it was]. And I really feel that at the end of the day I enjoy talking to the parents. In the morning's it's typically just news. In the evenings—I don't know if the parents miss those kids during the day and are worrying about them or what. But the end of the day tends to be more of the counselor time. "I've noticed that John's been doing this," or "I've noticed that Molly's been doing this." And that's when you are the most tired [laughter] and when you're dealing with the biggest problems—at the end of the day. Because that's when [parents] want to talk. And they do tend to be more in depth.

Like the other women I interviewed, Janice stops providing direct care for children between 5:00 and 6:00 P.M. But even if parents pick up their children by 5:30, Janice's family child care work does not end then. Her end-of-day conversations with parents continue into the evening.

> If we're getting really in depth, I mean if I can't talk to [parents] real briefly, then I'll tell them, "Well, I'll call you this evening. What's a good time?" or "Call me tonight." So I'll let them know my schedule. I will typically talk to a parent each night. About things I've observed and things that I feel need to be done—that I think would be helpful. Or can they give me a clue of what's going on? Because I need help, too. I can't read the little guys' minds.

The women I interviewed noted that child care work expands beyond the time in which they provide direct care for children. As Janice says, "I need help, too" in order to understand the children and their needs. Getting this help involves the invisible work of planning and preparation as well as the education required of licensed providers: enrolling in early childhood education courses, talking with parents and other providers, and accessing resources available through community networks and government offices. In addition, on weekends and in the evenings providers shop for food and cook in preparation for the upcoming day and week of care and prepare and plan activities for the children. Thus, although providers report that their direct care ranges from nine to thirteen hours each day (with a median of eleven hours), their work day is actually much longer. Synthesizing the preparation, planning, and record keeping (reported at seven to ten hours a week) with the hours of providing direct care to children (a median of eleven hours), the women I interviewed reported a work week of family child care that ranged from sixty-two to sixty-five hours, a figure consistent with family child care providers nationwide (Center for the Childcare Workforce 2000, Haack 1998).

In describing a typical day of family child care work, Janice reflects what theorists of care work tell us: that care work incorporates a "double characteristic"—a combination of both feeling and doing (Cancian and Oliker 2000, Himmelweit 1999). Care work involves directly providing for the physical and material needs of others who are dependent—in Janice's case, young children who cannot provide for their own emotional and material needs. But caring involves more. Time and again, care work theorists tell us that care work is not something one does *to* another. Caring is not the "emotional servicing of people who remain strangers" (Himmelweit 1999, 35). Rather, caring exists in relationship. It involves sensitivity, being present and prepared to help, acting in the best interests of others, and fostering the independence and development of others (Tarlow 1996). The providers I interviewed commonly discussed this experience of family child care as both material and relational work involving the qualities inherent in each. Regardless of their cultural and racial ethnic identities and country of origin, regardless of their location in lower- or middle-income neighborhoods, providers described the tasks, skills, and responsibilities of family child care in similar terms.

We see these qualities reflected in Janice's work day. She provides for the physical and material needs of the children by preparing food, feeding, ensuring sufficient rest, and planning and coordinating activities. At the same time, her work clearly is relational. She speaks of listening and talking to parents about their concerns regarding their children and sharing with parents her own observations about their children. She speaks of attending to children's emotional and personal needs (for example, enabling them to "do nothing," to explore options, to play). And she also speaks of teaching children to understand their relationships to others and enabling them to value others—to become caring people.

CONFLICTING PERCEPTIONS OF THE VALUE OF CARE

Because she understands that her provision of family child care work requires education and skill and she views this work as having social value, Janice expresses frustration at how little respect society extends to family child care providers and their work. She is past president of the state's Association for Family Child Care and is active in policy discussions regarding family child care. She serves on local and state committees and testifies frequently before local and state legislative bodies regarding child care policy.

> I have the ability to present what I do with some sort of credibility outside of the child care community. . . . And I dislike having to defend this as a profession. And I *do* defend it. It's really hard to have credibility and respect. I see it when I go to the legislature. I see it when I go talk to the fire marshals. I see it in any sort of professional setting. Say I'm going to an attorney's. I went to a meeting with a local government association. And I mean, it was like I had to try to make sure that I was coming across with big words because they would constantly dip down like they thought they needed to get down to my level so I would understand. And yes, educated people do choose to do this. And I was real irritated with it. And I get a lot of that at the legislature.

When I asked Janice to explain, she said, "When they're trying to make a point and explain things to me, they assume they have to [she begins speaking in a slow, soft voice] explain things and lean forward and talk a little bit slower to me so I'll get it. And I just—it's *very* frustrating. It's just an attitude. And maybe it's just because you're a woman. Maybe it's got nothing to do with child care."

Like Janice, other family child care providers told me of the anger and frustration they felt when they and their work were devalued. Nearly every provider used phrases such as "no respect," "no dignity," and "a stigma" to describe the public perception of and response to their family child care work. Jennie Davis, an African American provider who has worked in the field for three years, is clear about her commitment to family child care work and its public value.

> Children are my passion. And this is my way of [being] the nurturer. Because the children are just like your own children. The difference is that they go home every day. The difference is that you're with them eight, nine, and ten hours a day. You know, you teach them everything. You teach them to wash their hands. You teach them how to brush their teeth. You teach them to be independent, which means picking up toys and putting everything back. You potty-train them. You teach them etiquette. You teach them social skills—how to get along with everybody and respect everybody. So [family child care] is my way of teaching.
>
> And it's such a *joy* to see it when they learn something. You know, you're teaching them their ABCs. You're teaching them how to count. You're teaching them colors, shapes. [Family child care providers are] teaching. We're also mothers. We're their friend. There's a whole gamut that people don't even look at. They look at us as babysitters. And there's a *lot* more to it than that.

Like Janice, Jennie views her work as having public value and importance. These women believe that teaching and socializing children through developmentally appropriate activities is skilled work that is worthy of respect. Yet family child care providers consistently speak of the lack of respect and value their work garners. As a licensed family child care provider who offers government-subsidized care for children from low-income families, Jennie has contact with not only parents but also a variety of government personnel. Her experience teaches her that "the home day care providers do not get respect from the state, from social workers, or parents. The only ones who respect us are the children."

"Why don't people respect family child care providers?" I ask.

"Because they still have a mentality that we're babysitters. It's an *old* stigma. They think that we're just sitting here babysitting and watching TV. And this work is a *long* ways from that. Trust me!

It's much more in depth than *I* realized until I got in it. You're on your feet twelve hours a day—all day. [But] they just don't think that we're doing anything. I just really resent that. I really do."

The women I spoke with all discussed this issue as one of the primary difficulties they experience in their family child care work: the conflict between their own perception of their work and the public perception of it. They believe that family child care work requires skill and involves a high degree of responsibility. They believe that their work contributes to the development of healthy children and, as such, that it has social value. But their daily experiences testify to a "lack of credibility," "no professional recognition," "low prestige," and "low wages." One of the primary dilemmas we face as citizens is this disparity between the lack of public value accorded to child care work and our dependence on providers for the care, education, and socialization of our children.

Despite the clear social and economic need for child care, providers earn one-half as much as other comparably educated women (Whitebook et al., 1993, 1998). In our conversations, providers offered their analyses of the source of the low public value accorded to their work. As Jennie says, "People have a mentality that we're just sitting here babysitting." And although Janice says, "Maybe it's just because you're a woman. Maybe it's got nothing to do with child care," we know that child care is historically identified as women's work. To separate the two (women's work and child care) is to fly in the face of both historical and contemporary ideals and practices that identify women with care yet devalue care.

The devaluation of women's care work and the concurrent devaluation of care workers are linked to historical ideologies regarding work (Gordon 1990a, Daniels 1987). Definitions of work, as we know them in the contemporary United States, are rooted in the political theoretical tradition of Jeremy Bentham, J. S. Mill, and John Locke: the philosophy of liberal individualism (Macpherson 1990). Liberal individualism provides us with the ideology of the rational economic man who is the idealized actor in both the market economy and the polity. Feminist theorist Suzanne Gordon (1996) summarizes the characteristics of the rational economic man and liberal individualism, which "base individual identity and worth on the possession of individual rights and property; emphasize the pursuit of success and power in the marketplace; promote self-control through psychological, social and political theories that stress disengagement from others and radical self-reliance and autonomy; and contain only the most limited concepts of moral obligation to those others who might pose pressing claims on the self" (258).

In summary, the rational economic man is an inherently self-centered and independent individual seeking to satisfy his own needs at the expense of others—the very qualities needed to compete and succeed in the market economy. This ideal of the rational economic man sets up a dualistic model of work and worth. Work, associated with the extrinsic rewards of prestige, power, and financial gain in the marketplace, is constructed to exist in contrast to care, a gendered and racialized "natural" feminine activity. The ideal of the rational economic man exists in opposition to that of the emotional relational woman, and care is defined as something other than work. Within this ideological bifurcation, attention to the needs of others and facilitating the development of another (that is, the activity of care) can only hinder one's individualistic and autonomous pursuit of financial success and power in the market economy. As such, the work of care is devalued because it restricts the rational, market-oriented individual from competition and success.

As a result of such ideologies, child care lacks status and value, even when it becomes paid work. This lack of value is demonstrated most clearly in its low wages. Just as two-thirds of child care workers nationwide earn below poverty-level wages (Whitebook and Phillips 1999), fully two-thirds of the women I interviewed earned wages well below the poverty threshold. The most common theory used to explain the low wages of care workers generally and child care workers in particular is human capital theory, which considers low wages to be a result of a perceived lack of skills required to perform child care labor. This explanation is clearly linked to liberal political philosophy—its lack of recognition of care as skilled work and subsequently its devaluation of those who provide care.

Gendered ideologies associated with care and work identify women as naturally nurturant with an instinctive ability to care. In addition, cultural stereotypes of women of color as more emotional, loving, and less skilled than whites also contribute to the devaluation of work (Cancian and Oliker 2000, Glenn 2000, Romero 2002). Since (the argument goes) no education, training, or formal skill are needed to perform child care work, low wages are to be expected. Such arguments have long been debunked by analyses of comparable worth in which established job evaluation techniques are used to assess the skill levels required in jobs. Jobs are evaluated using techniques that control for education, experience, cognitive and physical demands of the job, and the sex composition of the occupation. Those jobs determined to have comparable levels of skill (that is, comparable worth) are then compared to determine whether salaries are equitable. Are similar salaries paid in occupations that require comparable skill levels? Consistently these studies confirm the political nature of skill. Jobs in which the majority of workers are women, even if they are evaluated as being of comparable worth to jobs held by men, offer significantly lower wages (Remick 1984). Uniformly, these studies demonstrate that jobs requiring greater nurturance and caring skills are penalized when it comes to wages (England and Folbre 2002). Paula England (1992) has come to call this phenomenon "the care penalty"—a net wage penalty of between twenty-four cents and $1.71 an hour that is directly associated with caring occupations. Together, the gendered and racialized composition of the child care work force, the ideologies associated with care, and the perceived lack of skill required in the provision of care play a role in the low wages of care workers, including child care providers (Nelson 2001). Ideologies that bifurcate care and work and associate them as gendered and racialized activities contribute to the social devaluation of child care providers and their work and subsequently to the economic devaluation and low wages paid to women who undertake the work. This devaluation, in turn, contributes to the "care gap"—the difference between the low value assigned to care workers and the high dependency we as citizens have on care providers. It is care providers who pay the price for this gap, which is filled largely by providers through their low wages and long hours.

THE CHALLENGE OF SYNTHESIZING IDEOLOGIES AND PRACTICES OF THE FAMILY AND THE MARKET

Clearly, the bifurcated ideologies of care and work present real challenges for family child care providers, ideologically, economically, and politically. Family child care providers live and work on the boundaries, in the intersection, between the historically dichotomous worlds of the family and the market. For providers, the work of family child care is a continuous negotiation between the meanings and practices historically associated with the dominant ideology of the family (relationship and care) and the meanings and practices historically associated with the market (competition and contracts). As a result, providers experience a conflict between their responsibilities as caregivers and their rights as paid workers.

While family child care workers provide care (work historically identified with women) and do so within their own homes (the historical site of women's unwaged care), they do so for pay. As such, they challenge the ideology that child care is unwaged activity motivated by women's love for children. Nonetheless, the struggle between the seemingly dualistic values of love and money is an ongoing one in the daily lives and work of family child care providers. Quite literally, they pay the price for this conflict between love and money, not only economically (in the form of the care penalty) but also emotionally and materially. These conflicts emerge from the empathy experienced by providers for the families for whom they care and the exploitation they experience as a result of both empathetic relationships and ongoing ideologies regarding women's care work.

Elena Molinero, a Mexicana and a family child care provider for the past eight years, is the mother of four children who range in age from twelve to seventeen years. Before entering family child care, she worked as a seasonal agricultural worker in local orchards, "thinning apples and picking apples. . . . Then in the packing shed for another five years." As a mother who worked for pay outside the home, Elena was a child care consumer before she became a provider. Thus, she understands the concerns of parents in need of child care and empathizes with mothers who entrust their children to the care of another in order to engage in paid work: "I know how it feels to give your kids to somebody else." Elena's enjoyment of her family child care work and her empathy for parents reflect the experiences of other providers I interviewed. Their relationships with children and their empathy with parents are the source of both significant challenges and primary rewards.

As providers spoke with me, I was struck by the seeming contradictions within their daily work. The very aspect of the work that proved most rewarding and engaging to the providers—relationship—proved the most challenging as well. While providers experienced the greatest rewards in their relationships with children, relationships with parents produced the greatest conflict. The tension between advocating for their own needs and rights as paid workers and the needs of the children and families for whom they cared was also a primary conflict. In addition, offering paid care in their own homes at times seemed to compromise the unpaid care they provided for their own family members.

Relationships with Children

Consistently, the providers I interviewed reported that their relationships with children were the greatest reward in their work. In fact, when asked what they liked most about their work, well over half of the women responded immediately with a phrase relating to the kids. Kay Schilling, a Euro-American and a licensed family child care provider for eleven years, has completed her child development associate certification and is working to complete her A.A. degree in early childhood education. When I asked, "What do you like most about family child care?" she thought for a moment before answering, "Playing with the kids. There's the moments that it's just fun with the kids. And it makes you feel lighthearted about life. It reminds you to stop and look. You know, if you look at the world through a child's eyes, it's a lot of fun."

Other providers, while not engaging in a direct analysis of why they enjoyed children, nonetheless spoke clearly on the topic. "I've always loved kids. I can't explain it any other way," says Annette Bradley, an African American family child care provider. Similarly, Isabel Inofuentes, a Mexicana provider, spoke of the affection she receives from and gives to the children and of the relationship she developed with a particular child.

> I like the job. I like the children. I like to be with the children. . . . It is rewarding when I'm in town and the children are with their parents. They see me, and they come to give me a hug. And when their parents come to pick them up, they don't want to go home with their parents. They want to stay here. "No, mama. No home. Stay with Nana," they say. They call me Nana because

they can't say Isabel. You get attached to them. I had a little boy through DSHS [Washington State's Department of Social and Health Services] named Robert who I cared for. He was really little. And the mother left the child. She left him with her father. But the grandfather had to work and couldn't take care of Robert. So he left him here, day and night, and I watched him. He paid me. DSHS paid me during the day, and the grandfather paid me for the night care. I got really attached to Robert.

Paula Shelton, coordinator of the state-funded Seasonal Child Care Program through which Isabel provides care and a friend of Isabel's for several years, spoke about Isabel's relationship with Robert. "She got really attached to that kid, I remember. He was like one of the family. And she loved him. She wanted to adopt him real bad. She got *really* attached to him. . . . Then they decided to take the boy. The grandfather moved to Oregon, so he took Robert with him. He took the little boy and moved over there, and it was really hard on Isabel."

Here, we begin to see the ways in which, for family child care providers themselves, the boundaries between paid and unpaid care become obscured through relationship. While Isabel provided paid care for Robert, she also developed a personal and emotional attachment to him. In accordance with market norms, her relationship with Robert was a market exchange: a rational exchange of money for care. But while the relationship began as a paid care relationship, it grew into something more. This is common in paid care work because "the process of caring is itself the development of a relationship" (Himmelweit 1999, 29). Care is always more than simply doing. It is more than instrumental. Care is also feeling. As a result, in the parlance of market ideology, paid care work is an oxymoron. Caring, which involves relationship and attachment, is antithetical to market notions of the dichotomy between work and care, between reason and emotion.

While rationality and autonomy are assumed and valued in the market economy, relationship and attachment are the norms associated with the world of families. Therefore, the challenges of doing paid care work are especially heightened for family child care providers whose site of paid care is their own families. Because of its location within families, the ideals of relationship and reciprocity associated with families are central to the work of family child care and are especially important to providers. Although the women I interviewed asserted their identities as paid, professional care providers, the frequency with which they described their emotional attachment with children was common. Given the women's experience of family child care as an occupational and professional identity, I was struck by the frequency with which they used the language of family to describe their paid work relationships and the regularity with which many equated their work with mothering.

Valerie Holton has provided child care for fifteen years in her suburban home. An African American woman who is working to complete her A.A. degree in early childhood education, she spoke about her relationships with the children for whom she cares:

> And these children, they are close to you. You're like a second mom to them. And you being there when they come home after school—you listen to the different little things they want to talk with you about. It becomes a personal thing. Where, you know, they can't get to Mom right away. But they can get to you. And it's nice to have those conversations. And it's nice to be able to be trusted by these children. I think that's real important. If a child feels that he can trust you. And he can talk to you. And you're there for him. That's a *big* plus.

In ways similar to Valerie's, Laura Mayfield spoke of the children for whom she cares as "like my own kids." Laura is a Euro-American who has been providing state-subsidized, licensed family child care in her low-income rural community for eleven years. When I asked what she liked most about family child care, she responded, "Being with kids. . . . It sure ain't for the money because you don't make that much. But I think all kids need someone that they can depend on. Get the love that they're not getting at home when their parents are both working. Instead of running up and down the streets. There's too many of them kids that's left out there like that. They're like my own kids. And I try to teach them like I did my daughter."

Like Laura, Segunda Cortez, a Mexicana who has provided family child care for eight years, told me, "I like children. I have children that I have cared for a long time. To me, they are like my own children." This practice of equating their family child care work with mothering by many (but not all) providers should come as no surprise. As Barbara Tarlow (1994) tells us, social perceptions of caring have become so closely identified with family life that "caring as experienced in family life has come to act as the metaphor and standard for all forms of caring" (56). While likening their work to mothering is common among providers (Fitz Gibbon 2001, Nelson 1990), using the metaphor of family and kinship and words such as "love" to describe their work relationships is common among other sorts of paid care workers as well (Stone 2000).

Although not all providers I interviewed likened their paid child care work to mothering, all spoke about their long-term commitment to and emotional connections with the children for whom they cared. And whether or not they liken their work to mothering, the emotional attachments that providers establish in paid care work blur the perceived dualistic distinction between private, emotional, home-based caring relationships and public, formal, workplace professional relationships.

Relationships with Parents

When I asked each provider, "What do you like least about family child care work?" their most consistent response was "parents." The most common concern they related about parents was labor exploitation: attempts to extract additional hours of labor without paying for them (such as parents who continually arrive late to pick up their children). Isabel Isofuentes reported, "Sometimes the parents do not pick up their children on time. I want to go buy something at the store, and they don't get here till late. And by the time I get to the store it's closed." Gloria Zuñiga, a Mexicana who has provided licensed home-based care for four years, described what she likes least about her work: "The parents get off work, go home, and rest for a while. Then they come and pick up their kids later. Sometimes I don't mind, but sometimes I have an appointment or something." Brenda Beall, a Euro-American and a provider of care for nine years in her suburban neighborhood, reported, "There's a lot of parents that like to go shopping and go home after work and then come back [to pick up their children from child care]. I have a lot of that. . . . And you're at a point where you don't want the children in your home more than ten hours. There's no need for it. . . . I have a contract that says I work ten hours."

Brenda went on to tell about her confrontation with one mother who consistently violated the contracted agreement for ten hours of care per day: "I even took a self-esteem class to *boost* me to be able to talk [to her]. But, she came back with "Well, I'm sorry. I'm not going to pay you overtime. And I would hate to take little Johnny out of here just because I'm an hour late." I asked Brenda how she responded to this statement by the mother.

> I said, "I really love your little guy, but we *have* to stick to [the contract]." And she said, "Fine." So the last three days she's been right on time. But the first day she was testing me again by saying, "I would *hate* to take him out because you don't want to keep him over ten hours." So my perfect answer was "Well, do what you feel you have to, but I think you can come back here within ten hours." So far everything is working.

The threat of the mother to remove her child from Brenda's care reflects, in a very overt form, one of the primary difficulties inherent in selling child care labor. While providers are conscious of selling their labor, the emotional attachments that emerge in care work increase the complexity of the market exchange. But despite the complexity that ensues, both parents and child care providers typically assume that emotional attachment is central to the work of child care (Hertz 1997, Nelson 1990, Uttal and Tuominen 1999). Providers of in-home child care report strong emotional attachments with the children (Macdonald 1996), including "highly motivated caregivers [who] themselves describe the work as something that should be done only by those who love children" (Wrigley 1995, 86). Wrigley goes on to state that parents "expect an emotional investment for a small salary. Parents look for caregivers who put children first and money second" (86). Herein, we find another dynamic common in the provision of family child care. Counting on providers' emotional attachment to their children, some parents seek to extract additional low-wage or unpaid labor from providers. And the centrality of relationship, as we soon see, causes providers themselves to violate their contracts to meet the needs of the children and families for whom they care.

Providers' Responses to Families' Needs

While reporting frustration with parents, many providers simultaneously described a genuine concern for many of the families they serve. Their commitment to the work of care and the relationships that are inherent in such work create a tension for providers between caring for families and setting limits to protect and care for oneself. According to Valerie Holton, different providers address this tension in different ways.

> And in this last class I found that it's important for us as providers to set goals—to help parents be educated toward children and play. There's just a lot of things that we can do as providers to help parents out. . . . Me, myself, I'm into the kids and into the parents. I reach out there. I like to reach out. And sometimes I know if a parent is misusing me. But if I know it's a parent that's struggling and catching buses, I'm very lenient because I believe in helping the other person. And well, I'm not into child care for gung-ho being rich. I know that these kids benefit from my care. And I'm like, "What is thirty minutes?" It's not every day. And I don't mind. Where other providers say, "Oh, no. No way."

Valerie wants to "help parents out" and is willing to be somewhat flexible in her hours of care, depending on parents' needs. Thus, the exploitation of providers by parents (discussed previously) takes an interesting turn when providers themselves violate the terms of their contracts to meet the needs of families.

A sizable number (one-third) of the family child care providers I interviewed reported consciously choosing to alter the rates they charged for care to help meet the financial needs of the families they served. When asked how she sets her rates, Annette Bradley, who provides unlicensed child care to subsidize her public assistance grant explained, "With Dominique, we started out with $300 a month, but I went ahead and went down to $150" [laughter].

"Were you caring less for him?" I asked.

"No. His mom is trying to move. And she's trying to sell all the furniture and trying to get all the bills paid before she leaves, so—." Here, Annette, who herself lives below the poverty level, reduces her own wages out of empathy to assist another member of her community. Similarly, Allie McGinnis, a Euro-American unlicensed provider, told about her process for determining the rates she charged for care: "It was negotiated. It fluctuated. Especially with the two single moms—depending on what was happening with them financially."

In addition to adjusting their rates based on families' financial circumstances, providers reported additional changes they made to their contracts in order to respond to families' needs. Patricia James, an African American and a licensed provider for eight years, reported:

> I prefer parents to drop off and pick up their own children. I have a mother at the present time who's having car trouble, and in order for her to get the kids here, I have to go and pick them up and bring them down, or else we'd have to look at her looking for other child care. And she thinks it's a temporary situation, and so I'm willing to work with her for a month. It's strenuous, you know, to have to do that. . . . It's taken a lot out [of me] right now. But we're doing it.

By increasing their work responsibilities and reducing their rates, providers such as Patricia, Annette, and Allie step in to fill the care gap between parents' need for child care and the limited resources (both money and time) available to devote to care.

These providers clearly experience a conflict in constructing their care relationships as formal and contractual market exchanges. Those I interviewed were conscious of their identity as workers and professionals worthy of respect and a living wage. At the same time, they empathized with the struggles faced by other employed mothers and, as a result, reported difficulty in enforcing the terms of their contracts. This conflict demonstrates the real struggle providers experience between their roles as paid workers and as empathetic caregivers.

The relational connections that providers experience with children and families are, however, different from the "emotional labor" described by Arlie Hochschild (1983) in her analysis of the centrality of emotion in paid service work. While Hochschild defines emotional labor, in part, as the creation of "a publicly observable facial and bodily display" (7), the emotional qualities of family child care work, as described by the providers, appears to go beyond the display of emotions she elucidates. In contrast, providers report a genuine attachment that complicates a straightforward exchange of their labor for wages. In the case of those I interviewed, emotional connections with children increased providers' willingness to violate their own contracts and working agreements; and they did so by providing additional and unwaged labor that they believed would benefit both children and families.

In her study of family child care Margaret Nelson (1990) acknowledges that "the challenge for these workers is to find a way to dampen acknowledged affections, to make their feelings appropriate to the structural conditions of their work" (110). She coined the term *detached attachment* to describe the tension they experience in the provision of paid care, and it accurately describes the experiences of the women with whom I spoke. Detached attachment means that, even though attachment persists (and is desired by providers), paid providers create a space that keeps them from developing an overwhelming attachment to the children they care for. It enables women to maintain the dance, the balance, between paid market exchanges and caring relationships with children and families.

Although relationship and emotional attachment are central to family child care work, providers' relationships with children and emotional attachment to them must always be balanced with the material and economic reality that providers are paid workers. While they liken their work to mothering they are not, in this case, mothers; and their relationships with children can be terminated at any time by parents who seek paid care elsewhere. Once again, providers find themselves caught between the boundaries of market and family norms; and they struggle to balance the norms of care in relationship with the norms of a market exchange. In discussing a typical day of family child care work, Janice Newman explicitly acknowledges both the importance of and the challenge to providers of maintaining this balance. She asserts that family child care providers need to learn to establish boundaries in providing care to children and families and reflects on the challenges of negotiating with parents regarding children's and families' needs.

> So you really have to be a diplomat. You really do. And the survivors [among providers] learn that skill. And you *also* need to learn when to cut it off. In terms of "I no longer have ownership of this. I've told you. I'm really sorry that you're stressed out at work, but you need to take control of this. I'm doing what I can in day care. You now need to handle it at home." . . . It's rough. But you do learn that at some point, even though you feel bad, parents still have to be responsible for those kids. And you have to learn to turn it off. But it's hard sometimes.

The ability to establish limits within relationships is difficult in care work, which synthesizes concern for others with fostering their well-being (Waerness 1996). Identified as a relational process that involves both reciprocity and putting others' needs before your own (Tarlow 1996), paid care work flies in the face of conventional theories of paid labor that identify the worker as a rational, economic actor whose sole motivation is extrinsic, material gain. Personal attachments do develop in market relationships. And family child care providers experience the struggle of balancing a commitment to caring for others with the need to acknowledge and advocate for their own needs.

THE CHALLENGES OF BLENDING PAID WORK, HOME, AND FAMILY

Although establishing emotional boundaries is a challenge for all paid care workers, it is a particular challenge for family child care providers, whose workplace is also their home. For them, establishing boundaries between home and family is difficult at best. As I interviewed family child care providers, I became increasingly aware of the challenges of simultaneously providing unpaid care for one's own family while providing paid care for the families of others. Again, providers experience the complexities that arise when the historically bifurcated worlds of care and work, of families and the market meet and merge. In this case, providers experience this synthesis in the form of tensions that arise between their two arenas of care.

All of the providers I interviewed entered family child care to support their families financially. (See chapters 3 and 4 for a more detailed discussion of this process.) At the same time, they appreciated and valued the opportunity to be available to their own children while engaged in family child care work. Patricia James is the mother of three children. Her youngest son is six years old and, as Patricia says, "was born into the day care." She was providing family child care at the time he was born and has continued to do so since his birth. I asked her what she liked about family child care.

> You can be with your own kids. You can watch your own kids. And then watching them get attitudes. They get kind of jealous of all the kids loving you. And my littlest son, he says, "I don't like it when you let the other kids do this and have my stuff." Or "You hold that baby too long" [laughter]. Or little things like that. . . . [But] I give him his special moments. I give him his

special times. As I said, I allow him to crash on my private time, too. We read that extra story or get that extra hug . . . because I know he's sharing. And then I talk to him. I say, "I know you have to share Mommy right now. But when all these kids go home, then you won't have to share Mommy. Mommy will be just here for you."

Although Patricia appreciates being available to care for her own son, she recognizes the challenges inherent in sharing her care with her own child while caring for the children of others. Other providers spoke about these challenges and the drain they experience as a result of blending their paid work with unwaged care for their own families. Julia Deavers, a Euro-American provider, voiced her struggle in caring for her own children after a day of caring for the children of others. In our interview, I asked, "You mentioned your own two children. When do you have time to be with your family?"

It's a struggle. It's a real struggle. It's a real dichotomy because I got into day care so that I could stay with my kids. And . . . over four years of experience what I realize is that it's a real blessing up until my own children are about three [years old]. And then I find that I'm at the short end of the stick. I mean, I see that the other parents, having been out to work all through the day, they come home refreshed—fresh and really ready to see their kids and happy to see their kids. And they have the weekends to spend with their kids. And it's real quality time. But for me, all these kids leave, and my own kids want attention. I can barely give it to them because I'm so saturated with kids. And so my need for personal time extends into their, supposedly, time with just me. And so it's been a real struggle.

Julia articulates the conflicts that providers experience when the responsibilities and site of paid work intersect with the responsibilities and site of their family life. While parental involvement in family child care is important and valued by providers, their home becomes an "open book." Even though family child care makes it possible for them to be with their own children, providers express concern that their own children's care may at times be compromised. What appears, at first glance, to be an opportunity to remain available to one's own family can prove to be one of the most complex elements of family child care work.

Sometimes providers report that their own children resent the other children in the house and that family members resent disruption caused by paid child care (Hofferth and Kisker 1991). Not only is family child care disruptive for family members, but providers themselves report powerlessness and frustration when they are unable to effectively synthesize caring for their own family members while caring for others' children (Rutman 1996). While both home- and center-based child care workers must balance their home and family responsibilities (Kontos 1992; Nelson 1988, 1990; Saraceno 1984), this struggle is most pronounced among family child care providers, whose work challenges the supposed split between work and family, between public and private.

This historical, ideological, public-private dichotomy fails to recognize that work might straddle or even synthesize those boundaries, but family child care is one such form of work. As such, the work of family child care not only reveals the inaccuracy of the public-private and work-family dichotomies but also enables us to explore the tensions that exist when the ideologies and practices associated with the market economy collide with those historically associated with families and households.

THE VALUE OF CARE IN A FAMILY SETTING

The providers I interviewed consistently spoke of the benefits they experienced because their paid care work was located within their own homes. This location facilitated flexibility and creativity in the care offered, qualities providers valued and believed to be lacking in more routine institutional care. Valerie Holton spoke of these intersecting qualities of flexibility and creativity as well as the autonomy she exercises in her work. She acknowledged, however, a tension in that autonomy. I asked her what she enjoyed most about the work.

> What I like most is you can set your own pace. You can set up things the way that you want to have them set up according to whatever type of children you have at that time. And I think that's important. Whereas if you're working in a day care center, you have to go by whatever *they* want you to do. [At home] you can do things the way that you want to do things. Being your own boss. To a *degree*. Sometimes I look at that, and it depends

what kind of parents you've got. Because they're actually the boss. Sometimes you forget that you're working for them. You're working for yourself, but you're working for the parents to please them and see that things are set up and things are going in the right direction.

Although Janice Newman reported a similar conundrum in her family child care work she, too, appreciates her autonomy. In particular, she contrasted the constraints she experienced as a public school teacher in an institutional setting with the flexibility she experiences in family child care—and the quality of care that results. I asked her why she continued in family child care after fifteen years as a licensed provider.

I like my independence. Which is a real conundrum as far as talking about family child care. Because you're independent, but you're not free [laughter]. You're not. I mean, I am more free because I have somebody working for me now [her assistant Debbie]. I enjoy the independence. I like being my own boss. I like deciding what is going to happen. I like the flexibility in schedules. The independence is wonderful. I enjoy working with the kids, as I did with school. But it's just different. There's more nurturing going on in family child care than in school. . . . In family child care you're so involved with their daily lives, and you watch all their little triumphs. You watch them go from infant to achieving walking. It's like you raise a lot of kids. And I enjoy that a lot. In school I enjoyed teaching the skills. I enjoyed watching the personalities emerge among those kids. But the sad part was that I didn't have them long enough to make a really big impact on them. . . . [In family child care] I let these kids be kids. And I enjoy being able to do that. When you're teaching school, all the basic insecurities and the sad things, they're set with those kids. And in family day care you can really make a difference. A huge difference. Because you're just one-on-one with those kids all day long. And if you're got a kid that's a Nervous Nellie, you can help get them over it. And there's all kinds [of kids] out there. They're scared. They're nervous. Happy. And some of them are clowns. And you encourage it. You let them be that way. You can't *have* a big clown in your classroom [laughter]. It's very disruptive. So I guess that's why I like it. I know that I make a difference. And I was frustrated with teaching as far as being able to make a difference. . . . They don't get to just *live* at school. They have things they *have* to do and all this stuff. But when they're in child care they just sort of live here all day [laughter].

Julia Deavers recounted beliefs similar to both Valerie's and Janice's: valuing the opportunity to provide personal and individualized care to children through family child care. When I asked what she enjoyed most about the work, she affirmed, "What I like most is that I can make it up. That I can create it. That it can be changed in a moment. I can change my mind. That I'm the one saying that we can be spontaneous. If it's a sunny day, we can go outside. Get on our bikes and go to the park, if they want. That kids can play in the swimming pool. I like that it's a home."

"And does that it's a home relate to the spontaneity?" I asked. "Are those related to each other?"

"Yeah," Julia explained. "That the kids can still be *kids*. And that they're not funneled off into a regimented program."

When I asked Julia why she stayed in family child care, she expanded on the importance of the flexibility and nurturance she provides in family-based care and contrasted it with center-based care.

> First off, I believe that family child care is the way to go in terms of child care. That putting children in centers at this young, young, age is—personally, I don't like the institutionalization of it. I don't like the fact that kids are corralled off into their own age groups. Here's the two-year-olds. Here's the three-year-olds. Here's the four-year-olds. And also centers, because of the volume, the number of kids, they *really* have to put in a lot of structure. And they're so focused on liability that [it's like] kids are in school. They're institutionalized from a very young age. And so my own belief is that kids, at this young age, need to be in a home. They need to still be in the structure of a family. And so I've continued doing [family child care] because I *believe* in it. I *believe* in family home day care.

Consistently, the providers with whom I spoke affirmed the distinction between family child care and more institutionalized forms of child care (such as care in centers) located within the formal market economy. They confirm that the organizational context, the setting in which care occurs, affects the care process—be it care in households, in the marketplace, or in bureaucratic settings governed by market principles (Fisher and Tronto 1990). Care located within the home draws on values and practices of kinship and community and can "lead to a relatively integrated caring process" and put women in a "relatively empowered position"

(46). The providers I interviewed invoked family ideologies identified with household and family settings and felt themselves to be in a "relatively empowered position" in the performance of their daily work, experiencing autonomy, creativity, and flexibility.

The organizational context of providing paid care within a family is central for family child care providers who, upon entering the work, identify a primary goal of providing a warm and loving environment (Hofferth and Kisker 1991). Providers' vision of good care is care in a homelike atmosphere. "[Children] should be at home here," one provider observed (Nelson 1990, 82). These values and practices are pivotal to the care that the women I interviewed seek to provide, and they stand in sharp contrast to the values and practices the providers identify with more bureaucratized forms of care in centers. Annette Bradley worked in a child care center before becoming a family child care provider. When I asked her what she liked most about family child care, she responded, "Well, giving it a home. Giving other children a home environment instead of that day care [center] where everything has to be set . . . [where] everything is structured. This way the children seem more comfortable to me. More at home." Segunda Cortez explained, "I want this to be like a family, not like a business."

Martha Buxton, a Euro-American, worked as a teacher in the public schools for five years before becoming a family child care provider. Although she is an unlicensed provider, she is familiar with the regulations that licensed providers are required to follow. "I know you can have up to eight children in a setting like this, but I choose not to," she reported. When I asked why she limits the number of children she cares for to four, she spoke of the more personalized care, the increased individual attention that she can provide in a home setting that serves a limited number of children.

> To me, [having more than four children] is not a whole lot different than having them in KinderCare, where there's a whole ton of children, a hassled day care person, or whatever. . . . With family care I see more time for individual attention. More time for hugging and loving and for them to get to know one person [and] my family, as opposed to a whole stack of different people who are there. With [fewer] children it's more like brothers and sisters as opposed to [the] many, many children that [center providers] have to deal with. Or to not deal with. And they can nap here, and sometimes in day care centers it's impossible to

have naps or quiet time. [Here] they can go sit by themselves if they need to or want to. [Here] it's more like a family setting.

I asked how she would characterize center care as opposed to family care.

Probably more of a school-type setting [in centers] with more emphasis with the older children on activities. More learning and teaching just to keep them busy. And I see a problem of having so many children in one space. And everything scheduled. "Now we're going to do this. Whether you want to do this or not, we need to clean up. It's time for lunch. And it's time for potty. And you have to wash your hands now." You know, things they have to do to keep order.

Cora Jenkins, an African American provider, was quick to voice concern regarding relationships and staffing in center-based care. "That's one part of [center-based] day care I've never liked is that fact that people aren't concerned enough about who's handling that child and how often. Is it five or six people handing the child? Or is there just one main person who takes care of that child? I think children need that [one main person] because not only do they need to bond with their parents, they need a type of bonding with their caregiver."

Providers believe that, in contrast to family child care, care provided in centers often reflects and re-creates an exchange mentality and a bureaucratic model of caring. While all paid child care work incorporates some characteristics of each location, different organizational contexts both enable and reinforce differing care values and practices. And research confirms that child care in centers more fully approximates a school setting in which care is associated with teaching, the day is fragmented into structured activities, and a form of deskilling creates an organizational hierarchy among staff (head teachers, teaching assistants) (Fitz Gibbon 2002).

Individual attention. Quiet time. Interaction with a limited number of people. Long-term relationships. These are all qualities that family child care providers value and see as essential to their provision of care. Sharon Fleming describes how her understanding of the value of family child care has grown as she takes college courses in early childhood education and gains experience as a provider.

> Just going to school, I feel really confident in having [an] in-home [child care]. Because at this age, this is what they need. They need to be at home. They need a home environment. And I can feel good about offering this. At first I was kind of shy: "Well, this is just an in-home [child care]. But now I can say, "I'm an in-home day care. They're going to get a home atmosphere. Give them one-on-one. Give them more attention. . . . It's mixed-age group. . . . Because it's a small home, they're like brothers and sisters." And I feel it's very important for them. They don't need a structured school classroom. They need a home. I feel good about that.

The development of relationship is integral to the work of caring, so the routine and rigidity often required in paid employment is less effective and hence less evident in care work (Himmelweit 1999, Stone 1998). Because of the flexibility and relationship required in good care and family child care providers' perception of the increased availability of these qualities in a family setting, these providers clearly distinguish between the care they are able to provide in a home environment and the quality of care they believe is available to children in more structured and institutional settings.[2] Family child care providers locate their descriptions and the importance of their paid care in a discourse of values and practices ideologically associated with women in families: nurturance, relationship, flexibility, attentiveness. In so doing, they draw on these ideologies as a way of claiming the value of their care work. Their paid child care is valuable *because* of its location in families and the caring practices associated with and believed to be derived from a family setting. For these providers, family child care has increased market value because of the qualities they associate with care in a family environment.

In contrast, for the public and for parents, family child care providers' choice to frame their child care work in the language of home and family may result in a devaluation of the work. When child care work is performed in a family setting, it is readily associated with mothering, work often believed to be natural to women, unskilled, and of little if any economic value (Crittenden 2001,

Harrington 1999). The providers I interviewed, however, did not experience an ideological contradiction between drawing on ideals of family as a means of promoting the social and economic value of their paid care work. They saw both skill and a family setting as essential elements in the quality of care they offer. They viewed themselves as skilled workers and professionals who are worthy of respect and a living wage. And they experienced frustration when others, equating their work with conventional ideologies that devalue women's care work in family settings, failed to respect their work. The providers consistently spoke with genuine passion about the lack of both social and economic value their work inspires.

When I asked Martha Buxton if she ever considered leaving family child care, she responded immediately, "Oh yeah."

"And what makes you think about leaving family day care?" I asked.

> Well, low pay. That's probably the main thing. And then also there's somewhat of a—not a stigma; that isn't the word. Some people don't consider it work when you're at home working with day care. I mean, they sort of do. But not *really*. They think, "Well, you're at home. You're doing your *own* thing. And you just sort of have the children there." But that's not how I consider it. The children are my work. My own things are secondary during the day when the children are here. . . . It's a low prestige type of a job, too. It's low pay. There's no benefits. Nothing for it. . . . And that's sad [because] the most important thing we have in the world is our children.

Valerie Holton, a provider of family child care for fifteen years, describes attitudes very similar to those confronted by Martha— that family child care fails to qualify as not only a profession but as work. As Valerie recounts, these attitudes begin at an early age and may be promulgated by families, among others.

> And things I don't like. When you're talking to parents, some of them think of you as just a regular little old babysitter. You're not respected as a person who goes to work. And sometimes you find that out through the kids. Because one of the kids one time asked me, "Do you ever go to work?"
> And I'm like, "Yes. This is my job."
> "This is not a *job*," [the child said]. And it made me wonder, where does this kid get this from? Are his parents thinking that I'm not working?

I tried to explain to him. I said, "My job is to see that you get from point A to point B. To and from school. My job is to see that you have your meals and that you are treated right and that things go right for you. I have things to do and keep you busy while your parents are at work." I said, "This is *my* job. Even though you may not think of it as a job."

Thus, we find that both the meaning of family and the location of households shape the provision and the experience of family child care. Women who provide family child care report that they value children. They speak of the importance of the development of healthy children and believe this development occurs most fully in the context of a family setting and family relationships. They draw on these values and practices in understanding and claiming the social and economic value of their work. The paradox is that frequently these same values and practices may cause parents and the public at large to devalue family child care and the women who provide it. Families, existing outside of the market economy, are viewed as the site of unpaid care provided by women as a result of their natural propensity to love young children. As such, paid care work that occurs in families—in particular, child care work—is antithetical to historical ideologies that extricate care from the market economy (Folbre 2001, Himmelweit 1999, J. Nelson 1999). While family child care providers report that the location of their paid child care within families and the values and experiences children receive as a result of care in a family setting actually increase the quality and economic value of the care they provide, they report that parents and the public do not concur. Child care in a family setting is commonly viewed as something other than real work and therefore lacks status and value, even when provided as paid work. As a result of this social and economic devaluation, providers are unable to achieve economic stability for themselves and their own families through their paid child care work. Despite our reliance on family child care to facilitate parents' employment (and economic security for their families), family child care providers (and other paid care workers) continue to pay the price for the disparity between the public need for care and the lack of public value granted to care workers.

3

"YOU'RE JUST A HOUSEWIFE"

Contesting Stereotypes about
Motherhood, Marriage, and
Family Child Care

Contemporary folk wisdom affirms the belief that women choose to provide family child care out of their desire to be full-time, at-home mothers. Among the women I interviewed, the responsibilities of caring for their own children did prove to be an important factor in their choice to enter family child care. Nevertheless, their understandings and experiences of motherhood proved much more complex than the dominant ideology of the full-time, at-home mother would have us believe. How, then, did the women I interviewed define their responsibilities as mothers? Did their racial ethnic identity and social class inform their understandings of motherhood? Did their earlier beliefs and practices about motherhood change as providers became mothers? And did their provision of child care for pay affirm or conflict with their understanding of motherhood?

STEREOTYPES AND ASSUMPTIONS REGARDING
MOTHERHOOD AND FAMILY CHILD CARE WORK

Patricia James, an urban, African American woman, began providing paid group child care in her home more than eight years ago. While Patricia tells me how much she has enjoyed her work, she is also quick to answer when I ask, "What do you like least about family child care work?"

> The stereotype. The babysitter. [People think] you're a babysitter. There's no education needed for that. There's no reward. There's no real appreciation. You know, when you go to a bank and say you have a job [in family child care], they say "Oh, does your husband work?" You know, you're not considered a really employed person. That's one thing I dislike about it. Unless you can show tax receipts or someone else's signature on your stuff, you're really just a housewife that's just watching kids.

Patricia's anger and disgust at the devaluing of her employment as a family child care provider make sense. She entered family child care as her chosen profession and is making this work her career. She has provided licensed child care for more than eight years and plans to continue in the field. She is taking courses toward an associate's degree in early childhood education at a local community college. With an annual net income of $20,000, Patricia's work is equal to that of her husband's in supporting their family of five. Yet she's seen as "just a housewife," not an "employed person."

Like Patricia, all but three of the providers I interviewed were married and all but one were mothers of school-aged children when they entered family child care work. Thus, I began to wonder if the dominant ideology of motherhood had served as a primary force influencing the employment options and choices available to these women workers and their decisions to enter family child care. But my questions went further. Did women's desire to be full-time, at-home mothers actually draw them to family child care work? How might cultural meanings of motherhood interact with other values, identities, and responsibilities so as to draw women to the work?

Although providers' relationships with children are ones in which women provide care for pay, providers frequently use the language of motherhood, not the market, to describe their work, as we learned in chapter 2. ("You're like a second mom to them," said Valerie. "They're like my own kids," explained Laura.) Providers' use of the language of family and motherhood is not surprising. Given the historical power of the separate-spheres ideology, caring has become so closely identified with family life that family and, in particular, idealized motherhood have come to serve as the standard by which we judge care. Given the many similarities between the work of mothering and the work of family child care, it is not surprising that providers liken their work to mothering.

Qualities inherent in care work, whether paid or unpaid, are those associated with mothering. For example, care is a relationship in which dependents cannot provide for their own needs. Attention must be directed toward the needs of the dependent to foster their well-being and development. In this process relationships are developed and sustained between care workers and dependents; and emotional attachment is often assumed. The needs of the dependent must often be given priority in the care relationship because that is the foundation of a relationship of care: one is entrusted with the well-being of another (Himmelweit 1999, Kittay 1995). Clearly, these qualities of care work accurately reflect those of both mothering and family child care. Given that providers engage in care work, that their care work is a process in which relationships develop, and that these relationships are between women and young children located within families, it is not surprising that family child care providers liken their paid child care work to mothering. And given the centrality of family life in our cultural understanding of care, mothering is the relationship that most closely resembles family child care. "We are the surrogate mothers," explains Jennie Davis. There is no other language currently available to frame an explanation of the work. Nonetheless, my conversations with providers and my analysis of these conversations led me to an increased appreciation of the ways in which women interpret motherhood and the responsibilities of motherhood in different ways, depending on their own social location. While the women I interviewed often described their work in the language of mothering, their own understandings and experiences of motherhood differed considerably from the gendered and racialized ideology of the full-time, at-home mother.

MOTHERHOOD AND PAID WORK AS CONTIGUOUS RESPONSIBILITIES

Kim Phan was one of two providers I interviewed who was caring for her own children at home when she was asked by another mother to provide family child care. Kim, a Vietnamese immigrant, began providing unlicensed care shortly after her arrival in the United States. I asked, "How did you first get started in family child care?"

Kim answered, "My neighbor; she's Vietnamese. She got a state job. She had her son before I had mine—about a month before. And then she came to ask me, 'You don't have a job. Will you babysit my son also?' And I said, 'Oh, yes. That's a good idea! I can make money, and I can take care of my children also.'"[1]

Kim's experience reflects that of the other women I interviewed who explicitly identified motherhood as a primary factor in their decision to enter family child care but did so in a manner different from the ideology of the full-time, at-home mother. These women did not report any conflict or compromise in values when women with small children (themselves included) engaged in paid labor. Kim's identification, within the same sentence, of her simultaneous need to care for her children and to make money mirrors the ways in which the providers I interviewed defined motherhood in their daily lives. Belying the dominant ideology of full-time, at-home motherhood, the women I interviewed did not separate a mother's responsibility for providing emotional and physical care from providing for her family economically; nor did they privilege one over the other. We begin, through Kim, to see the ways in which the providers I interviewed perceived their responsibilities of paid work and motherhood as contiguous and how they experienced family child care as a solution to their convergent responsibilities as mothers. Their identities as paid workers and mothers were not distinct and conflicting responsibilities between which they were forced to choose.

Like Kim, Elena Molinero, a Mexicana who has been providing licensed family child care for eight years, did not experience an ideological conflict between mothering and paid work, including her family child care work. Yet Elena did express a commitment to caring for her own children as a factor influencing her decision to enter family child care. I asked, "Why did you get started in family child care?"

She replied, "My kids were smaller. And then I liked to be with kids. And now I still do it because when my kids come home [from school], I'm here. And I enjoy kids."

Later Paula Shelton, a long-time friend of Elena's and coordinator of the program under whose auspices Elena provides care, commented, "See, that's the culture. That's the way that we were raised. To stay home and take care of children. Not to be out in the work force."

Yet Elena has always been in the work force. While she values caring for her children, she has also consistently worked full time for pay, even after the birth of each of her four children. Before entering family child care, she worked in a factory for one year and then as an agricultural worker: five years thinning and picking apples, and five years in the packing shed. When she considered leaving agricultural work, she made a conscious decision to enter family child care specifically as a business. She canvassed her neighbors to assess the market demand for services before she opened her family child care: "I asked my friends. At that time I was living in the housing of the Double R Orchards. They have maybe twenty homes. I asked my friends, 'Well, if I decide to do day care would you be interested in placing your children with me?'"

Paula observed, "So she set up her business before she got into it. That's a pretty smart way to do it. She found her clients before she got licensed."

Thus, while caring for her children was important to Elena, her adherence to the ideology of full-time, at-home motherhood is insufficient to explain her entry into family child care. She worked outside the home for a number of years before she researched and subsequently acted on the option of becoming a licensed provider—employment that enabled her to simultaneously care for her own children and earn money to support her family.

Like other providers I interviewed, Jennie Davis expressed no reservations about full-time employment and experienced no conflict between the roles of motherhood and paid worker, either as a family child care provider or in other positions in which she's been employed. Jennie is an African American, single mother of a fourteen-year-old daughter and worked for pay both before and after her daughter's birth. She drove school bus for ten years and, after her daughter was born, worked at a child care center for two years. She then drove a Head Start bus for two years ("Door to door transportation," Jennie explained) until an injury required her to leave that job and she began to provide foster care for children in need. After providing foster care for two years, she entered family child care. Jennie explained her employment history: "I just always had jobs that deal with children. I didn't have the education as far as college and all that, but I did have the experience. I just never had a chance to get [the formal education] because I was always trying to survive and take care of my family."

For Jennie, "taking care of my family" and "trying to survive" are synonymous. Like Jennie, providers' definition and practice of motherhood as one that synthesizes affective, physical, and economic care make the care penalty they pay all the more ironic. Family child care providers work for the same reasons that other parents do: to support themselves and their families. Yet the work of family child care that facilitates the economic security of other parents and families contributes to the economic vulnerability of providers and their own families.

In embracing and synthesizing the economic responsibilities of motherhood and care, the women I interviewed contest the gendered and racialized ideology of the full-time, at-home mother as well as the assumption that women enter family child care work to live up to this ideology. In providers' understanding of their roles and responsibilities as mothers, I found constant confirmation of West and Zimmerman's (1987) analysis of "doing gender." Gender is not an essential or universal characteristic (as the historical separate-spheres ideology would have us believe) but is an emergent feature of social situations. Gender and its myriad manifestations, including motherhood, are not cast in stone. While we do gender (by acting on ideologies that define what it means to be a woman and a mother), we can also undo or redo it by redefining or re-creating the meaning of gender and gender roles, including that of motherhood (Gerson 2002). The providers I interviewed experienced motherhood in a much more complex way than the racialized and class-based ideology of the full-time, at-home mother would have us believe. While motherhood served as a primary identity in the lives of providers, their daily lives teach us about the ways in which women redefine the role and the responsibilities of motherhood in accordance with their own social location.

Not only do the lives of family child care providers such as Kim, Elena, and Jennie clearly conflict with the ideology of the full-time, at-home mother, so do the lives of the majority of mothers in the United States today. By 2001, more than 74 percent of mothers of school-aged children worked for pay, as did nearly 60 percent of mothers with children under six years of age (U.S. Department of Labor, Bureau of Labor Statistics 2002). Clearly, a conflict exists between the ideology of the full-time, at-home mother and the reality of women's lives. How do mothers experience and address this conflict?

Recent research regarding mothers and motherhood within the contemporary United States confirms the tenacity of the dualistic gendered ideology that continues to identify women with nurturance, moral sensitivity, and motherhood, albeit in somewhat modified ways (Gerson 1987, Hays 1996, Vogel 1993). Most recently, Anita Garey (1999) documented that women experience an overt conflict between the two distinct roles of paid worker and of mother-wife. In her thoughtful analysis of the meaning and negotiation of motherhood, Garey speaks of a consequence of the separate-spheres ideology as "the orientation model of work and family." Because of the dichotomy between work and family, women identify themselves as being either work-oriented or family-oriented. The gap between the two spheres is too great for one individual (in particular, one mother) to bridge. Using the metaphor of weaving to capture the interconnectedness of work and family, Garey analyzes the strategies women create in order to reconcile their identities as mothers with their identities as workers. What struck me in my interviews with family child care providers was that, unlike the women in Garey's study, the women I interviewed did not consciously work to reconcile their identity as mother with their identity as worker. With the exception of one provider, the conscious need for reconciliation was not evident specifically because they failed to experience a conflict between these roles. Their lives confirmed continuity, not conflict, in their understanding and experience of motherhood as a role that embraced both paid work responsibilities and unpaid care for family members.

Evelyn Nakano Glenn (1994) articulates the ways in which these women's experiences and, more broadly, women's historical and contemporary realities conflict with the dominant ideology of motherhood: "mothering is contested terrain. . . . it has always been contested terrain. However, a particular definition of mothering has so dominated popular media representations, academic discourse, and political and legal doctrine that the existence of alternative beliefs and practices among racial, ethnic, and sexual minority communities as well as non-middle-class segments of society has gone unnoticed" (2–3).

An emerging body of scholarship recognizes that, in fact, the ideology of the full-time, at-home mother is a historically race- and class-specific ideology (Abramovitz 1989, Amott and Matthaei 1991, Michel 1999, Mink 1995). Consistently, studies of mothers of diverse racial ethnic identity and economic status challenge the perceived existence of women's historical and contemporary commitment to the ideology and practice of full-time, at-home mothering. These challenges carry implications for the belief that women's commitment to this ideology is the only or primary reason for their decisions to enter family child care work. My findings confirm those of a number of scholars of immigrant mothers and mothers of color. For example, Chicana and Mexicana immigrant mothers interviewed by Denise Segura (1994) did not adhere to the dualistic ideology of the full-time, at-home mother that separates waged and unwaged caregiving. In her investigation Segura found that

> Mexicanas, raised in a world where economic and household work often merged, do not dichotomize social life into public and private spheres, but appear to view employment as one workable domain of motherhood. . . . Raised in rural or working-class families in Mexico, the Mexicanas described childhoods where they and their mothers actively contributed to the economic subsistence of their families. . . . Motherhood in this context is both economic and expressive, embracing both employment as well as childrearing. (212, 224–25)

Patricia Zavella (1987) found similar experiences of motherhood and its meaning among Chicana cannery workers who sought out paid employment specifically because they wished to be better wives and mothers. When asked why she entered cannery employment, one woman responded, "I did it for my family. We needed the money, why else?" (88). For African American, poor, and immigrant women, economic support of their children is an essential part of their definition and experience of motherhood (Brewer 1988, Dill 1998, Michel 1999). Because of the racial ethnic and economic context in which women experience motherhood, the family forms of poor families "do not exhibit the radical split equating private with home and public with work" (Collins 1990, 47). Subsequently, among many women of color, economic self-reliance has long been integrated with motherhood; and for black women, paid work "has been an important and valued dimension of Afrocentric definitions of Black motherhood" (Collins 1987, 124).

My research confirms the ways in which multiple social forces entwine to give meaning and definition to motherhood among family child care providers. Because of their social locations, the women I interviewed experienced motherhood and subsequently their family child care work in ways different from the white, middle-class ideal of motherhood. They understood their paid child care work to be not only compatible with but also a means by which they fulfilled their multiple responsibilities as mothers.

THE PROVISION OF FAMILY CHILD CARE AND CONTESTED IDEOLOGIES OF MOTHERHOOD

Of the women I interviewed, only one, Martha Buxton, expressed an explicit commitment to her primary social role as a full-time, at-home mother. Martha is a graduate of Brigham Young University, a former public school teacher, and, like the family child care providers in Nelson's (1990, 1994) studies, white and native-born. A mother of five, she has been providing unlicensed care in her home for eight years. Consistent with the rural, white, native-born providers that Nelson studied, Martha adheres to a white, middle-class cultural ideal of mothering.

> I think children need a family environment. I *really* do. I've always believed that, and I continue to do so. It gets frustrating sometimes. I've tended a number of children who are adopted children. And the parents have waited for years and years and years before they would get children. Then they'll wait a few weeks or however much [time] they have and then either they have to or they *choose* to—most of the people I deal with, they *choose* to—put them in day care and go back to work. And it always surprises me a little bit [laughter]. I'd think that they'd want to be home.

Martha is genuinely perplexed by parents who struggle for years to create a family and then, upon the arrival of a child, immediately put the child in child care so as to return to paid work. Such a practice is inconsistent with her ideal of parenting and in particular of mothering. In our interview Martha went on to speak about her own decision to stay home with her first child and how, when her oldest son was in second grade, she began providing unlicensed paid child care: "It started out when a friend of ours needed someone to watch their child. . . . It didn't start out as a conscious decision because I didn't do day care when I had my own children. I had five little boys and that was enough [laughter]."

I said, "So, your friend needed somebody. And why did you say yes?"

> Because I was at home, and I preferred to be at home. And that's one of the obvious things about why a lot of people do day care. And why I do. Even though my children are older now, I still feel it's important for them to have me [at home]. I prefer to be at home when they go to school and when they come back from school. And they know that I'm available if something comes up—if they need something or other. And that's always been important to me. I can do child care at home and still accommodate that.

Martha's view of motherhood is one in which a mother is always accessible to her children. She can "do day care at home" without violating her primary social role and responsibilities as a mother. Her experience of being a full-time, at-home mother approached by a friend to provide care and thus informally entering family child care work is commonly perceived as the primary way in which women enter the field. Martha herself voices her own belief in this perception: "I preferred to be at home. And that's one of the obvious things about why a lot of people do day care." In fact, however, her assumption that her experience reflects the experience of "a lot of people" in family child care is inaccurate. Among the women I interviewed, only Martha and Kim Phan were already at home providing full-time care for their own children when they were approached by other mothers to begin providing family child care. So how did Martha come to believe that women prefer to be at home full time with their own children, and that women enter the work of family child care because it doesn't interfere with their primary responsibility for full-time, at-home mothering?

Family Child Care Research and Ideologies of Motherhood

The public perception that family child care providers are, like Martha, dedicated first and foremost to being full-time, at-home mothers is directly linked to historical ideologies that identify women as nurturers, caregivers, and mothers. As I discussed in chapter 1, ideologies are systems of thought that are directly linked to social organization and action. It is no coincidence that the responsibilities of child care work, whether paid or unpaid, are likened to motherhood. We see this ideology that links motherhood with family child care work further played out in research studies. A number of studies of family child care, while not overtly seeking to identify the motivations that initially draw women into the work, identify motherhood as a primary factor organizing family child care. In the most comprehensive analysis of family child care to date (now more than twenty years old), the National Day Care Home Study identified two groups of family child care providers: one a group of young mothers caring for their own children while providing paid care for other children, the other a group of middle-aged and older mothers whose children were grown (Fosburg 1981, 38). In her study of family child care providers in New York City, Mazur (1981) found two groups of providers similar to those identified by Fosburg: "later motherhood care-givers" and "early motherhood care-givers." Kappner (1984), in her study of family child care in New York, further delineated the "life cycle groups" of caregivers into four statuses: childless caregivers, early motherhood caregivers, middle motherhood caregivers, and later motherhood caregivers.

All three research studies describe providers in relation to their status as mothers and explicitly use various stages of motherhood as a means of characterizing diversity between providers. That choice alone affirms the common assumption that motherhood is central to the organization and provision of family child care. In her extensive study of family child care, Nelson (1988a, 1988b, 1990, 1994) identified a number of motivations for women's entry into family child care work, including financial motivations. At the same time, she said, "The family day care providers in my study clearly construct their role in line with the white, middle-class cultural ideal of mothering" (1994, 185). Fully 85 percent of the providers she interviewed (1990) stated that they started offering family child care because they wanted to stay home with their own children. These women also perceived that their family child care work intruded into their lives in ways that jeopardized their mothering. The native-born white providers reported that the presence of other children in their homes limited their ability to enact and required them to compromise their own ideal of motherhood (1994, 193).

> [F]amily day-care providers in this study choose to provide family day care in order to enact a "traditional," at-home, mothering ideal. In doing so, they inevitably offer a service in which they do not believe. That is, to the extent that they have chosen not to seek employment outside the home because they feel strongly that a mother should be available to, and fully engaged with, her own children, the family day-care provider offers to other people's children a service that she could not accept for her own. . . . Not only does she redefine the "traditional" mother as someone who can combine both productive and reproductive work in the home, but in doing so she inevitably compromises her ideal of good mothering. (Nelson 1994, 183)

Among the providers I interviewed, motherhood emerged as a factor influencing their entry into family child care—but not in a manner consistent with the white, middle-class cultural ideal of mothering embraced by the providers Nelson (1994) interviewed. As a result of racial ethnic, cultural, and social class location and their experiences of motherhood within these locations, the women I interviewed, unlike the rural, native-born, white providers in Nelson's study, failed to experience their paid family child care work as an "inevitable compromise" of their ideal of good mothering. In contrast, providing family child care became the means by which they were able to enact their own ideal of motherhood: one that synthesized their responsibilities as mothers to provide economic, affective, and physical care for their families.

The Historical Emergence of the Ideology of Motherhood

Understanding the ideology of motherhood—specifically the tenacity of the ideal of the full-time, at-home mother—is key to understanding the social organization and perceptions of family child care work. In the mid-nineteenth century, industrialization in the United States fostered a dualistic and newly gendered view of social and economic life: a gendered division of labor in separate spheres of family and market. As production moved from families to factories, households took on a new identity. Perceived as existing in the private sphere, they increasingly served the social and economic roles of consuming rather than producing. In contrast, the market became identified as the sphere of production: the public sphere (Abramovitz 1989, Kessler-Harris 1982, Matthaei 1982). What emerged from this public-private distinction was an ideology of the family as the symbolic opposite of the market. The market emerging as the material site of production in a capitalist economy, became identified with values of the rational, the impersonal, and the bureaucratic. The market became the site of business: competition and financial exchange buttressed by laws and contracts. In contrast, the family was viewed as the site and source of opposite values—love, relationship, and intimacy based on personal commitment. A dualistic construction of market versus family emerged: competition versus cooperation, laws versus love, contracts versus personal relationship—in sum, a public sphere forged by market-driven values versus a private sphere forged by family-driven values.

These transitions in the location of work and work practices resulted in an ideology that not only distinguished the family from the market but also identified these two spheres as gendered. The workplace, a place of paid labor, rationality, and competition, became identified with masculinity; and men's behaviors and values were increasingly explained by their market-based working conditions. In contrast, women's behaviors and values were increasingly interpreted to be the result of their relational family experiences; and home and family became identified with women's work sanctioning so-called feminine values and practices of nurturance, affection, and caregiving. This idealized notion of womanhood (often called the cult of domesticity or the cult of true womanhood) identified women with domesticity and moral sensitivity, a clear alternative to the competitive drive needed by male breadwinners to succeed in the market economy.

With the growth of industrialization and the subsequent emergence of the ideology of separate spheres in a small but growing white middle class, the social role of children (and subsequently of mothers) began to change. In contrast to their previous role of pro-ductive worker in an agrarian economy, children were redefined as needing indulgence, attentive care, and guidance. Who better to assume this role of guide than the white, middle-class mother newly assigned to the home and imbued with a "natural" moral in-stinct to offer love, care, and compassion? The ideology took root and began to dominate. Motherhood was regarded as incompatible with labor-force participation, mothers and fathers were assigned distinct family and market responsibilities, and child care was un-derstood to be the responsibility of individual family members (that is, women) in private homes. This gendered and racialized di-vision and location of labor contributed to the social and eco-nomic devaluation of care that remains with us today. If, as the logic goes, women are nurturant by nature (not by skill) and their care is motivated by love (not by money), then care must be some-thing other than work.

This racialized and class-based ideology held sway for de-cades—well into the 1960s, when large-scale economic, political, and social transformations drew middle-class mothers into the paid labor force and spurred the need for paid child care. Between 1950 and 1970 divorce rates nearly doubled. Divorced, formerly middle-class mothers seeking to enter or expand their participation in the paid labor force found themselves in need of child care. In-flation necessitated an increased income to maintain a family's standard of living; and among two-parent, middle-class families, women's labor force participation provided this needed income. In addition, economic restructuring resulted in the decline of high-wage, male-dominated manufacturing jobs and a commensurate growth in low-wage, service-sector jobs. Thus, a variety of sources of male income previously available to white, middle-class families declined. As their economic need grew, these families became in-creasingly dependent on the paid employment of previously at-home mothers.

As a result of these social and economic transformations, the idealized gendered division of labor in families reached an im-passe. Increasingly, white, middle-class families were confronted with a social reality inconsistent with the dominant ideology of family life, with its male breadwinner and female homemaker models. How did this conflict between social reality and belief systems manifest itself in the families of the family child care providers I interviewed? How did these women as young girls in the mid-1950s and mid-1960s experience (or fail to experience) the idealized gendered division of labor in the homes and families in which they grew up? What impact might their experience have had on their subsequent values and practices regarding the roles of women and men, mothers and fathers, in families? And how might those values and practices have influenced these women's choices to enter family child care work?

Providers' Early Experiences of Motherhood and Care

As children growing up in the mid-1950s and mid-1960s, few of the women I interviewed lived in families headed by the male breadwinner and female homemaker and caregiver idealized in the separate-spheres ideology. Martha Buxton, the only family child care provider to adhere strictly to the ideology of the full-time, at-home mother, was one of only a few women raised in such a family and interestingly was the only provider who reported a father with a white-collar occupation: banking. Most of the women were raised in middle- or lower-income families, and in only four of these families did parents assume distinct male breadwinner and female homemaker roles. In fact, the majority were raised in families in which both parents were employed or in families in which they were raised by a single parent. Employed fathers generally held blue-collar or service-sector jobs. Of their fathers, providers recalled: "He was a laborer." "Dad worked for the post office." "He always worked in shipyards." Mothers generally worked in service-sector, pink-collar, or agricultural jobs. Providers described their mothers' employment: "Mom was a counselor with mentally disturbed kids." "She was a nutrition aide." "She worked every day as a caretaker in private homes."

Allie McGinnis, a Euro-American family child care provider for three years, recalled her father's death when she was fifteen and how her mother formally assumed responsibility for the family business that she had been running for several years.

> My parents owned and, together, ran a shoe repair shop in Seattle. They owned it when I was born. So that's all I ever knew that they did. And my dad died when I was fifteen. And my mom had a very big decision to make. And she said, "Pffft, I ran this

by myself half the time anyway" [laughter]. Especially in the beginning. My dad was an alcoholic. I never knew him as a drinking alcoholic. He stopped drinking long before I was born. But my mom learned very early on. My dad always "had the flu." So she learned very early on.

Patricia James was also raised in a family in which both parents worked outside the home. Under circumstances somewhat different than Allie's, Patricia's mother also assumed primary caretaking and economic responsibility for her family.

My father worked on the railroad. He worked for the Burlington Northern. He used to take me to work with him. They'd keep me on a blanket. He was a laborer. He worked on the track, putting track down. Repairing them and things like that. Then my mother. My mother was a jack of many trades [laughter]. She was a mortician. She was a hairdresser. A nurse. A social worker. My father and mother separated when I was five. So I commuted between the two of them. So summers I spent in Tacoma with my dad. And in Seattle the rest of the time with my mom.

Like Patricia and Allie, the women I interviewed experienced, from an early age, a disjuncture between their daily lives and the gendered and racialized ideology that endorsed a male breadwinner and a female homemaker with distinct responsibilities performed in distinct locations. These women did not grow up in families in which fathers worked full time earning money to support their families while mothers engaged in full-time homemaking and caregiving for family members. In fact, the lives of these women taught them that motherhood involved a variety of responsibilities, including that of supporting one's family economically.

Early in life, these providers also learned about the gendered responsibility for direct care work within families. While their mothers worked outside the home, the providers themselves, as children, were often responsible for caring for the other children in their families. Laura Mayfield is a Euro-American woman who has been providing family child care for eleven years and whose entrance into family child care is rooted in her early responsibilities for her siblings. When I asked Laura why she began providing family child care, she responded, "Well, to me it just felt natural—watching kids. I mean, I enjoy being around them. They're fun to be with."

"Had you been around kids much?" I asked.

"Oh yeah. I'm from a big family. There's ten in my family, and I was the oldest. We're from a split family. My mom and dad were separated when I was about ten years old. So it was just mom and me and the kids. I helped with the cooking and helped with the household chores. I watched the kids while my mom was working."

Like Laura's, Janice Newman's mother worked outside the home while Janice assumed responsibility for care work within the home. Janice, a Euro-American provider, recalled:

> I was the eldest of six kids, and I ran the household. My mom was not typical of a family in those days with six kids. She worked in a factory. We lived in England in those days. And she worked in a factory—a day shift. And my stepfather worked like 3 P.M. to 11 P.M. And so I was running my day care when I was ten [laughter]. I got the kids up and got them off to school and got myself off to school and went to school all day. And then I came home, and I fed the kids. School gets out at four [o'clock] in England. I'd come home, and I'd get tea. And my stepfather, he worked three to eleven, but he would make sure that sandwiches had been made and the fruit and everything had been put out for teatime. And then I'd put it out for the kids and then clean that up. And then I'd jump on my bicycle and run to my grandmother's and take care of her and get her supper. And then I'd come home and do my homework.

I asked, "Your grandmother was frail?"

Janice said, "Well, she was still living in a house. But when I look back on it, I realize that she had Alzheimer's disease. She was not quite with this world. But she was harmless, and so I would get her something to eat and get things put together for her. And then I'd come home and do my homework and get the kids to bed."

Like Laura and Janice, family child care providers learned early on that mothers worked outside the home and assumed responsibility for supporting their families. At the same time, while mothers worked outside someone had to assume the work of caring for young children; and mothers frequently transferred this family care work to their daughters. As a result, daughters soon learned the responsibilities and skills needed for caring for others, particularly young children. Thus, the socialization of women in their families of origin and the lessons they learned about women's work in and for families were not as simple as learning that mothers worked for pay outside the home. They also learned aspects of the gendered organization and provision of care work in families, which enabled providers to enter family child care work thinking that it "just felt natural."

The commonly held belief that women enter family child care because of their adherence to an ideology of full-time, at-home motherhood fails to accurately explain the motivation of women to enter this work. Just as their daily work as family child care providers synthesizes the perceived ideological and material distinction between work and family, so does their definition of motherhood. For these women, the economic care of one's family is the responsibility of a mother or, in a two-parent family, the responsibility of both parents. Early on they observed their mothers' care work for family members, and they also assumed these responsibilities. Thus, while they learned of women's responsibilities to care for their families economically, the providers also learned about the gendered division of labor within families. They learned about the double day of women's paid work and care work and incorporated this experience into their own understandings of motherhood. As a result, while they do not adhere to the separate-spheres ideology, motherhood remains central to their identities and, as we will see in later chapters, to their employment options and choices.

MARRIAGE AND THE PROVISION OF FAMILY CHILD CARE

Although the providers I interviewed did not adhere to the dualistic ideology of separate spheres, seventeen of the twenty providers were married at the time they began providing paid, home-based child care. Two of the three unmarried providers were living with men in long-term relationships. Only one of the three (Jennie Davis) was single when she entered family child care. Of the nineteen providers with a husband or male partner, seventeen reported that their husbands or spousal equivalents were employed. Thus, marital status or its equivalent, as well as a household's adult male employment, seemed as if it might influence the choice or ability of women to enter and remain in family child care work. Although providers' adherence to distinct family gender roles of breadwinner and homemaker failed to explain their entry into the field, could other structural elements of gender in marriage influence the organization and provision of care?

Valerie Holton, an African American woman providing family child care for fifteen years, spoke of the importance of the additional resources a husband provides to a family child care worker: "If you're single, [family child care work] is not great. It is not great. I couldn't make it without a husband in a profession like this at all. There's just no way. We use all his [health care benefits]. Because if you start taking out of your [family child care] income and you've got to pay health [insurance], some kind of dental, . . . and all that, you'll be a broke cookie."

Valerie's experience exemplifies that of the providers I interviewed. A second source of income is essential, given their low wages, and that income almost always comes through marriage and a husband's employment. As I began to analyze their family income, the centrality of marriage as a structural economic necessity for the provision of family child care began to emerge. In 1999 the annual net income of the providers I interviewed ranged from a low of $4,175 to a high of $30,000.[2] Their median 1999 annual net income totaled $15,280, well within the range of the annual earnings of licensed family child care providers in Washington State.[3] At this rate, the income of all of the providers would fall well below the state median income without the additional income provided by their husbands. Despite a sixty-to-sixty-five-hour work week, thirteen of the twenty providers would live below the federal poverty level were it not for an additional source of family income. In all cases but one (whose second income comes from public assistance), a husband provides this income.

Throughout the country, family child care workers earn poverty-level wages; and the providers in this study are no exception. Just as two-thirds of child care workers nationwide earn below poverty-level wages (Whitebook and Phillips 1999), fully two-thirds of the women I spoke with earned wages below the poverty threshold. The $4.82 hourly wage earned by the providers I interviewed is well below the $5.15 federal minimum wage and 25 percent below the $6.50 minimum wage in effect in Washington State at the time of my interviews. Each year, national data tell us that parking lot attendants and animal trainers earn double the wages earned by family child care providers (Center for the Child Care Workforce 1998, 1999, 2000).

As Gloria Steinem (1983) observed twenty years ago, "Most women [with children] are only one man away from welfare" (8). This is certainly the case for women who are family child care providers. Marriage or its economic equivalent provides the necessary second income to enable them and their families to live at or above the poverty level. As such, a husband's income is a structural necessity to the provision of care. Otherwise, family child care as we know it today would not exist.

In addition to a living wage, health care is essential to family economic stability and survival. Among the providers I interviewed, marriage played a central role in the availability of health insurance for providers and their families. Only two of the twenty women I interviewed reported coverage under private health insurance plans that they had purchased; and each of these women expressed concern about its high cost. Sondra Ames, who reported one of the highest annual incomes among the providers I interviewed ($21,000), was one of the two providers who could afford to purchase health insurance. When asked about benefits such as sick leave, Sondra, an African American woman who has worked as a provider for two years, voiced incredulity, a response common among the women I interviewed: "Sick leave? [laughter]. What's that? [laughter]. Make believe? I don't know about sick leave. I am on Group Health [an HMO]. I belong to the King County Day Care Association, and through that they offer a medical and a dental plan. It costs me a mint. $300 a month for me and my daughter. You got to have health insurance, though."

Ten of the twenty providers would be without health insurance were it not for their husbands' employment, When I asked Patricia James, "Do you get any employment benefits?" she responded, "No. But, I still work!"

"What about health insurance?" I asked.

"That's available," Patricia responded, "but the rate is so outrageous it's like, 'I don't think I can afford that.'" Patricia, like many of the providers I interviewed, has health insurance only because of the employment benefits received by her husband.

Four of the providers earned so little money from full-time family child care employment that their families qualified for government-subsidized health care intended to aid working-poor families. Three of the four women whose families received state-subsidized health care are licensed providers and offer state-subsidized care for the children of low-income families. As a result, they are de facto state employees. For each of these women, all or a large portion of their income is derived directly from the state as payment for providing subsidized child care. As a result, their qualification for state-subsidized health care is particularly ironic. As indirect government employees, they earn so little providing government-subsidized care to low-income families that their own families qualify as low-income families and are entitled to government-subsidized care.

Six of the providers reported that they are in even more dire straits than those receiving government-subsidized health care. These women have no health care coverage. Because their husbands do not receive health care benefits through employment, providers cannot access husband's plans as dependents and, as a result, are entirely without insurance. Clearly, a husband's employment benefits and status directly affect the economic well-being of providers and their families.

For the majority of the women I interviewed, marriage provides an essential source of not only income but also the health care benefits needed to supplement the low wages they receive as providers. These findings confirm the precarious economic status of providers nationwide as well as the reality (and necessity) that "a sizable proportion of [family child] caregivers come from households in which there are two wage-earners, and caregiving is not the only source of income" (Fosburg 1981, 42–43). In her study of providers of diverse racial ethnic identities, Kappner (1984) reports similar findings: "Economically, it would appear to be difficult for single parent providers to earn a wage from family child care which would be sufficient to bring their families above poverty level incomes" (105–6).

While it may appear a coincidence that the majority of family child care providers are married and members of two-income households or that providers aspire to live in an approximation of a male breadwinner and female caregiver household, the reality is that marriage is an economic necessity for them. The low-wage work of family child care is invariably linked to marriage and the additional economic stability that a second adult income brings to a household.

Family child care providers are almost uniformly married women with at least one child of their own. These characteristics are a product of different aspects of the experience of working in family child care. First, family day care rarely can pay enough to support a woman living on her own; the occupation thus relies heavily on the population of women who, because they are married or living with someone, have access to a second means of support. (Nelson 1990, 27)

Marriage is a structural necessity not only for individual providers but also for the organization and provision of family child care as a form of paid care. Without access to a husband's income, the ability of women to enter family child care and thus parents' (and indirectly employers') reliance on family child care as a source of paid care would be substantially reduced. When we understand the ways in which marriage is integral to the organization and provision of family child care, it becomes clear that husbands of family child care providers, as well as providers themselves, work to fill the care gap. A combination of the low wages of family child care providers and their husbands' wages enable providers and their families to address the discrepancy between society's high reliance on paid care providers and the lack of resources allotted to pay for care.

Here again we see that the dominant ideology of the family shapes family child care work in ways that are, at first glance, invisible. The work is organized by gender, and gender is inherent in the structure of contemporary (as well as historical) family life because, in large part, of the tenacity of the ideology of the separate spheres. This ideology informs multiple practices that contribute to the devaluation, low status, and low wages of family child care work. First, the racialized and class-based separate-spheres ideology historically affirms women's primary role as that of full-time, at-home mothers. Care work within the home is viewed as unskilled work motivated by women's love for children, and the work has little (if any) economic value. As a result, if child care work must enter the market economy, it is viewed as worthy of little compensation. Second, the tenacity of the separate-spheres ideology is manifest in the belief that, if women do enter paid work, family child care work enables them to do so in a way that allows them to continue living out their belief in a family composed of a male breadwinner, a female homemaker, and dependent children. Ascribing women's entry into family child care work as motivated by their own adherence to the ideology of the full-time, at-home mother makes it possible to further devalue the work. Third, the persistence of the male breadwinner and female homemaker ideology and its companionate family wage (a male wage sufficient to support an entire family) further devalues women's care work (Barrett and McIntosh 2000) because, when women work outside the home, their wages are believed to constitute "pin money"—to play a secondary role in a family's economic self-sufficiency.

Together, these beliefs contribute to the lack of status and the low wages that are paid to providers and reinforce both the belief in and practice of providers' reliance on a male income as essential to family survival. Again, we see that an ideology is not solely a system of belief but one that reproduces the social organization it endorses. While dynamic and subject to change, dominant ideologies are extremely tenacious, as we see in the organization of family child care. The class- and race-based ideology of the family becomes the frame around which family child care is organized. As such, marriage and an adult male income become necessities in the lives of family child care providers.

REFLECTING AND CHALLENGING IDEOLOGIES OF MOTHERHOOD

As married women providing care for children within their homes, family child care providers appear to reinforce the ideology of the gendered division of labor identifying women with nurturance, home, and family. But a powerful social dynamic is at work, one in which economic necessity reinforces the gendered division of labor within families, the larger economy, and family child care work. While providers resent that they are seen as "just housewives who are watching kids," they are themselves dependent on their economic status as housewives. Without the second income provided by a husband (or, in some instances, government-subsidized benefits including Medicaid and food stamps), a provider's family can rarely approach economic self-sufficiency—the very self-sufficiency that she facilitates for other parents by caring for their children so that they can engage in paid employment.

As the need for paid child care grows, ideologies of care, motherhood, and marriage continue to organize the provision of child care. Both the historical practice of mothering and the dominant ideology surrounding women's caregiving continue to associate women with nurturing skills and thereby with nurturing, low-wage occupations. As Francesca Cancian and Stacey Oliker (2000) remind us, while women take on more care work than men, "the reasons have more to do with cultural beliefs, duties assigned by gender and opportunities in the job market than with instincts" (48). Thus, when care work is transformed from unpaid labor into a service to be purchased, it is predominantly women and dispro-portionately women of color who provide paid care. Consistent with the historical ideologies and socially reinforced practices re-garding motherhood, the majority of workers who emerge to pro-vide family child care are women and, not surprisingly, themselves mothers.

Clearly the class- and race-based ideology of the family and motherhood play a primary role in structuring the organization of family child care work. At the same time, close attention to the lived experience of women of diverse racial ethnic identities and social classes enables us to understand the power of ideology, structure, and individual agency in a more complex way. As both an ideology and a larger social structure, the gendered and racial-ized division of labor serves to organize our lives. At the same time, within this context, women make active choices about their identities, their responsibilities, and their daily work. In so doing, they demonstrate that ideologies, including those of motherhood and family, are persistent but dynamic, social forces. Among the family child care providers I interviewed, motherhood and paid employment are contiguous, not competing, identities. Support-ing one's family economically is part and parcel of what it means to be a mother. While the providers did not overtly seek to chal-lenge the historical ideology of motherhood, they in fact do so on a daily basis. By envisioning and acting on motherhood as a syn-thesis of economic and expressive functions, they call into ques-tion the racialized and class-based ideology of motherhood that distinguishes care from work and motherhood from paid employ-ment. In addition, they contest the contemporary manifestations of the ideology of full-time, at-home motherhood in which em-ployed mothers reconcile the conflict between motherhood and employment by choosing between an identity rooted in domestic responsibilities and one rooted in paid work. The family child care providers with whom I spoke did not perceive a conflict between motherhood and paid employment. In contrast, by defining paid employment as integral to their identities and responsibilities as mothers and transforming unpaid care work in families into paid employment, they help us perceive the ways in which women confront and challenge historical ideologies of gender, work, and family in their daily lives.

4

"WHEN YOU HAVE YOUR FAMILY, YOU NEED YOUR MONEY"

Employment Opportunities and the Meaning of Family Child Care Work

Given the low wages and low status of family child care work, why do women choose to enter the work? While those I interviewed made choices about becoming providers, these choices were not isolated, individual ones. Women's location in larger social contexts shaped the employment opportunities and options available to them and thus their decisions to enter, remain in, or leave family child care work. Regardless of racial ethnic identity, country of origin, or social class, providers shared common experiences of economic need, limited employment options in local labor markets organized by sex- and racial ethnic–segregation, and a lack of available and affordable child care. These external forces were common to all the providers I interviewed.

Just as the women I interviewed shared common experiences in which ideological practices (both their own and those of larger social forces) drew them to family child care work, diverse opportunities and varied access to resources shaped each woman's life and choice of work. Although structural forces influence the opportunities available to us, we make active decisions about our lives. Family child care providers are no exception. Within the options available to them, each of the women made the best choice possible—the one that most enabled her to engage in meaningful work that would support her and her family. How women experience that choice to enter family child care is informed by their social location, a context that includes an interaction of ideological and material forces of gender, race ethnicity, country of origin, family economic status, and local labor markets. As a result of these forces, each woman chose to enter family child care for quite different reasons: as stable and permanent employment, as a source of professional identity and continued mobility, or as an alternative form of professional employment. In the second section of this chapter I explore these meanings women ascribe to their status as family child care providers.

COMMON STRUCTURAL FORCES IN THE LIVES OF FAMILY CHILD CARE PROVIDERS

What external forces influence the occupational choices available to women? And how do these structural and ideological factors inform their decisions to enter family child care work? Gloria Zuñiga's story exemplifies the power of ideological and structural forces to influence providers' decisions to enter family child care work. For all the women I interviewed, these ideological and material forces influenced both their employment options and choices.

On a hot, sunny afternoon, I drive to Gloria Zuñiga's small, well-maintained house on a busy street in a residential neighborhood in the small town of Wenatchee, Washington. A gardener myself, I am immediately aware of the well-cared-for trees and flowers and the tall cornstalks in Gloria's garden. Inside, the house is clean and neat—and quiet. Today Gloria is caring only for her own children: her son, Miguel, age five; and her daughter, Maria, age eight. She has no other children in the house because the parents of all of the children she currently cares for are seasonal agricultural workers, and the cherry crop has recently ended. In a few weeks the pears will be ripe, parents will return to the orchards, and the children will return to Gloria's home, which will no longer be nearly as quiet.

Gloria is a soft-spoken and gracious Mexicana. She invites me to sit down and offers me a large glass of lemonade. Several pictures hang on the wall and adorn shelves in the living room: a wedding portrait of Gloria and her husband, several photos of their two children at various ages, and pictures of the entire family. Gloria begins to tell me about her work as a family child care provider. As our conversation progresses, she talks about the different jobs she held in the years before becoming a family child care provider: the one job she says she will never leave. Given her experience in other forms of paid employment, I ask why she was drawn to family child care work. Gloria responds, "This is a very stable job. It's better than working on the outside [of the home]. I can stay home and take care of my children." Short and to the point, Gloria's answer nevertheless tells us a great deal about the multiple and interrelated forces that attract her as well as other women to family child care work. It offers stable employment, is personally rewarding work when compared to other available options, and enables women to care for their own children.

While neither Gloria nor the other women I interviewed are committed to the gendered and racialized ideology of the full-time, at-home mother, ideological practices inform labor markets, employment options, and women's responsibilities for their families. As Gloria continues to speak, I come to understand more about how these three factors work together to draw her and other women into family child care work. Before entering family child care, Gloria worked outside the home. I ask her to tell me about the kinds of jobs she did before providing licensed family child care. She recounts that, after immigrating from Mexico, she arrived in Texas and began to work as a cook.

> I worked in a restaurant in the kitchen, cooking. I would come out *really tired* at the end of the day. I worked there for three years. I had the children and I used to take them into the day care before I worked. I did other small jobs before that. The restaurant work was in Texas. I learned *a lot* [in that job]. What I didn't like is that I had to work long hours and weekends, and I didn't see the children. . . . When I was young, I just left them with people who didn't have any training. Now it makes me nervous to think that we had left them with just anyone without any previous training. I have a sister-in-law that leaves her children with a person that is not licensed, and it scares me. I try to tell her that it's a kind of scary situation to leave them with someone who doesn't have any type of training or anything. It really bothers me. It worries me a lot.

I asked about her other jobs. Gloria said, "I worked in a nursery. I worked with the plants in the spring. It was temporary. Arranging—cut flower arranging. And it was temporary. Six or seven months. I liked [the job], but it was just that: it was temporary. It ended in the winter, and then I went to work at the restaurant."

"Why have you stayed in family child care for the last four years?" I asked.

> I like it. I feel very good about it. I like caring for the children. When the children were younger, I used to work outside of the home. And I used to come home and I'd be tired, and I couldn't spend any time with the children. I'd be nervous and had to fix dinner and had to spend time with them. It's very different [now]. The children tire me out right now, but it's different. Rather than feeling just exhausted, I feel like I can move. I have a little bit of time to rest and everything. . . . It's different than when I was working outside.

While the details of the stories differed somewhat among providers, the themes Gloria raised in our interview were frequently voiced by the other women as well. They experienced common structural forces, which led to a similar pattern in their lives. A cycle emerged: the responsibilities of motherhood included working for pay to support one's family as well as ensuring that care was available for one's own children while working outside the home. But when working outside the home, women had difficulty securing reliable child care. In addition, care was unaffordable when compared with the low wages available to women in local labor markets. Hence, the women experienced a shared quandary: how to provide for their families economically by working outside the home when child care was unavailable and unaffordable because of women's low wages.

When women make choices to enter family child care or other forms of employment, they do so in a context of employment options and child care services that are made available (or not) in accordance with dominant ideologies. As I listened to the providers' stories, I developed a greater appreciation for the ways in which the gendered and racial ethnic ideologies that inform our understanding of motherhood also inform labor markets and other institutions in the lives of women. Specifically, women consistently sought to work outside the home; but when they did so, they were invariably confronted by limited employment options in sex- and race-segregated labor markets, a lack of affordable and available child care, and the material and biological responsibilities of motherhood.

Employment Turnover in Low Paid, Sex- and Race-Segregated Jobs

While family child care may not be "a very stable job" for middle- or upper-class women, Gloria and many of the other women I interviewed see it as an attractive employment option in light of other available employment opportunities. Before entering family child care, Gloria worked long hours and weekends as a restaurant cook and in a temporary position in a flower shop. The characteristics of her previous employment were comparable to those of the other women I interviewed: short-term employment in service-sector work, and jobs and labor markets organized by gender and race ethnicity. Valerie Holton's employment history reflects short-term, service-sector work as well. Before entering family child care fifteen years ago, Valerie, an African American woman, worked as a teaching assistant in a government-subsidized job training program, an unlicensed family child care provider, a dishwasher, and a file clerk.

> I used to work for the school district for two years. I was on the CETA program, which at that time they had people riding on the buses.[1] And it was called a "deseg [desegregation] affiliate." When I got off the bus, I went into the school, and I would work with a first-grade class teacher. Any children that needed extra help, I was responsible for tutoring them. And my program ran out. That wasn't supposed to happen. When the funding was out, the district was supposed to pick us up. But the district wouldn't pick us up.

So Valerie enrolled in early childhood education courses at a community college and began to provide informal, unlicensed child care for her sister and sister-in law: "What I started with was just strictly doing it for family." When she left informal family child care, she took two jobs for which she had training, one in food service and one in insurance. But in both positions she was underemployed and found the work unrewarding.

> I stopped providing [unlicensed family child care] and went to work for the airlines for a little while. When I was in high school, I had taken a chef class. Doing foods and stuff. So I had that behind me. And I thought I would be strictly dealing with food. I didn't know that I would be *stuck* in the dishwashing area. I was working in the kitchen, and they had me shuffling these trays back and forth. Back and forth I took them out. And

in the process of doing that I ended up with tendonitis in my arms within six days. And I had to stop, . . . and I thought, "What else can I get into?"

[Then] I worked for an insurance company for like one year. And I wasn't impressed with that either. . . . I went to a school to learn to read medical terminology, and actually what I was trying to do was be a claims adjuster. It was like working through Medicare, and you're adjusting these people's care forms and bills and stuff that are coming through. And when I went in, of course, you would start at the entry level. So I was a file clerk.

Like Gloria and Valerie, all of the women I interviewed demonstrated what economists call "long-term labor force attachment." As young women, many worked for pay during junior high and high school in telemarketing, food service, clerical work, and child care. Women who enrolled in college reported working while they attended college, primarily in food service or clerical work. Although they experienced these jobs with different degrees of permanency given their social location and opportunities, the women shared a common and lengthy employment history in low-wage, race- and sex-segregated, female-dominated jobs. All of them had "always worked": before and after the birth or adoption of their children, with limited breaks in paid employment. Among the women who were mothers, only four reported taking more than three weeks of maternity leave following the birth or adoption of a child. Their families needed them to return to work to pay the bills. As Patricia James, an African American provider, reported, "When you have your family, you need your money."

Only three of the twenty women worked in full-time, permanent positions with employment benefits during their late twenties to mid-thirties. The others all worked in low-wage jobs with few, if any, employment benefits and little, if any, opportunity for advancement. Typical jobs before entering family child care included seamstress, salesperson at Kentucky Fried Chicken, data entry operator, janitor, seasonal agricultural worker, teaching assistant at a child care center, and bookkeeper. Although the women demonstrated long-term attachment to the labor force, the available jobs involved long hours, low wages, and few personal or professional rewards. As a result, these women tended not to stay long in one position. Jobs ended because of the structural nature of the work (seasonal and temporary work), or workers left to seek employment with higher rewards.

The low wages, long hours, and sex- and racial ethnic–segregation that might cause some workers to shy away from (or never consider) the option of family child care employment did not appear to play a role in the employment decisions of the women I interviewed. Even though it was another form of sex-segregated, low-wage, service-sector employment, it held the promise of greater employment stability and a steady source of income as well as the likelihood of greater autonomy and personal rewards not available to the women in other forms of paid work.

Occupational Segregation and the High Cost of Child Care

Given the employment options available to them, the high cost of child care relative to their low wages emerged as a factor that influenced women to enter family child care work. While their earnings were low, the relative costs of child care were too high for work outside the home to be a viable economic option. By listening to the stories of family child care providers, we can learn more about the social processes that shape women's employment options. Gendered ideologies of motherhood and family have material consequences, including limited public investment in child care services, which in turn lead women to return home and care for children—this time, the children of others for pay.

Cora Jenkins, an African American mother of four and foster mother of a two-year-old son, discussed why she began working as a family child care provider nineteen years ago. She spoke explicitly of her difficulty in finding what is commonly referred to by child care advocates as "accessible, affordable, quality care": "I had three kids. I couldn't afford the cost of day care back *then*. So it was better for me to stay at home and take care of my three kids and other children than to go out to work. The wages were a lot lower then than they are now. So I preferred to stay at home and take care of my kids and then do child care, too."

Cora's reasoning acknowledges a concern commonly experienced by employed mothers: after deducting the cost of child care, what portion of women's historically low wages will remain? When working outside the home requires a woman to place her children in paid child care, at what point does the cost of child care exceed her own income? Given the employment options available to them, these were vital questions that the women I interviewed had to answer for themselves.

Janice Newman, a Euro-American family child care provider for thirteen years, discussed this dilemma when she spoke of her decision to leave her work as a kindergarten teacher after the birth of her third child. She calculated the cost of placing her three children in child care and determined that by caring for one or two children for pay, in addition to providing unpaid care for her three children, her net income would equal what she had been receiving as a full-time kindergarten teacher in the public schools. The cost of care in relation to her salary and the complex child care arrangements she would have had to coordinate to return to full-time teaching were enough to sway her from returning to the elementary school where she had been teaching for the past four years. Janice described her decision: "So financially, I said, 'Three kids in day care. I should just stay home. . . .'" I knew I had the skills to be around kids and that I could do [family child care] for a year. So it was no time, and I was full with six [kids], including my own. So I really enjoyed it, and I haven't looked back." Even for Janice, the woman with the most formal education among the providers I interviewed, including the highest-wage and -status employment and the most stable employment history, the cost of child care in relation to her income as a public school teacher caused her to reassess her employment options and costs and to enter family child care work. As Janice's and Cora's experiences attest, family child care is an employment option that enables women to counter the high cost of child care by providing unwaged care for their own young children while providing paid care for the children of others.

The experiences of these women make visible the larger social processes that influence women's decision to enter the work of family child care. Sex- and race-segregation in employment have long been documented, as have the effects of gender and race ethnicity on lowering wages. Women of color and white women form the largest proportion of employees in low-wage, service-sector employment. They historically earn less than their male counterparts in all jobs. Thus, gender and racial ethnic ideologies evident in the labor force and labor markets directly affect women's employment decisions. In making employment choices, women consciously consider their families' needs on multiple levels. What income can they earn through employment? And what costs accrue with employment? Specifically, what will child care cost (Hofferth and Collins 2000)? Even though they were responsible for supporting their families economically, the women I interviewed were also responsible for locating affordable, reliable care for their children (discussed later in this chapter). These two necessities—paid employment and affordable quality child care—directly conflict when low wages make child care inaccessible. Assessing the options available to them, family child care emerged as a means for them to earn money to support their families, while ensuring that care would be available to their own children.

Conflicts between Waged Work and Caring for One's Own Children

In addition to the relative high cost of child care, women also experienced conflicts when child care was neither stable nor readily accessible. Among the women I interviewed, the responsibilities of employment conflicted with the responsibilities of caring for their own children: bearing them, nursing them, and subsequently ensuring reliable care for them. Among a number of these women, the conflicts between caring for their own children and undertaking paid work outside the home proved insurmountable and resulted in their choice to enter family child care work.

Annette Bradley was one of these women. An African American mother of two, Annette provides family child care to supplement her income from public assistance. In our discussion, she related two specific instances in which difficulty in finding or providing care for her children resulted in her need to terminate her employment—once to return home to provide unpaid care for her daughter; the second time, to enter family child care work. Annette completed a six-month training course in barbering at a vocational school and began working at a local barber shop: "And then sometimes I just couldn't find a babysitter. I didn't have a steady babysitter."

I asked, "Would you have stayed on the job if you could have gotten child care?"

"At the time, yeah. But then I got into a car accident. . . ." Two years later Annette began working at a child care program for homeless children sponsored by her church. She took unpaid maternity leave from this position for two and a half months. After returning to work part time, "I just could not wean Adonica. . . . So that's when I said, 'Oh, well, forget it. I'll just stay home a year with her and see what happens after that.'"

Kay Schilling is a married Euro-American mother of two. She spoke of the challenges of finding quality child care and how the logistical conflicts of coordinating child care with paid work led to her decision to enter family child care.

> I had my first child. In that year I was trying to juggle work and get her to child care. I took her to a lady that wasn't licensed. I just had a really bad feeling about her. So I ended up [taking her to my mother's for care]. And my mom lives about a half an hour drive from here, and I would drive her to my mom's house and then drive to work. So . . . . I just had a really hard time.

Like Annette and Kay, other family child care providers spoke of conflicts in finding care for their own children as a factor that caused them to enter family child care work—in particular, difficulty in finding a single provider who would care for all of their children (especially if one of the children was an infant). Their experiences teach us that, counter to popular opinion, these women did not choose to become family providers out of a commitment to the ideal of the full-time, at-home mother. In fact, staying home to care for their own children was not their first choice. Instead, the lack of structural supports in the form of stable and reliable child care drew women into family child care work.

Patricia James is a licensed provider who is currently working toward a college degree in early childhood education. She discussed how she entered family child care work after the birth of her son. Both her pregnancy and the subsequent birth of her child affected her employment options and choices. When she became pregnant, she worked as a seamstress, sewing women's clothing at a small shop.

> And then I became pregnant in 1981. So it was like, "When you're physically able to come back to work, then you can come on back." So then after I had my son I was kind of like in limbo. I really didn't want to go back to [sewing]. It really wasn't *me*. I could do it, but it really wasn't what I had all my education and stuff in. . . . And I went to work at [the child care program sponsored by] the Jewish Community Center with my son. A job I

could take my son to. So I took my baby to work with me at the Jewish Community Center.

I asked, "Was that considered one of the benefits? They said, '. . . one of the things you can do is bring your baby?'"

Patricia said, "Yeah. You could bring your baby. I would have to *pay* for it, but still I could bring my baby. And that made it kind of nice. And that's what got me back into child care." But after working at child care centers, she realized, "Well, shoot. I could do this myself. I could be my own boss." Patricia subsequently decided to become a licensed provider and has provided paid child care in her home for the past eight years.

Workers also spoke about long hours and weekend work that required them to be away from their families and led to their decision to enter family child care work. Gloria Zuñiga recalled, "I didn't see the children."

Brenda Beall, a Euro-American provider, voiced similar concerns: "I worked Thanksgiving. I worked Christmas. And I wanted [work] where I could be home with my family on Mother's Day and holidays. It's real important to be with my family." Thus, while family child care also entails long hours and weekend work, the location of the work gives women increased flexibility and the opportunity to be more involved in the lives of their own families.

The experiences of family child care providers teach us that the gendered ideologies and social and biological realities of women's care for children explicitly shape their employment options and choices. While the women I interviewed did not intend to be full-time, at-home mothers, the biological and social responsibilities of mothering explicitly altered their employment options and subsequently their decisions to enter the work of family child care. For workers who experienced biological motherhood, pregnancy and nursing at times inhibited their participation in paid labor outside the home. Additionally, for many women the social childrearing (as opposed to the biological childbearing) aspects of motherhood conflicted with waged labor outside the home. Clearly, the values and choices of individuals led to their decisions to enter family child care work. At the same time, these choices were made within a larger social and economic context. In the lives of the women I interviewed, the lack of public resources and structural support to ensure the availability of reliable, accessible child care contributed to mothers' decisions to leave employment, provide unpaid care for their own children, or redefine their employment options and enter the work of family child care.

Individual Choices That Affirm Gendered Ideologies and Family Child Care Work

Although external constraints promote the gendered ideology and practice of women's care for children within families, the women I interviewed also made decisions that at times reinforced these ideologies. While paid labor was an essential component of their motherhood, structural conflicts clearly arose as women attempted to carry out their contiguous responsibilities as mothers: arranging for and coordinating the provision of care for their children so that they could work outside the home. The structural constraints of low-wage work and inaccessible, unaffordable child care were heightened in their lives by the child care responsibilities they assumed within their own homes. Gendered ideological practices of motherhood and family are facilitated in institutions and institutional practices outside the home (such as labor markets and public policy), but individuals also act in ways that both contribute to and challenge these ideological practices. Although providers struggled against dualistic and gendered ideologies of family versus market and care versus work when providing paid child care in their own homes, they also contributed to these ideologies.

This understanding emerged as I spoke with providers about their daily lives and work. As is frequently the case in interviews, silence can be as telling as conversation. Eighteen of the women I interviewed were mothers and lived with the fathers of their children when they entered family child care. In none of the interviews, however, did the issue of the fathers' responsibility for caring for or locating care for their children arise. As I reviewed interview transcripts in which women described their work day, which spanned the hours between rising in the morning until going to bed at night, patterns began to emerge. While a small number of husbands assisted their wives in the provision of family child care (either informally or, when not engaged in their own paid employment, as licensed assistants), fathers assumed very little responsibility for the care of their own children. This gendered division of labor within the families emerged with clarity as providers described their day of paid care work for the children of others combined with care work for their own family members.

Because their paid work day begins between 6:00 and 7:00 A.M., most providers rise at 5:00 or 5:30 A.M. In the mornings women care for their own family members: getting breakfast ready, preparing and packing lunches for their children and husband. "Cleaning and picking up. Empty the dishwasher. Those kinds of things," Martha Buxton reported. Following their day of paid family child care work, women reported another three to four hours of work in which they cared for family members: preparing and serving dinner, washing up after the meal, cleaning the house, doing laundry, shopping, helping children with homework, and bathing children and getting them to bed.

Annette Bradley described what happens after her day of family child care work has ended: "After I've gotten dinner ready and everybody has eaten, we sit around and watch [a TV show]. And then it's time to clean up. Time to wash clothes, vacuum, wash the dishes, and stuff like that. And that usually takes until about eleven o'clock at night. Then I sit down for about another half an hour. I usually fall asleep on the couch, or I go to bed . . . around 11:30 or 12:00." Annette's evening responsibilities also include nursing her eight-and-a-half-month-old daughter, putting her down for the night, helping her six-year-old daughter bathe and get ready for bed, and preparing her home for the next morning's arrival of family child care children.

Patricia James also spoke about her responsibilities after her day of family child care work ends: "By seven o'clock I'm through with the day care basically. And then I have to become Mom. And that might be taking my daughter to a friend's house to retrieve some clothing or return some clothing. Or going to the library with my son to do research for him. Or reading a story to my little one because he might want to hear his own story that he got from school. And then by nine o'clock I'm just my own self. I don't want to be bothered with nobody. I get one hour in for me."

Women's descriptions of their unpaid morning and evening work offer an important insight into their lives. While their paid care work contests the distinctly gendered ideological boundaries that separate market from family and care from work, in their own households providers consistently maintain a gendered division of labor. Like the vast majority of employed mothers, family child care providers put in a double day, in which a day of paid work is preceded and followed by several hours of care work for family members (Crittenden 2001, Harrington 2000). When they enter paid labor, family child care providers—and other employed mothers—continue to maintain primary responsibility for caring for their own children.

Research consistently confirms this gendered division of labor in families. Women spend from two to four times as many hours in domestic labor as do husbands (Coverman 1989). Over the past thirty years men have gradually begun to spend more time assuming child care responsibilities within families. Nevertheless, mothers continue to outspend fathers on time with children by a ratio of four to one (Rubenstein 1998). Confirming the experiences of the women I interviewed, social class appears to do little to mediate the gendered division of labor in households, specifically women's responsibility for children (Wright et al. 1992).

The gendered division of labor evident within the families of employed mothers particularly intrigued me with regard to family child care providers. Despite providers' daily struggle with gendered ideologies that associate women with care and thereby devalue their family child care work, providers themselves adhere to gendered ideologies and practices regarding women and care within their own families and households. This does not contradict my previous assertion regarding their perceptions of motherhood; among the providers I interviewed, their responsibilities as mothers were contiguous with their responsibilities as paid workers. Neither did these women adhere to newer manifestations of the ideology of full-time, at-home motherhood experienced by many employed mothers as intensive mothering (Hays 1996) or as a conflict between being either work- or family-oriented (Garey 1999). Nonetheless, ideologies of gender and motherhood remained central to the identities of the family child care providers I interviewed and had clear effects on the employment options they considered and the employment decisions they made. While providers viewed economic care for their own family members as the responsibility of both parents in a two-parent family, they did not view child care as a mutual parental responsibility. It was the women who were responsible for locating child care when they were employed outside the home. It was the women who juggled the responsibilities of coordinating care outside the home with their own employment. It was the women who considered entering family child care as a means of ensuring care for their children when their own low-wage jobs made child care unaffordable.

Here we see, once again, the ways in which gender is central to the organization of families and paid work and therefore central to the organization and provision of family child care work. In the lives of the women I interviewed, external constraints promoted the gendered ideology and practice that identifies women as the primary providers of care for children within families (both unpaid care for their own children and paid care for the children of others). These external constraints were a common experience regardless of women's racial ethnic identity, country of origin, or social class. Low wages in labor markets organized by race ethnicity and gender, coupled with a lack of reliable child care, a lack of affordable child care, and the social and biological responsibilities of motherhood, contributed to women's decisions to enter family child care—after attempting, unsuccessfully, to work outside the home. This experience clarifies the ways in which the gendered institution and dominant ideology of the family is re-created in our daily lives through a variety of social forces, including employment practices, the structure of local labor markets, and public policy (or, in this case, a lack thereof) that provides affordable, accessible, quality care for the children of employed mothers. Because women bear primary responsibility for child care within families and structural supports for employed mothers are, at best, in short supply, women return to the home to provide paid child care when labor markets (organized in accordance with gendered and racial ethnic ideologies) fail to pay wages sufficient for families to afford reliable child care.

THE DIFFERENT MEANINGS OF
COMMON EMPLOYMENT DECISIONS

Gender ideologies, both structural and those consciously and subconsciously adhered to by individuals, shaped the decisions of the women I interviewed to enter family child care. At the same time, other forces were equally active in drawing them to family child care work; and I became intrigued by the ways in which women in very different social locations came to a common decision to enter the work. My conversations with providers gave me an increased appreciation for the ways in which ideologies and processes of race ethnicity, culture, family economic status, and local labor markets interweave and influence not only the employment options available to women but also the choices they make regarding their employment and the meaning they ascribe to those choices. Regardless of social location, the women I interviewed made active choices about the employment that would best meet the economic and social needs of themselves and their families. Despite differences in racial ethnic identity, country of origin, and social class, their choice was to enter the work of family child care. Although each believed strongly in the social value of her work and enjoyed personal rewards from it, the women represented their reasons for entering the work very differently. Providers' social locations influenced their experience and representation of their work as a means of achieving stable and permanent employment, as a source of professional identity and continued professional mobility, or as an alternative form of professional employment.

Family Child Care As Stable and Permanent Employment

Seven of the twenty women I interviewed experienced family child care as the attainment of both stable and permanent employment. Primarily immigrant women (Mexicanas and one Vietnamese woman) but including one African American and one Euro-American, the women in this group all provided family child care in communities in which their employment options were severely constrained as a result of their country of origin, culture, race ethnicity, and formal education. Given limited employment opportunities and previous employment in temporary, part time, or seasonal jobs, family child care seemed to be a particularly viable form of employment. These workers actively chose to enter family child care and do not envision leaving it for other employment.

Isabel Inofuentes is a provider who sees family child care as permanent and stable employment. As we drive to Isabel's house, Paula Shelton, coordinator of the Catholic Family Services Seasonal Child Care Program, tells me that Isabel has been providing licensed family child care for the past eight years. Isabel greets us on the front porch of her small home, which she and her husband bought a few years ago. She is quiet, calm, and welcoming. She seats us at a dining room table covered with a hand-crocheted lace tablecloth. The air conditioner hums in the cool room as we sit sipping lemonade and talking about Isabel's life and work. I ask her about her history; and she tells me about her childhood in Mexico, her work experience before her family child care work, and the explicit experiences that led her to decide to enter family child care.

Isabel grew up in Tampico, Mexico, where her father worked as a fisherman and her mother "washed clothes and ironed" for other families. She attended school there, completing *la primaria* and *la secundaria*—the equivalent of American elementary, middle, and high schools.

> Then [I completed] two years of a business course, secretarial. Then I worked in an office. It was for a grocery store. I did the books, and I also did shorthand, transcribing. I did that for two years. . . . Then I came across to Texas. I came to work here. I worked for a time, and then I started the restaurant. . . . I had two restaurants. . . . I lived in Texas for twelve years. When we decided to make the move over here, we closed them down. We wanted to change our lives.

I ask, "And then why did you decide to come to eastern Washington?"

> We didn't plan to come to eastern Washington. But we knew some people who were coming to Wenatchee, and they invited us to come here because they said there was a lot of work up here. We came in an old car we had, and [the car] burned down on our way here. And somebody gave us a ride into Orlando. Then we got another ride. We got here with the children, and we didn't have a place to live or anything. So we went straight to the welfare office. They didn't want to give us any assistance because we didn't have our permanent residence because we were just transients, you know. We stayed at the Salvation Army. We stayed there a couple of days. I don't know how long. And then we stayed at the park. We were living in the park with five kids and nothing. Then we met Victor from the employment office, and he helped us find a room. Then we started looking for work. I found a job cooking at a restaurant. I only worked for

two months, and then it closed down. Then I went to work in the orchard.

"And how long did you work in the orchard?" I ask.

She answers, "One year. We started at five o'clock in the morning. We worked usually till four o'clock. We [thinned and pruned] cherries, apples, pears. I also picked pears and cherries and apples under contract. You could make anywhere from $100 to $120 per day."

When I ask Isabel why she started providing family child care, she describes the working conditions and the demands of seasonal agricultural labor: "The work in the fields was very heavy. Very hard. Picking cherries and apples." Then, while balancing on a ladder and picking fruit, "I fell and hurt myself. I was picking cherries when I fell. I fell from a ladder and broke my foot. And then I was on crutches." Unable to return to orchard work, Isabel heard through friends that the local Catholic Family Services program was recruiting child care providers. She contacted Paula, the program coordinator, who helped her through the process of becoming a state-licensed family child care provider. As a licensed provider, Isabel now offers family child care for children through various state-subsidized child care programs. When I ask her why she stays in family child care, she explains, "I like the job. I like the children. It is rewarding." She is emphatic that she will never leave family child care work and again speaks of the personal rewards and her commitment to her work: "The children I have right now—I started taking care of them when they were little tiny babies. Since they were first born, I've been caring for the same children—all through these years. They're still at the age where they need care."

Like Isabel, Laura Mayfield sees family child care as rewarding, permanent, and stable employment. In our interview Laura, a forty-one-year-old Euro-American provider, spoke of her schooling, her employment before becoming a licensed family child care provider, and the ways in which changes in agricultural employment have shaped her employment: "I finished eleventh grade. And then I quit and got married. I got my GED [high school General Equivalency Diploma]. And then I took a typing course at Trend Business College while I was in the CETA program."

I asked when she got her GED.

That was when I was working in the support enforcement office. I had to get my GED before I could work in that position with the state. . . . I worked at a support enforcement office in a [CETA] training position. I was a secretary and worked on the computer. And I've done migrant work. Picking and thinning and pruning. And I worked at a restaurant as a teenager. . . . I done orchard work until the time I started at the enforcement office. So I did that about ten years.

"Did you work all year or primarily during harvest?" I asked.

Well, I picked and thinned. Sometimes I'd be off. And sometimes we'd work for a different orchard. We'd go out and prop or pick up the props or do summer pruning. Stuff like that. To be honest, I liked the money. We made real good money then. . . . We could make anywhere from $100 to $150 a day. You can't do that now though. Or we couldn't. Everything's more expensive now. But wages is still the same thing they was back twenty years ago in orchard work. Wages haven't increased. . . . [But] it was hard work. It's real hard work.

Laura's and Isabel's descriptions of their education and employment experience characterize those of the women who see family child care as a source of steady employment. Formal education and the unwillingness of employers to recognize the formal education of immigrant women in their country of origin influence the employment options available to women. For women with limited formal education, the decision to enter family child care is an empowering decision—a means of experiencing advancement in employment status and stability. Among the providers I interviewed, women who experience family child care as a source of fixed employment have the lowest level of formal education. While several women had not finished high school (or a GED high school equivalency), some had completed high school or vocational training. These levels of formal education were generally lower than that of the adult population in communities where providers live (U.S. Department of Commerce, Bureau of the Census 1990b). As such, these women were not as competitive as more highly educated workers, and their employment options were limited to jobs that required minimal formal education.

In addition, the women who had grown up and completed their formal education in Mexico were affected by the difference in the recognition of their education and that offered in the United States. Victor Rodriguez, an outreach worker with the Washington State Migrant and Seasonal Farmworker Outreach Program, spoke with me about employment options for Mexicanas in the Wenatchee Valley. For agricultural jobs requiring physical labor, few, if any, formal education requirements exist. But if women workers seek to advance to a supervisory job in agricultural employment or a job requiring clerical or computer skills, employers look for a U.S. high school degree or a GED. Thus, even though Isabel and other Mexicanas had completed the equivalent of high school in the United States and had received vocational training in Mexico, their education was not recognized or valued in jobs that require a high school diploma.

Kappner (1984) confirms that the educational levels of family child care workers "are likely confounded by the variables of ethnicity, age, and agency affiliation" (101–2). Kappner goes on to tell us that, while the median years of education among a racially and ethnically diverse population of New York providers is twelve years, only 23 percent of Hispanic providers had completed a high school education. The twenty-year-old National Day Care Home Study remains the most comprehensive study of a large population of family child care providers of wide racial ethnic diversity. It, like Kappner, finds a relationship between race ethnicity and levels of formal education among providers. While the majority of providers (57 percent) had completed high school, the median education for Hispanic providers was 9.6 years. Hispanic providers had two years less education, on average, than black providers and almost three years less than white providers. While researchers go on to explain that "educational attainment has traditionally been considered the least relevant index of competence for family day care providers, [n]evertheless, it is still held by some to be an index of professionalism" (Fosburg 1981, 44). Formal education may be an inadequate reflection of job competence, but it remains a powerful social indicator of skill and ability. As a result, formal education (or a lack of it) affects the employment options available to all workers, including family child care providers.

Paula Shelton discussed the types of employment that the majority of family child care providers in her community held before their family child care employment: "The majority have worked in orchards or packing sheds in the past. . . . A lot of them have been working in hotels as maids. That's one of the biggest jobs they have around here. A lot of women work at [motels] and the orchard."

Thus, family child care is an attractive occupation and one that providers with severely limited employment options plan to continue. When I asked Isabel if she ever considered leaving family day care work, she replied emphatically, "No. Never. No." When I asked Laura the same question, she responded "No. No. Never have." Consistently, these women clearly state that they never consider leaving the work. The providers offer differing but related reasons for remaining in the work. Segunda explained, "Because I like children. I have children that I have cared for a long time. To me, they are like my own children." Gloria Zuñiga reported, "This is a very stable job. It's better than working outside [the home]."

Immigrant women's experience of family child care as desirable and rewarding employment is informed, in part, by the social context of both their country of origin and their immigrant status in the United States. As Hondagneu-Sotelo (2001) determined in her study of immigrant women who work as nannies and housekeepers, immigrant women use their society of origin as a point of comparison regarding their employment. As a result, "the low pay may seem acceptable when they compare it to what they had previously earned in Mexico or El Salvador" (65). When one's country of origin is coupled with limited employment opportunities in the United States, women view their entry into family child care work (otherwise regarded as low-wage, low-status work) as a means of increasing their employment status by achieving both occupational mobility in rewarding work as well as employment stability and permanence in an otherwise precarious labor market.

In her study of the occupational mobility and work history of forty Mexicana immigrants and Chicanas, Denise Segura (1986) offers analysis that sheds light on Mexicana providers' view of their work as permanent and rewarding employment.

> [W]omen who had limited occupational options saw employment in a stable job arena as a form of mobility. Similarly, women who were unsure of whether or not they could obtain any job at all felt mobile when they found employment. . . .

This interplay between objective and subjective aspects of occupational mobility underscores the complex character of Chicanas' and Mexicanas' experiences in labor markets, which are themselves shaped by the structures of race and gender. (cited in Dill and Zinn 1990, 10)

Given their previous employment in temporary, seasonal, and part-time jobs, women actively choose family child care employment and experience it as not only permanent but also rewarding employment. Annette Bradley spoke of the ways in which she saw the work as personally rewarding, especially compared to her previous employment as a telemarketer for a cable television company. When asked why she planned to continue in family child care, she smiled and spoke with enthusiasm:

> I've always loved kids. I can't explain it any other way. Because they're all at the learning stage. They're so energetic. I mean, you can never sit down at a desk and say, "Oh, I don't have anything to do." I've done that. That's one of the reasons I left [the cable company] was because there was a whole lot of time when I had nothing to do, and that's when me and the supervisor used to conflict: "Do something. Do something."
>
> "You give me something to do and I'll do it." But if I don't have nothing to do and I'm bored, I'll just sit there.

Annette plans to stay in family child care; but rather than continuing as an unlicensed provider, she has begun the process of becoming licensed. "Why are you interested in being licensed?" I asked.

Annette explained, "Oh, because I want to be in charge. I like the responsibility of being in charge. It's exciting. And I'd get more kids and more money, of course. I'd make a living at it. I might as well be making a living at it." For Annette, entering family child care and becoming a licensed provider are active decisions that enable her to experience greater autonomy and power within the social context and structural constraints of her life.

Like Annette, many providers appreciate the rewards, responsibility, and stability of family child care employment. By working in their own homes, women gain increased control over their work environment. In addition, they engage in work they find personally rewarding, achieve employment stability through permanent work, and earn a stable (though limited) income with which to support their families.

Family Child Care As a Source of Professional Identity and Continued Professional Mobility

Ten of the twenty women I interviewed identified their entry into family child care as a source of professional identity and a means of professional development. In addition, given that no career ladders are available within family child care, many women chose to use their family child care experience as a means of facilitating continued professional mobility. These women, all of whom are native-born and native-English speakers, include seven African American and three Euro-American women who live in small towns, suburbs, and urban settings. Julia Deavers is one of these women, a licensed Euro-American provider for four years, who lives and works in a small town. Like other providers for whom family child care serves as a source of professional identity and mobility, Julia's level of formal education is higher and, having been received in the United States, is more widely recognized than that of immigrant providers. Julia completed high school as well as one year of college and is certified as a child development associate. Among providers like Julia who choose family child care as their source of professional identity and development, all have completed high school or received a GED certificate in the United States. Two of the ten have completed a college-level associate of arts degree, two are working toward completion of that degree, and three have completed college coursework (but not toward a specific degree). Three are certified by the National Association for the Education of Young Children as child development associates.

Their higher levels of formal education, native-English skills, citizenship, and location in larger labor markets give these women access to more employment options than are available to providers who experience family child care as permanent employment. Within the array of options available to them, providers such as Julia identify family child care as their chosen profession and, in some instances, as a career springboard to other forms of professional employment in early childhood education or related social service work.

At age thirty-seven, Julia has one of the most varied employ-ment histories of the providers I interviewed. Like the history of providers for whom family child care is a means of achieving per-manent and stable employment, Julia's employment history before entering the field is composed of short-term jobs. But she repre-sents her employment history in a different way—as one moti-vated by a self-conscious search for meaningful work and a source of professional identity. Like her peers, Julia held jobs primarily in sex-segregated, service-sector employment. In our interview she of-fered a chronological summary of her employment history:

> I was a hairdresser for ten years. That was my first career. Then I was a cook for a year at Celestial Seasonings. It was like a store/deli. And then I managed an office for a year. And then I joined the Peace Corps and raised goats in the Philippines. And then I groomed dogs for a year. And throughout all of that I've always done waitress work. . . . I have found that every single job that I've done has prepared me for [entering and providing] child care.

I asked Julia to tell me more about the jobs she had held— what she liked, why she left, and what specifically she gained that helped prepare her for becoming a family child care provider. Julia represents her work history as one actively motivated by a search for meaning. Although providers who entered family child care work from a social location of severely constrained employment options may also have experienced their choice as a search for meaning, they did not consciously represent it as such. They re-ported that, once they began providing family child care, they found it to be personally rewarding but did not discuss their deci-sion to become a provider as one motivated by a conscious search for such a reward. Julia discussed her own employment history differently:

> Basically I've left all of [my previous jobs] because I've always searched to have meaning in my jobs. So the time I started in hairdressing, I knew I would not last in it. I stayed a long time because I made a lot of money at it and just didn't know what else to do. But the whole time it just did not have enough mean-ing for me. But what I loved about it was the intimate involve-ment I had with everybody and the fact that it changed all the time. I really liked that.

I love cooking. That was a wonderful job just because I love to cook. Managing an office—it gave me some good organizational experience. I didn't like it much. . . . I'm not good at sitting at a desk. I like to move. I like to have a lot of different things [happening]. I find that I work best at a high-stress level.

Peace Corps. I really liked it a lot. It was total hell. But [the] experience [it] gave me [was like] having an uncarved block— where it was up to me to create what it was. It was totally and completely up to me. I wasn't walking into a situation that was already prearranged for me. And so as overwhelming and hellish as that is, to have to create [something] out of nothing, it was a really valuable experience to have to rely on myself. Oh, and then grooming dogs. Oh, god. That was *hard*. But the experience was in learning to control my own emotions. I mean, it's the same thing in child care. I cannot control these kids and make them into something I want them to be so that my job is easier. So I had to learn. I have an ability to not need to have the control that a *lot* of people need around kids. I can handle chaos really well. And I can accept reality very well. So that job helped a lot.

Throughout her employment, Julia sought jobs that were meaningful and rewarding to her. And when she found them unrewarding, she tried to glean what she could and chose to move on. After working in several such jobs over a period of thirteen years, she decided to enter family child care. In listening to her describe her decision, we learn that Julia's active search for meaningful work is shared by her husband: "It was apparent that [my husband] *really* wanted to change occupations. He was in construction for many years and did *quite* well at it. But he *hated* it. He wanted to go back to school and finish his degree." So Julia's husband left his well-paying construction job to return to a former massage therapy practice and to school. He had been the primary economic supporter of their family after the birth of their daughter, but with his return to school Julia's employment became increasingly pivotal for her family. While she needed to support her family economically, she was also the adult responsible for child care in her family. How could she ensure quality care for her daughter, support her family economically, draw on her previous employment history, and engage in work "where I could be happy"? Family child care emerged as the answer. "I got licensed at the beginning. I entered [family child care] as a profession. I entered it wanting it to be a business right from the start. I wanted to do a business of day care. So I started by getting licensed."

Like Julia, Sondra Ames held a variety of positions before entering family child care and came to the work as part of a conscious search for personal and professional identity. But unlike Julia, Sondra climbed a career ladder with a single employer until an economic downturn led to her early retirement and her search for new employment and a new source of professional identity. A thirty-eight-year-old African American provider for two years, Sondra described her employment before entering family child care.

> At eighteen I graduated from high school, had a baby, went to [a vocational training center] to get some typing skills. And then I started at PNB [Pacific Northwest Bell] making $475 a month. I started entry-level typing. I was in that [position] five years until my promotion to first level of management as an instructor. I was there for eighteen months. And then I went into supervisor. And then the split came [the court-ordered separation of AT&T and its regional companies]. Then I went to the AT&T side as a sales manager and stayed there for five more years. Then AT&T was reorganizing. You know, cutting back. And the opportunity came to take early retirement or probably get laid off. I was on the list to get laid off if I didn't take early retirement. I took the early retirement.
>
> I left AT&T in August of that year. . . . I didn't know what I wanted to do after that because I didn't have any formal education and I was trying to think, "What do I want to do?" There were a lot of changes going on. Looking for jobs. Looking for jobs. Looking for jobs. Nobody was willing to give me anything close to what I was making.

I asked, "So there were jobs . . . , but they weren't at a reasonable salary?"

> Yeah. And I did some temporary work, and I really liked temporary service. But I had to take a real job [laughter]. I had done some temporary work for the university, so I took a [permanent] job at the University Hospital. [In 1985] I was in management at AT&T making $3,000 a month. And I ended up taking a job as an accounts worker at University Hospital making $1,200 a month.

The career ladder Sondra climbed during her years at AT&T reflects the opportunities available to many workers, both women and men, in the primary labor market in the postwar period of the 1970s and 1980s. But as the U.S. economy declined in the 1970s and moved into recession, workers like Sondra increasingly experienced job loss, declining wages, or early retirement. After twelve years of stable employment with expanding job responsibilities and income, Sondra found herself in a labor market with increasingly limited job opportunities. Previously working in management, Sondra found that her new job as an accounts manager entailed much less responsibility and a salary cut of 60 percent.

She stayed at the hospital for five years, but throughout that time she anticipated her entry into family child care: "I just believed through my relationship with God that I was going to have a business. And I didn't know what kind."

"Why did you pick family child care?" I asked.

Well, I had been thinking of social work because of my interaction with the cancer patients [at the hospital]. And at one time I was going to go back to school at the university and try to get a degree in social work. I took a couple of classes and then—it just didn't seem like it was happening. And my mom had been in day care. We were raised by a day care mom. And so I got to thinking about it, and I thought, "Well, I want to do it." I went to my husband and asked him. That was like October 1. And we set the wheels in motion immediately. And we were ready and waiting for licensers in December. I quit my job as soon as my licenser got out and approved [our home]. I had already gave my job notice and everything.

Sondra's job as an accounts manager before her entry into family child care is typical of the employment histories of other women who describe family child care as their chosen profession. Before family child care employment, these women worked most often as clerical workers, sales attendants, food service workers, teacher's aides, or child care center employees. Sondra was the one woman who had climbed a career ladder to a management position; but as a result of large-scale economic and corporate transitions, she found herself in a clerical position similar to the one she first held when she began her career twelve years earlier.

Given their employment experience in lower-wage, and sex-segregated jobs, workers such as Julia and Sondra consciously sought opportunities for personal and professional growth and

represented their decision to enter family child care as the culmi-
nation of a self-conscious search for meaningful employment and
a professional identity. Among the women I interviewed, commitment to family child care as a profession is manifest in their
longevity in the field. In contrast to the high turnover in family
child care (estimated at 30 percent annually) (Kontos 1992), women
I interviewed who described family child care as their chosen professional identity have remained in the work for a median of eight
years—significantly longer than the statewide average (Miller and
Schrager 2000).

In contrast to the women who report that they will never leave
family child care, these women often see the work as a means of facilitating continued professional mobility. For women with more
formal education, native English skills, U.S. citizenship, and access
to larger and more diverse labor markets, leaving family child care
is a viable option. Providers who plan to leave the work (or have already done so) consciously build on their family child care skills
and experience as they seek other employment in social services or
early childhood education.

Julia and Sondra are among the providers who are using family
child care as a professional springboard. Julia told me about her future plans. Having recently separated from her husband, she is increasingly conscious of her need to support herself and her family
and is attentive to this need as she prepares to move into another
form of work with young children.

> Just this last December I finished a degree called a CDA, which is
> a child development associate. Well, now I have this credential
> that I wanted. It's a real valued credential in the field of early
> childhood [education] because it's such a new field that they're
> really pushing to educate people who are already in it. So that
> credential I have, although it's not a lot, means a lot in this
> field. And what I want to do is I would like to open a child care
> in a high school. They're opening up child cares in high schools.
> And I would like to do parent education with the teenage girls
> and run the child care. Manage the child care. And so I need to
> research that. My plan is to research it and see what the pay is
> and what it would take for me to get into it. I need to see how
> much they pay. I mean, can I make a living? Can I support my-
> self? And I want summers off and Christmases off. I've been
> working at an ungodly pace for four years.

Sondra, like Julia, plans to make the transition from family child care to other employment. While building her family child care business for the past two years, she has expanded the transportation service originally incorporated into her family child care as a separate business.

> When we set up the child care, it was set up with providing transportation for our child care clients. That was what was going to be different about us. We were providing extra services above and beyond the call. And so transportation was provided for my child care kids. And we were getting calls from people wanting transportation for other child cares. Kids in school that [parents] didn't want to ride the school bus for whatever reason. Or kids that parents thought had to walk too far. And so I decided to expand [our transportation services]. And so in March we decided to go into transportation [more fully]. So immediately we incorporated and did it. Just did it. . . . It has grown so much. We have five vehicles. . . . We contract with some [social service] agencies to provide transportation to some of their clients.

While some providers report they will never leave family child care, providers such as Julia and Sondra are making different choices. In contrast to those with severely constrained employment options, women with a greater array of opportunities elect family child care work as a source of meaningful professional identity and continued professional mobility. Having different personal resources as well as structural opportunities, these providers, when they choose to do so, are able to use their professional family child care experience as a career springboard into other early childhood education or social service employment.

Family Child Care As Alternative Professional Employment

Three of the women I interviewed chose to enter family child care as an alternative form of professional employment. Of these women, two are native-born and one emigrated from England with her family when she was fourteen. All are of European descent, live in small towns, and are native English speakers. Each of these providers completed a B.A. degree, making them, of all the women I interviewed, the providers with the highest level of formal education. Before becoming family child care providers, they had the most stable employment histories and the highest-status employment among the women I interviewed: all worked as public schoolteachers. Allie McGinnis is one of these women. She spoke about her lifelong goal of being a teacher as well as the rewards and challenges of employment as a teacher.

> I had always known that I had wanted to work with children. I had very positive experiences in school. And I loved my teachers, and I just thought it would be the most wonderful job in the world. . . . I went to college off and on for nine years. And did a lot of traveling in between. I eventually did get my teaching certificate. And I got the first teaching job I ever applied for! Which just shocked me and petrified me. And I thought, "Oh God! Do I even *want* it? It's a fifty mile [one-way commute]." But I took it. It was a second-grade position. And it was one of the hardest years of my life. Also, one of the most rewarding. It was *very* challenging. So I taught second grade for a year, and the commute was really hard on top of it being first year teaching.
>
> And teaching—people say, "If you get through the first two years, you'll make it. You'll have your curriculum all set up, and you'll just breeze through it." Well, first of all it doesn't work that way. You're *constantly* revamping your curriculum. You have new kids and new problems and new parents. And I just realized that I was not willing to devote that much of my life to one thing. It took me two years to truly make that decision. . . . It's hard to give up a dream you've had since you were eight or nine years old. It really was a dream. And something I knew I would do. My whole life, I just knew I would teach. So giving up that dream was really, *really* difficult.

I asked, "And why did you have to give up that dream?"

She replied, "[Teaching] was all I did with my life. I just did not want to devote all this time to one thing. And [the decision not to teach] is hard for me to accept sometimes. . . . And I still second-guess myself sometimes. I still say, 'I think I'll go back to teaching part time some day.' And you know, I may. Part time may work."

While Allie thoroughly enjoyed her work with children, the demands of preparation, teaching, curricular design, and curriculum revamping were further exacerbated by the lack of institutional support she experienced as a public schoolteacher. Both Allie and Janice Newman, another former schoolteacher and current family child care provider, spoke about their love of teaching; but they also spoke of their dislike of the institutional practices and philosophies that constrained their teaching styles and the pleasure they gained from teaching. Allie reflected, "The school system isn't changing as fast as I'd like. And that was one of the other things was dealing with the administration. The constraints that I found on myself that I did not enjoy."

"What were those constraints?" I asked.

> I didn't have kids in desks very often. And I got a lot of very undermining [responses]—nothing direct [like] "Your children will only learn if they sit in their desks." But lots of jabs. . . . And I think it was threatening. A lot of the older teachers who were there were *very* settled in what they were doing. I think it was a little threatening to them to have someone come in and do something *totally* differently. And have a classroom that was not quiet very much of the time. There were kids who worked well in quiet, so I had that, too. But most of the kids didn't. They didn't like sitting in desks all day, and so we didn't. We did lots of other things. We still did the curriculum but just in different ways. So that was hard, too. The pressure [on me] from people to do something in a way that's been done for a long time. And that was partly the school and the school district. I'm sure there's schools that encourage that, but I wasn't in one.

Janice, a kindergarten teacher in the public schools before entering family child care, recalled similar dislikes about teaching in a public school setting.

> I disliked how much my hands were tied. You had curriculum, and that's what you were to follow. And I'll tell you what else I disliked. I disliked the "in" stuff amongst the teachers. I like people a *lot*. And I like my parents coming in and out. But with teaching, the territorial stuff, like "You can't teach that because that's a second-grade thing and you can't do that." And "If you do that, then they're going to think we want to do this every year." Like I would want to put on a spring program. Or we had a mother-daughter tea. And it was like "You're making us all look bad. Why are you doing that?"
>
> "Well, because it's fun! Let's just do it." Christmas programs, that kind of thing. And so I was always getting in trouble for that kind of stuff.

As a result of frustration with the institutional constraints and practices of the public schools, both Janice and Allie eventually left their jobs. Allie reflected on her subsequent decision to enter family child care work.

So [leaving my teaching job] brought me to not knowing what I was going to do—and being a little concerned about it. Especially with [my husband] in school. It was like, "Okay. I'm still the breadwinner here, and we've got to make some bread" [laughter]. And it was right about that time when [my neighbor] came to me and asked me to care for her son. And it went on from there. And [family child care] meant still working with kids. And I think for me that made the transition easier. "I'm *not* giving up my dream to work with children yet. I'm *still* working with children, and so it's okay."

For Allie, family child care emerged as alternative professional employment. She could continue to draw on her education and skills as a teacher, experience the most enjoyable parts of teaching ("working with small groups or one on one was my favorite"), and earn the wages she needed to support her family.

Allie was the only provider I interviewed who entered family child care work when she had no children of her own. The other women I interviewed were mothers when they entered the field; and as we have learned, motherhood played a central role in their employment options and choices. Janice Newman and Martha Buxton, the two other women who chose family child care work as an alternative to teaching in the public schools, were no exception. When faced with the need to leave the public schools because of personal choice and the structural constraints related to their own child care needs, both women identified family child care as a form of employment where they could use their professional skills, carry out their commitment to early education and care for young children, and contribute to their own families' economic support. Martha spoke of her personal and professional commitment to making sure that children receive "good, quality care" and the rewards she experiences in family child care.

I think tending children is a real important job. And in fact, I can't think of anything more important that working with human beings. . . . I like children. I think it's important that they have good-quality care. [That they have] attention. And lots of time. Playing with and talking to. Just spending time with [them]. I love all of the children. And if I didn't love them, I don't know if I could—I don't know if you'd even want to do [this work].

Janice also spoke of the ways in which she is able to facilitate children's development in family child care work and the benefits of doing so in a family child care environment rather than a school environment. "I enjoy working with the kids, [just] as I did with school. But it's just different. There's more nurturing going on in family child care than in school."

"Can you tell me about that?" I asked.

> Well, in family child care you're so involved with their daily lives, and you watch all their little triumphs. You watch them go from infant to achieving walking. It's like you raise a lot of kids. And I enjoy that a lot. In school I enjoyed teaching the skills. I enjoyed watching the personalities emerge among those kids. But the sad part was that I didn't have them long enough to make a really big impact on them. Sometimes family child care is the best thing that happens to a kid. . . . When you're teaching school, all the basic insecurities and the sad things—they're set with those kids. And in family day care you can really make a difference. A huge difference. Because you're just one on one with those kids all day long.

For all three women, family child care offers an opportunity to continue to work with children but in an alternative environment that provides greater professional opportunity and rewards. Each of these former teachers appreciates the more personal and flexible environment of family child care, where they believe they can provide higher-quality care and service than they could as teachers in the public schools. The stories of these providers and their decisions to enter family child care foreground the differences between women who represent their decisions to enter the field as a means of achieving permanent and stable employment (often immigrants and former agricultural and food service workers) and those who represent family child care as a form of alternative professional employment (white, former public schoolteachers). While earlier in their lives, all of the women I interviewed worked in similar jobs (primarily service-sector and often clerical jobs), the women who eventually became public schoolteachers viewed these jobs as temporary, a stopgap measure on the way to more permanent, professional employment in the public schools.

Family child care enabled Martha, Allie, and Janice to continue to use their professional skills and education in a setting that allowed more independence and creativity. This opportunity to leave one higher-status, higher-paid job for one with lower pay and lower status but greater professional reward (family child care) reflects the employment opportunities that these providers perceive to be available to themselves—and that *are*, in fact, available to them. In contrast to providers who reported, "No. I will never leave family child care," providers who chose family child care as a form of alternative professional employment have all considered leaving the work. After three years as a provider, Allie explained her decision to leave the work as one motivated by a need to distinguish more fully between her work life and her personal life.

> I'd had it [laughter]. . . . I wanted adult contact in the work. . . . The diligence it took to do [quality care]—just in terms of physical energy and emotional energy. *Lots* of emotional energy expended. And I was ready for something that would leave me with more of my emotional energy for my personal life. . . . If I ever am working with children again, which I *still* am drawn to just *passionately*, I think I would have a much easier time having my own life separate from—not completely separate; certainly they're going to overlap—but being able to meet my needs away from my job and have the energy for that.

Allie also spoke of the lack of social value and respect granted to family child care providers. "Certainly the people I did child care for had a great deal of respect for me. They were wonderful. But I didn't get much support from other people around me. There were some people I knew who thought that it was wonderful and looked upon it as a job—and most of those people were women with children. But it was not looked upon by a lot of people as my work—[work] that you had to have skills for."

Unlike Allie, Martha has chosen to continue in family child care. But like Allie, Martha voiced concern about the lack of public value accorded to child care and providers. When I asked if she had ever considered leaving family child care work, she responded immediately, "Oh yeah." As I queried her further, she spoke of the low pay, the perception that anyone actively choosing to engage in family child care was "nutty," and of the "stigma" attached to the work. Janice voiced similar concerns: "I have often fielded questions from providers, 'Is this worth it?' I personally have thought about 'Is it worth it?' when I've had to deal with parents that aren't supporting me. With parents that don't take me seriously." But after twelve years of "having to defend this profession," Janice rarely thinks of leaving family child care. During her tenure in the field, she has become an active child care advocate, serving as past president of the state's Association for Family Child Care. As she says, "Now I'm able to meet people head-on and not apologize for what I do."

DIFFERING SOCIAL LOCATIONS, SIMILAR DECISIONS

As former public schoolteachers who have chosen to remain in family child care work, Janice and Martha differ in significant ways from providers with severely limited employment options, primarily immigrant providers for whom the choice to enter family child care is a means of achieving permanent and stable employment. Clearly, both Janice and Martha could make more money by engaging in work other than family child care. With their formal education, employment experience, racial ethnic identity, citizenship, and cultural access, more lucrative sources of employment exist for them in their communities. Yet they choose to remain committed to the work. This is partially because of the economic status and pooled resources available to them through their families. Martha's husband works as a psychologist in the public schools and has been employed there for more than twenty years. Janice's husband teaches and coaches at a public high school and has worked in the schools for more than fifteen years. Through marriage and the stable, professional employment of their husbands, both women have greater financial resources than do those women who report that they will never leave family child care. Although other, more financially rewarding employment is available to both Janice and Martha in the public schools, neither is required to consider leaving her less lucrative but more personally and professionally rewarding family child care work.

Why do women who vary so greatly in racial ethnic and cultural identity, social class, and employment opportunities choose to engage in the common occupation of family child care? The decisions can be explained, in part, by a process called "sending out," in which consideration is given to family members' ability to generate income.

"Sending out" is important. . . . How much labor power a working-class household needs to send out is determined by many things: the cost of reproducing (or maintaining) the household, the work careers and earning trajectories of individual members, and the domestic cycle (that is, the relations between the genders and the generations, which specify when and if wives and adolescent children are available to work outside the home). (Rapp 1992, 53)

The decision to send out labor clearly varies among families of the women I interviewed and depends, to a large extent, on the material resources available to them. The paid labor of former schoolteachers such as Janice and Martha need not be, proportionally, as financially rewarding to their families as the labor of former seasonal agricultural workers such as Isabel and Laura. In Janice's and Martha's families, the employment of their husbands provides a stable income as well as health insurance benefits for all family members. While their families depend on the women's income, they also have the option of sending out less female labor as a result of a stable and sufficiently sizable source of male income. Families such as Isabel's and Laura's also send out their adult female labor. For these families, however, family child care is one of the ways to ensure the maximum financial return from adult female labor. Women such as Isabel and Laura choose to engage in family child care work in part because it is the most stable and lucrative form of employment available in the race- and sex-segregated markets in which they must otherwise sell their labor. In listening to the stories of providers we learn that similar choices (in this case, to remain in family child care work) can emerge from very different social and economic locations. While financial resources differ dramatically when comparing families such as Martha's and Janice's with those of Isabel and Laura, the decisions regarding how to best use female labor are the same.

The stories of providers reveal the diversity of their biographies, their daily lives, and employment histories and help us appreciate that they are clearly not a homogenous group. The workers share a common experience of gender as an ideology and practice and share ways in which this ideology and practice informs their employment opportunities and choices. At the same time, these women differ dramatically in their racial ethnic identity, country of origin, citizenship, formal education, and the local markets in which they sell their labor. Interviews with diverse providers illuminate the ways in which these processes not only influence women's decisions to enter family child care work but the meaning that they ascribe to these decisions. Dill and Zinn (1990) describe these processes; the multiple forces that comprise them; and in particular, the ways in which constructs of race, gender, and class must be recognized "as fundamental analytical categories with complex and interacting effects on human social behavior. Nor [should] these constructs [be] seen as descriptors solely of Blacks, Latinos . . . the working class, or of women. Instead, they are seen as categories which classify *all* members of society. Everyone is affected by their location in each of these categories" (1).

While each has a degree of autonomy, race ethnicity, class, and gender do not operate separately. By viewing the decision to enter family child care work from the perspective of diverse providers, we see the ways in which immigrant status, racial ethnic identity, gender, and social class are in fact integrated processes that generate disparate opportunities, choices, and meaning within women's employment. This interaction of social processes is seen in the ways in which women from widely different social locations are drawn into a similar occupational choice: family child care. While the decision may be similar, it has significantly different meanings for the women who make this choice.

5

"IT'S WORD OF MOUTH"
Social Networks, Local Markets, and the Provision of State-Subsidized Family Child Care

Through my interviews with family child care providers I came to appreciate the ways in which both geography and social networks are key to understanding the organization and provision of family child care. Providers sell their child care services in markets bounded by local geography. And members of the geographic communities tend to share a common racial ethnic identity and socioeconomic status. Thus, social networks and local markets facilitate providers' sale of their services to families who are much like themselves as regards social class, racial ethnic identity, and cultural identity. These social forces play a primary role in a provider's determination about which clients she will serve. In particular, social networks and local markets influence providers' decisions about whether or not they will serve families for whom child care is government-subsidized. How does the geographic location of a provider's home (which doubles as her paid workplace) influence to whom she sells her child care services? How do this location and its relation to social networks inform her decision about whether or not providing government-subsidized care will work to her financial advantage? And how does the organization of family child care (including government-subsidized programs) by local markets and social networks both challenge and reinforce structural forces of race ethnicity and social class?

For providers in lower-income communities in which parents' ability to pay for care is severely constrained, the reliability of the government as a stable source of payment makes the provision of government-subsidized care attractive. Providers' decisions to offer government-subsidized care enable them to challenge the structural link between social class and race ethnicity that limits families' ability to pay for care and subsequently providers' own earnings. Because they understand parents' limited ability to pay for care, providers in lower-income communities are able to ensure a stable source of income for themselves and their own families by offering state-subsidized care. Although the decision to provide such care can challenge structural constraints of race ethnicity and social class, it also re-creates these relationships through the low rates paid by the state. By paying low rates for care in lower-income communities, government-funded programs reinforce structures of race ethnicity and social class within and between communities.

NEIGHBORHOODS, SOCIAL NETWORKS, AND FAMILY CHILD CARE WORK

According to all the providers I interviewed, word of mouth is the predominant mode of advertising their child care services. Despite economic, racial ethnic, and cultural differences, providers share a common attribute of informally marketing their services through the grapevine. Justine Reeves, an urban African American family child care provider for four years and certified child development associate, describes the importance of social networks in informally advertising her services: "All of my self-pay clients are clients that have been referred to me from past parents. [Clients] are coming from my friends who say, 'Oh, maybe Justine has an opening,' and they give me a call."

Martha Buxton, a native-born Euro-American woman with a bachelor's degree in education, provides family child care to middle-income families. When asked why she attracts these families, she replied, "Probably because I don't advertise. It's word of mouth. And so many of the people I tend are the neighbors. And my husband works, and the people he works with know that I do day care, and many times they refer children to me. And people that I have tended for, they will tell their friends and neighbors. That's how it's happened. Just word of mouth."

Kim Phan is a Vietnamese immigrant who arrived in the United States in 1978. "We are boat people," Kim said, identifying herself one of the refugees who came to the United States after the Vietnam War. "We escaped, and we came to the Malaysia camp for five and a half months." Kim began providing unlicensed family child care immediately after arriving in the United States; and for five years she offered paid, home-based child care to other Vietnamese families in her community.

"How did people find out you were providing child care?" I asked.

"Many people ask me to babysit[1] because the first one recommends me," explained Kim. "People hear about me from my friend. They ask, 'Who babysits your son when you go to work?' And my friend says me, and she talks about me."

While Justine, Martha, and Kim all advertise their services through word of mouth, each serves a distinct clientele. Each differs with regard to race ethnicity, cultural identity, and social class and reflects many of the qualities of the community she serves. Justine serves lower-income families who live in her urban, predominantly African American community—families who are referred to her by other parents for whom she has provided care. Kim provides care solely to other Vietnamese families referred through friends. Martha serves two-parent, professional, Euro-American families who come to her through neighborhood social networks and her husband's employment as a school psychologist. In my conversations I discovered that this is a common organizational principle within family child care. Thus, providers in quite different social locations and circumstances are drawn into a common organizational practice: social networks and neighborhoods organize the provision of their paid care work.

This organization is common not only among the women I interviewed but in family child care nationwide. Providers use friendship, family, and neighborhood networks to advertise their services far more often than they formally advertise in newspapers or through other sources (Kontos 1992, Nelson 1990). Providers are not alone in using these networks; parents in search of care use them as well (Nelson 1990). As we will see in this chapter and the next, social networks are used for both economic and cultural reasons and have both structural and social consequences for providers and the families they serve.

Social networks informed by social location are not the only forces used by parents and providers in the selection and provision of family child care. Because parents seek care that is conveniently located near their homes (Kahn and Kamerman 1987, Kontos 1992, Nelson 1990), geographic location structures care in community-based markets as well. Geographic and social locations are also linked to social class and race ethnicity, and these forces simultaneously contribute to the organization and provision of family child care. This link is evident not only among the providers I interviewed, who shared a common racial ethnic, cultural, and social class identity with the families they serve, but among providers nationwide (Kontos et al. 1995, Weaver 2002). Family child care reflects social class congruity between providers and parents (Auerbach and Woodill 1992), especially among low-income families: 75 percent of families with incomes lower than $20,000 select providers with similar incomes (Galinsky et al. 1994). Providers, as well as many parents, look for potential compatibility in their selection of clients; and social class is often a means used to determine potential compatibility (Nelson 1990). In her study of the race ethnicity, social class, and gender dynamics between child care providers and the families they serve, Uttal (1997) found that, in the majority of the relationships between mothers and providers, women share the same racial ethnic identity. The most recent study of family child care providers nationwide confirms that parents select providers who share their ethnic backgrounds, with 83 percent of Latino families selecting Latino providers, 87 percent of African American families selecting African American providers, and 96 percent of white families selecting white providers (Galinsky et al. 1994).

This similarity in social status and racial ethnic identity of providers and parents differs somewhat from that of employers and employees in other forms of paid home-based work—in particular, paid housework. The organization of paid housework as a structurally subordinate relationship between more privileged women and women of historically subordinate social classes and racial ethnic groups is well documented (Dill 1994, Glenn 1986, Hondagneu-Sotelo 2001, Rollins 1985, Romero 2002). By employing poorly paid maids with lower social and racial ethnic status, more privileged women purchase not only a material service (housecleaning) but also deference and higher social status. Like paid domestic work, child care work, also organized by gender, race ethnicity, and social class, can be structurally exploitative. Parents who employ private in-home child care providers, for example, "can create class and cultural chasms," particularly by hiring immigrant women and then by routinizing child care, thus minimizing expense and maximizing control over the provider (Wrigley 1995, 20).

In contrast, other parents seek more equitable relationships with home-based providers and "hire class peers [to] minimize cultural conflicts over child rearing" (Wrigley 1995, 48). When paid child care is provided in the home of the employer, the employer is more likely to retain greater control over the process. Parents' choice of family child care in the provider's home may therefore reflect their desire for a more peer-based relationship. Parents who seek a more equitable relationship may be more willing to consider family child care in the provider's home.

In addition, the social meaning of child care, as opposed to housework, is a likely contributor to the continuity between the social status of parents and family child care providers. In housework, the object of care is the house, an inanimate object. In the case of child care, the subject of care is a being. The responsibility of the provider is to give physical care but also to provide for the child's psychological well-being. Providers teach basic living skills and socialize children to cultural norms and values. As a result, despite its provision in the home, child care has a different meaning and a higher social value than housework (Uttal and Tuominen 1999). As Macdonald (1996) observes, "Children are considered more socially valuable than clean houses" (244).

While decisions of individual parents and providers contribute to their shared culture and social class, structural forces including the use of social networks in advertising and the desirability of a convenient geographic location contribute to social class and cultural similarity between parents and providers in family child care relationships. Thus, structural forces work in tandem with individual preferences and decisions and create a situation in which providers serve families who are very much like themselves. As a result, the organization and provision of family child care replicates racial ethnic, cultural, and social class identity and status within and between communities.

REFLECTING THE COMMUNITY: PROVIDING GOVERNMENT-SUBSIDIZED FAMILY CHILD CARE FOR FAMILIES IN NEED

Structural forces and individual choices have direct implications on the organization and provision of family child care generally as well as specifically on state-subsidized care for families in need. The geographic and social organization of family child care, including government-funded family child care programs, reinforces existing social class boundaries between families and communities. Simultaneously, the decision to provide state-subsidized family child care enables individual providers to challenge these boundaries by increasing their own economic self-sufficiency and thereby their social mobility.

Like most states, Washington offers a number of forms of child care to low-income families as a means of facilitating their movement toward economic self-sufficiency. While the effectiveness and the intent of these programs are strongly contested (especially under the 1996 devolution of welfare to the states, "ending welfare as we know it") (Heymann and Earle 1998, Meyers 2001, Scharlach and Grosswald 1997), subsidized child care is nonetheless essential to low-income families who are attempting to achieve self-sufficiency. In Washington, nearly 54,000 children each month receive state-subsidized care, including children from low-income working families, homeless families, and families eligible for public assistance while parents are enrolled in job-training or school programs (Miller and Schrager 2000). While providers make conscious choices about whether or not they will serve state-subsidized families, they do so within differing contexts of social opportunities and constraints. The cultural identity, racial ethnic identity, country of origin, and social class of a provider and her community help to determine whether serving such children puts her at a financial advantage or disadvantage.

Although family child care providers in Washington care for nearly one-third of all state-subsidized children, not all providers are equally willing to serve these families and their children. The organization of family child care by local markets is reflected in the decisions that providers make in regards to serving this population. Among the providers I interviewed, those who lived and worked in middle-income communities—in particular, middle-income, Euro-American communities—rarely served state-subsidized children; and, if they did, chose to serve a very limited number. In contrast, in lower-income communities and communities of color, state-subsidized children formed the majority of children served by the providers I interviewed.

The racial ethnic and socioeconomic organization of the provision of state-subsidized care is common among licensed family child care providers throughout the state. Although children of color make up 33 percent of all children in licensed family child care, they form a much larger proportion (45 percent) of children subsidized by the state through the Department of Social and Health Services (DSHS), the agency responsible for implementing and monitoring state-subsidized child care programs. In addition, race ethnicity and social class play a clear role in organizing the provision of licensed family child care for these children. The vast majority share the racial ethnic identity of their provider, and providers are more likely to care for children of similar race ethnicity. For example, nearly two-thirds of the children cared for by black and Hispanic providers are, respectively, black and Hispanic. And 85 percent of the children cared for by white providers are white (Miller and Schrager 2000).

Viewing the data from a somewhat different perspective, we see that, while providers serve children who share their racial ethnic identity, providers of color are much more likely to serve poor children than white providers are. Specifically, while 80 percent of licensed providers in the state are white, only 16 percent of the children they serve are state-subsidized. In sharp contrast, while only 2 percent of providers statewide are black, 56 percent of the children they serve are state-subsidized. Similarly, Hispanic providers make up 11 percent of providers throughout the state, yet 48 percent of the children they serve are from families who receive state-subsidized care (Miller and Schrager 2000). Thus, not only do children of color form a disproportionate number of children in subsidized care, but women of color care for a disproportionate number of state-subsidized children.

The findings of my interviews reflected this statewide pattern. Among the providers I interviewed, rural and urban providers living in lower-income communities (disproportionately African American women and Mexicanas) actively sought to care for state-subsidized children, while Euro-American providers living in middle-income small towns and suburban communities reported a variety of decisions regarding the provision of state-subsidized care. Although some refused to care for or limited the number of children for whom they provided subsidized care, others welcomed such families. Given the disproportionately higher number of women of color who served state-subsidized children and the disproportionate number of white women who refused to serve or limited their service to state-subsidized children, I was particularly interested in the forces that shaped the apparent racial ethnic organization of state-subsidized family child care. To explore forces that might contribute to this practice, I spoke with providers about their choice to serve state-subsidized children.

Providers viewed the benefits of caring for state-subsidized children in two ways. Isabel Inofuentes, a Mexicana licensed provider for eight years, spoke of the economic benefits of providing care for these children: "With these [state] programs you're sure that you're going to get paid." In contrast, some providers see state-subsidized clients as an economic liability. Those who refuse to accept such children or limit the number they serve report that their decision is most often rooted in Washington's policy of paying for subsidized care at less than the market rate. At the time of our interview the state paid family child care providers at a rate referred to as the *fifty-fifth percentile*.[2] After conducting a biennial survey of market rates charged by family child care providers and center-based providers throughout the state, researchers determine local rate variations and identify regions of the state in which market rates are similar. The state then pays providers who care for state-subsidized children at a rate that is higher than the market rate charged by 55 percent of providers in their region but lower than the rate charged by 45 percent. For example, in the region in which Isabel resides, the maximum monthly rate charged by a family child care provider for toddler care is $565 per month. The minimum charged is $206 per month. The state pays $385 per month. Thus, depending on whether the rates charged by a provider are closer to the maximum or the minimum in her community, she will view the state-subsidized rate as "a crime" or as a viable fee for her services. Isabel and other women (primarily women of color and immigrant women who serve lower-income communities) speak of the desirability of caring for state-subsidized children. In contrast, providers in middle-income and predominantly Euro-American communities either limit or refuse to serve "state-paid kids" or find that, while their unlicensed status prohibits them from providing state-subsidized care, providing unlicensed care is nonetheless more economically viable.

REFUSING OR RESTRICTING THE PROVISION OF STATE-SUBSIDIZED CARE

Julia Deavers is a Euro-American provider of licensed family child care in a middle-income Euro-American community. When I asked if she provided care to state-subsidized families, she replied immediately, "No. They don't pay me enough. It's a *crime*, the rate that they pay. . . . I have a full [time] rate of $445 a month or $23 a day. I just raised my rates. The last I heard, I think [DSHS] was paying $13."

Valerie Holton, the only African American provider who reported limiting the number of state-subsidized children she serves, has been providing family child care for fifteen years. While she reported that she does accept "DSHS kids," she offered the caveat, "A very limited number, though. Because you lose money."[3] Valerie reported that she charges more for family child care than DSHS pays: "Now I'm down to [earning] $223 a month [for a state-subsidized child] when I like to get $280." Like Julia, Valerie can earn significantly more by serving private-pay clients in her suburban community. Given the difference between what she charges ($280) and what DSHS pays ($223), Valerie's choice to serve a state-subsidized child reduces her monthly income by more than 30 percent.

When asked if she cares for state-subsidized children, Janice Newman, a Euro-American provider in a small town, responded, "I haven't really been approached that often. I had one child [once]— Jack. I did that. I wouldn't let [state-subsidized clients] be a bulk of my business." I asked why, and she answered, "Because of the money. It's just I can get a lot more than [the state pays] for my slots. And I want to be fair to people, but there's a point at which you quit subsidizing the state. And that's what I feel like I do. And I feel like a lot of people do. And it's not fair."

"You charge more than DSHS pays?" I asked. "Way more. Jack [a state-subsidized child] was seven months old. . . . I was getting $17 a day for him and typically I can get $22 to $23 for that slot.

I said, "So you would take DSHS kids, but you don't make a point of it. You would limit?"

She responded, "I would definitely limit. I *know* I wouldn't take more than two [state-paid children] out of the twelve."

Janice raised two primary issues in her discussion of why she limits the number of state-subsidized children that she serves. First, she "hasn't been approached that often" by parents who seek state-subsidized care. Second, the economic status of families in her neighborhood and social networks is such that, like Julia and Valerie, she makes less money by serving state-subsidized children. The fact that she hasn't been approached to provide state-subsidized care reflects her residence in a middle-income, Euro-American community. Like all providers, the rates that she charges mirror the community in which she lives and works. In determining her rates, Janice reported that she attends to "what the market will bear. That's about where I'm at. I keep in contact with what's going on around my neighborhood." And within Janice's neighborhood and social network, families are able to pay rates significantly higher than those paid by the state for subsidized care.

While the state bases its rates on a survey of local market rates, it most often pays less than what providers living in middle- and upper-income communities charge for care. When Janice discussed providing care for Jack, a state-subsidized child, she reported being paid by the state at a rate 22 percent less than if she were to provide her services to a private-pay client. At the time of our interview, several years later, the disparity between what she charged and what the state paid had grown even further. Janice reported her rate for infant care at $467 per month, close to the maximum charged by providers in her area. With the state paying $317 for infant care in her area, Janice's rate was 47 percent higher than the rate at which she would be paid by the state.

Although Janice reported that "a lot of homes won't take [state-subsidized] kids," the homes she refers to are those of middle-income providers who live in middle- and upper-income communities. Her reference point is that of families within her own social class and social network. Because she provides family child care to support her family economically, she recognizes the financial implications of serving state-subsidized children from low-income families. To do so reduces her own income.

Because of the disparity between the rates they charge for child care and the rates that the state pays, providers in middle- and upper-income communities often limit the number of state-subsidized children they serve. As Janice says, "there's a point at which you quit subsidizing the state." The analysis that family child care providers subsidize the low cost of child care is heard among providers in communities nationwide (Haack 1998). When those in middle-income neighborhoods, like Janice, choose to serve state-subsidized clients, they consciously reduce the income they would otherwise earn by serving higher-income, private-pay families. They see this income reduction as "subsidizing the state"—quite literally, the price they pay to serve state-funded children from low-income families.

While a number of the women I interviewed reported that they refuse to serve state-subsidized children or limit the number they serve, some providers are not legally able to serve state-funded children. At the time of my interviews, unlicensed providers were not allowed to care for state-subsidized children. But regardless of their inability to be providers of state-subsidized care, I found that Euro-American, unlicensed providers in middle-income communities, like their licensed counterparts, have no economic motivation to serve state-subsidized clients. Because of the middle-class and professional families they serve, they earn more (even as unlicensed providers) by selling their services to private-pay clients than to the state.

Martha Buxton is a former public schoolteacher who became a family child care provider eight years ago. When I asked Martha if she served any state-subsidized children, she responded, "None have ever asked. You know, I've not had the occasion to. I mean, nobody's asked." A number of forces interact to create this situation. Because she is an unlicensed provider she cannot, under state regulation, provide care to state-subsidized families. At the same time, because she currently serves middle-class, professional, two-parent families with sufficient financial resources to purchase her services, she has no economic motivation to provide services to state-funded families. I asked Martha how she determines the rates she charges for child care. She answered, "[I charge] what the [local] rate is generally. In some areas day care is more expensive than other areas. And I started out low. And then . . . I thought, 'Hey. This is ridiculous. This is important; and if [parents] want good care, they will be willing to pay for it.'"

While unlicensed providers generally earn much less than their licensed counterparts (Galinsky et al. 1994), as an unlicensed provider Martha's rates are still more than 46 percent higher than those the state pays to licensed providers. She is able to charge those rates because her community is composed of middle-class, professional, formally educated, two-parent, Euro-American families like her own. Clearly, there is no financial incentive for unlicensed providers serving middle- and upper-income communities to either become licensed or provide state-subsidized care.

Allie McGinnis, another Euro-American unlicensed provider, analyzed the rates she charged while providing home-based child care. She began by reflecting on her previous employment as a playground recreation leader with the Parks Department in Seattle: "I loved it. I was outside, and I was playing softball, and I was playing on the jungle gym. And I was getting paid for it. And at that time I was getting paid well. I think I was getting $6 an hour. And that was almost twenty-five years ago. Actually, that's about what I made when I did child care just a few years ago." While Allie's wages as an unlicensed provider were about equal to what she made twenty-five years ago as a playground leader, they still exceeded the wages paid by the state for state-subsidized children by more than 25 percent. I asked about the rates she charged when providing unlicensed care for parents who were full-time students at a local state college. She reported, "It was negotiated. It fluctuated. Especially with the two single moms, depending on what was happening with them financially. But it could not go below $2.35 an hour. And the highest I was paid was $3."

Providing care for the children of full-time college students, especially young, single mothers, is not a particularly lucrative profession. Nonetheless, even at their lowest, Allie's rates exceeded those paid by the state by more than 25 percent. And at their highest, they exceeded those of the state by more than 60 percent. Even though two of the three clients she served were single mothers (a primary population served by state-subsidized programs), as private-pay clients, those mothers paid more for child care services than the state would have. Like Martha, Allie had no economic motivation to become a licensed provider of state-subsidized services.

While disparities in income and education are generally recognized to exist between licensed and unlicensed providers (Kappner 1984), these disparities do not exist when unlicensed providers are Euro-American, have attained a high degree of formal education themselves (a college degree or some college study), and serve primarily middle-class and professional families who have completed or are in the process of completing their college education. Because of the financial resources of the families they serve and the local markets in which they provide care, it is more profitable for these providers, whether licensed or unlicensed, to refuse to provide care for state-subsidized children (as Julia does), to limit the number of state-subsidized children for whom they care (as Janice and Valerie do), or to continue to provide unlicensed care (as Martha and Allie do).

WELCOMING THE PROVISION OF STATE-SUBSIDIZED CARE

One government-subsidized child care program offered by Washington State is the Seasonal Farmworker Child Care Program. The state subcontracts with Catholic Family Services to staff this program, which is aimed at employed, low-income agricultural workers. Catholic Family Services, in turn, recruits women from primarily Spanish-speaking homes to provide services for the children of predominantly Mexican and Mexican American seasonal workers. Unlike providers in middle- or upper-income communities who refuse to take "state-subsidized kids," Gloria Zuñiga is a Mexicana provider who prefers caring for such children over private-pay clients. She explained that her preference comes from her understanding of the financial constraints faced by the parents she serves.

In a way [I prefer not to take private-pay clients] because in private pay the parents just don't want to pay much for day care. And I feel kind of uneasy asking for payment. I understand how hard it is to pay for child care because I had to pay for care for my two children. It's very expensive, especially when half of your check goes to child care. So I understand. It's very expensive. Sometimes in the case of an emergency I'll take private-pay kids for a day or two, but I'm always embarrassed to ask for payment. When you [care for] two or three children and you're asking $11 or $12 a child, that's a lot of money. But what I do is refer [the parents] to Catholic Family Services or DSHS to see if they qualify for the [subsidized] programs.

Like Gloria, Laura Mayfield provides state-subsidized family child care for the children of families in need. Laura is one of the few Euro-American providers who offer care through the Seasonal Farmworker Child Care Program. Living in a rural agricultural area several miles from town, she is the most geographically isolated of the providers I interviewed. At $7,000 a year, her earnings as a full-time child care provider are the lowest of the licensed providers I interviewed. Laura reported a willingness to serve state-subsidized children; in fact, half of the children she cares for are from state-subsidized programs. Like other providers, the rates she is able to charge are determined by the economic viability of the families in the community in which she lives and works. Laura explained, "I was charging $1.25 an hour up until the first of this month. And now I charge $1.50. I charged [$1.25 an hour] for eight years, so I decided it was time to raise it a little bit."

Despite her decision to raise her rates by 25 percent, Laura's rates remain well within those paid by DSHS. The fact that a 25 percent increase in her rates still keeps her within the DSHS range of payment indicates the poverty of her community. Remember that DSHS reimburses providers at the fifty-fifth percentile. Thus, after raising her rates by 25 percent, Laura still charges less than nearly half of licensed providers in her region. Because of the low socioeconomic status and the economic vulnerability of parents in her community, offering state-subsidized family child care is a viable economic choice for her.

Like Gloria, who finds herself "embarrassed to ask" for payment from families with limited economic resources, Laura feels guilty about the possibility of overcharging families for care. She needs a stable income to support her own family, yet families in her area have few financial resources with which to pay for care.

Me, I feel guilty if I go overcharge people because, like, I heard this one woman in town, she charges $2.50 an hour for a three-year-old. And to me, I can't see that. Maybe it's just me because I've been around kids and down south you'd watch them for $1 a day. And that's all you would get paid. And so I guess I'm stuck with southern ways, and it just seems like she's charging too much.

"You said you'd feel guilty if you overcharged. Would $2.50 an hour be overcharging?" I asked.

She answered, "It would in my opinion because most of the people, you watch their kids, most of them's got minimum-wage jobs. I know how tough it is on two parents. They've got two or three kids on a minimum wage, and the rent is $600 a month. They can't afford it. So occasionally when I run into somebody like that I will go ahead and cut my rate down."

Economic constraints faced by parents have economic consequences for Laura when families are private-pay clients. Even though she reported reducing her rates for families who can't afford care, she related, "I had a couple of [private-pay] people who didn't pay."

Like Laura, Segunda Cortez understands the limited ability of the families she serves to pay for care. Segunda serves families within her community who share her socioeconomic status as well as her cultural identity and history: migrant Mexican families in which parents engage in seasonal agricultural employment or families that have "settled out" in the area. When I asked Segunda if she accepted private-pay clients, she responded, "No. It's not worth it."

"Why isn't it worth it?" I asked.

"[Parents] pay very little," she answered. Segunda went on to describe the way in which the income of her private-paying clients directly relates to the amount of money they can afford to pay for child care: "If I care for three children and [the parents] make $35 [for a day of paid agricultural work], am I going to charge them $35 [for child care]? If they have three children, I would have to charge them $15 or $16 for all three children."

"So you would vary your rate depending on parents' ability to pay?" I asked.

"Yes," she responded. "Sometimes if the need is there and they don't have anyone to care for the children, I will take the children."

While Segunda prefers not to serve private-pay families because of their inability to pay, she demonstrates a thorough knowledge of their financial circumstances—a knowledge born out of experience. Her own husband is an agricultural worker in seasonal employment. "He works during the harvest through the picking. Then he stops for a month or two, depending when the thinning starts." Her empathy and concern for such families led her to report that she sometimes does serve private-pay families "if they don't have anyone else to care for the children." But she does so at an economic cost to herself and to her own family; for in serving private-pay families, she reduces her income substantially from what she could earn serving state-subsidized families.

Given that Segunda serves families who share her racial ethnic identity and culture, the likelihood of her serving low-income families increases. In the county in which she lives, the poverty rate is 10.8 percent. Among Hispanic families, however, the poverty rate is 40.4 percent, nearly four times as great (Washington State Office of Financial Management, Forecasting Division 1992). Segunda, like other family child care providers, offers her services in a local market. Thus, she knows that the families she serves will be low-income families and knows that these families' limited ability to pay for care has direct economic consequences for her. Segunda's adjustment of her rates to fit families' ability to pay, Gloria's embarrassment about asking for payment, and Laura's concern about overcharging all have at least a partial solution in providers' decisions to offer state-subsidized care. Serving such clients is a beneficial arrangement for these providers, both personally and professionally. Providers are assured of regular payment for their work, and families receive assistance in paying for child care that enables them to maintain their employment—albeit in minimum-wage jobs that perpetuate their low incomes and qualification for state-subsidized child care.

Urban African American providers also reported that they often serve state-subsidized children from low-income families. In fact, among the African American providers I interviewed, all but one reported that between two-thirds and all of their clients are government-subsidized. Sondra Ames is one of these providers. Sondra began providing licensed family child care in her community three years ago. When I asked if she serves state-subsidized children, she reported, "Most of my kids are state kids. In fact, all of them are right now. It has always been that way for us. . . . It just happens. It just happens that way. I said when I started that I would only do so many DSHS clients. And then the rest would be cash-paying folks. But for me it hasn't worked out that way at all. In fact, I can count the cash-paying clients that I've had in three years on one hand."

Although Sondra explains that "it just happens" that she serves state-subsidized children, it does not, in fact, "just happen." A number of factors contribute to Sondra's provision of care to low-income families, including the economic status and the racial ethnic identity of the members of the community in which she lives and works. Like other family child care providers, African American providers report that "word of mouth" is the primary mechanism by which they attract clients. As such, these women reflect the community in which their social network operates—geographic and social communities that are primarily communities of color. Among the urban African American women I interviewed, the poverty rate for all residents in the county in which they reside is 6 percent. In contrast, the poverty rate for African Americans living in this same county is more than 22 percent (Washington State Office of Financial Management, Forecasting Division 1992). In addition, the per capita median income of white families in this county is almost double the median income of black families (U.S. Department of Commerce, Bureau of the Census 1990c). Given the race-based disparity in income and poverty, it is not surprising that providers living in urban African American neighborhoods serve primarily lower-income, government-subsidized families. By offering care to these families in need, providers are able to ensure a stable source of income for themselves while caring for the children and families they are called to serve. (See chapter 6 for a discussion of the spiritual and political motivation to provide family child care reported by African American providers.)

Jennie Davis is an African American provider living in a low-income community. She reported that, in direct contrast to the Mexicana providers I interviewed, she can earn more caring for private-pay clients than for state-subsidized clients. When I asked why she continued to accept state-subsidized DSHS clients, she explained, "Well, I work with DSHS because with DSHS the income is timely. The only thing I hate about that is they don't take the taxes out. And once you sit down and figure out the taxes on that [income], we're not making very much money at all. I deal with [DSHS] because they're very consistent [in paying]."

Similarly, Patricia James, an African American provider for eight years, discussed her motivations for serving subsidized children: "I do [subsidized care] mainly out of a soft spot for single parents. As my husband says, 'She's a sucker for that single mom' [laughter]. On top of that, you know you're going to get paid. DSHS's timing may be off, but they will pay you. It might be three or four months, but you will get paid" [laughter]. Thus, like providers who serve families in rural, low-income communities, the urban African American women I interviewed recognize the benefits of providing state-subsidized child care. Providers such as Patricia and Jennie understand that offering state-subsidized care creates a mutually beneficial arrangement for both providers and parents: low-income families receive needed assistance in paying for care, while providers can count on steady income from their family child care work.

Kay Schilling is one of the few Euro-American women I interviewed who provides state-subsidized care. When I asked why, she explained. "Currently I'm a Head Start provider, and Head Start is reaching out to lower-income people. You know, they're people just like you and I." Kay's reference to Head Start families as "they" indicates that she does not personally identify with low-income families' social and economic circumstances. Yet she earns so little as a full-time family child care provider that her two daughters qualify for state-subsidized health care. Although Kay's motivation to serve state-subsidized families is in part humanistic ("they're people just like you and I"), it is also pragmatic. Understanding the limited ability of families in her community to pay for care, she described the benefits of serving state-subsidized families: "One thing I do like is that you don't have money issues [and] problems with clients that are on DSHS. Because it's not coming out of their pockets. Because that can put a strain on the relationship with the parent when they have financial [problems]—when it's hard for them to pay. So I like it, actually, when I get DSHS clients because it takes off that strain."

Family child care providers serve families who are like themselves, in large part because of the role of geography and social networks that organize the provision of family child care. Thus, providers such as Kay who live in working-class communities are more likely to serve low-income families. Because of this economic and social reality, providers in these communities, often communities of color, make active choices to serve state-subsidized, low-income families. For them, providing such care is a way in which to deal constructively and creatively with families' limited ability to pay. In so doing, providers also address the reality of the geographic and social networks that structure their provision of family child care, reducing tensions that arise as a result of parents' limited ability to pay for care while establishing a reliable source of income for themselves.

For immigrant women who are non-native English speakers, the economic decision to provide state-subsidized care is informed by forces of native language and culture as well as social class, race ethnicity, and country of origin. Recognizing the inability of immigrant or recently settled parents to pay for child care, Mexicana providers who affiliate with a local community agency offer their family child care through the sponsorship of the state-funded Seasonal Farmworker Family Child Care Program. In doing so, the immigrant women I interviewed are able to access paid employment in communities in which their employment options are limited not only because of the racial ethnic organization of jobs but by native language as well. For each of the Mexicanas I interviewed, her native Spanish language skills far exceeded her skills in spoken English. In the community in which these women reside, fewer than 9 percent of community members speak Spanish (U.S. Department of Commerce, Bureau of the Census 1990a), thereby severely limiting job access for these women. By becoming licensed family child care providers and affiliating with a local community service agency staffed by members who speak their own native language and share their cultural and racial ethnic identity, these women are able to access resources within an English-speaking community that would otherwise be less accessible to both themselves and the families they serve.

Segunda Cortez speaks of the ways in which affiliating with the community-based Catholic Family Services (as opposed to dealing directly with DSHS) enables her to obtain training as a provider. Segunda speaks of Paula Shelton, the local program coordinator, who is a member of the community, was also born and raised in Mexico, and whose family members were originally agricultural workers: "One of the differences [between affiliating with Catholic Family Services versus DSHS] is Paula always gives classes and there's always interesting topics like income tax. She brings in people to talk about children, child development. . . . The class is a lot easier with Paula because she speaks the language."

Isabel Inofuentes describes her own affiliation with Catholic Family Services. Her assessment of affiliating with the community-based organization is similar to Segunda's. "I like that Catholic Family has classes available in Spanish. Like the child development classes. There is a lot of training through the department [DSHS]. Mostly for Anglos, but they never offer a lot of training [for Spanish-speaking providers]. I would love to go to them. But they're all in English. At least now they have someone at the department who speaks Spanish. Before they didn't have anybody."

Paula Shelton also spoke of the limited opportunities that Mexicana providers have to affiliate with the local chapter of the Association for Family Child Care, the national professional organization of family child care providers. She reported that while the local association chapter has invited Mexicana providers to attend their meetings, none of the local chapter members speak Spanish, and no interpreters are available at the meetings. As a result, the opportunity to affiliate with other community providers involved in self-education and advocacy is limited for Spanish-speaking providers.

By providing state-subsidized care through affiliation with a local community agency, Mexicanas are able to gain cultural access to training and educational resources that would otherwise be unavailable to them. In addition, providing state-subsidized child care enables both native-born and immigrant women in low-income communities to create a mutually beneficial solution to address the employment and cultural constraints faced by parents as well as providers.

THE CARE PENALTY AND THE PROVISION
OF STATE-SUBSIDIZED CARE

Listening to the stories of family child care providers, we learn that geography and social networks are powerful structural forces that organize family child care work. The provision of care in local geographic markets and the marketing of care through informal social networks increase the likelihood that providers will serve families who are like themselves. Shared racial ethnic identity, native language, cultural affiliation, and social class are common between the providers and the families they care for, not only among the women I interviewed but among providers nationwide (Galinsky et al. 1994).

Cultural identity, race ethnicity, and financial resources within geographic communities also determine the rates that providers are able to charge for their child care services in local markets, influencing both the provision of family child care generally as well as the organization and provision of government-subsidized family child care programs. Because no provider is required to offer state-subsidized care, her decision to do so is a conscious choice informed by personal experience and the social forces of cultural identity, race ethnicity, and social class. These individual experiences and structural forces operating within communities help providers to determine whether serving state-subsidized children puts them at a financial advantage or disadvantage.

The conscious choice not to serve low-income, state-subsidized families is a sound economic decision made by providers who live and work in middle- and upper-income communities. Because parents are on a sounder financial footing in these neighborhoods, providers are able to earn more by serving families who pay directly for care than by serving parents for whom care is subsidized by the state. Providers in middle- and upper-income communities charge more than the state pays for care. For these women, a choice to offer state-subsidized care is a choice to reduce their own income by as much as 50 percent. As a result, providers in middle- and upper-income communities rarely serve state-subsidized children or strictly limit the number for whom they care. If they choose to offer subsidized care, their reasons are clearly not motivated by economic self-interest. Janice Newman, a Euro-American provider in a community of middle-income families, limits the number of subsidized children she serves. "And the reason I would [provide care to subsidized children] would be to put those kids into a quality situation. A lot of the homes won't take those kids. And I feel badly that they don't have equal opportunity to get into a good place. I really do. But there's also a bottom line for my family, as well."

The bottom line for Janice and her family is an economic one. She reduces her own income and that of her family when she chooses to provide state-subsidized care. Given the ways in which social class entwines with race ethnicity, the decisions made by Janice and providers like her have a cumulative social effect. They contribute to a pattern in which women of color in lower-income communities disproportionately become the pool of labor on which the state relies to provide government-subsidized family child care.

Class relations are also experienced in the context of race ethnicity in the work of family child care providers who offer state-subsidized care to the children of low-income agricultural workers. Paula Shelton spoke of the women who provide state-subsidized family child care.

> The majority [of providers] are Hispanics. I have very few Anglos. Very few. I have maybe ten [family] child care providers that are Anglos [out of seventy-five]. There [are] quite a few Anglo providers in the area, but they don't want to do child care for seasonal workers—mainly because of the hours that agricultural workers work. The Anglo providers have their set hours, which are usually six in the morning until six in the evening. Agricultural workers: their hours are anywhere from three, four o'clock in the morning till six, seven, eight o'clock at night. And also weekends. . . . Very few of the Anglos want to work on weekends or long hours.

Long hours is a relative term, informed by one's employment background and opportunities. Most of the Euro-American and African American providers I interviewed reported hours of service similar to those described by Paula, "from six in the morning to six in the evening." When viewed in the context of a conventional eight-hour work day, the twelve-hour work day of family child care is a very long one. But Paula reports that few Anglo providers, with their twelve-hour work day, "want to work on weekends or long hours." Thus, the decisions of individual providers to offer state-subsidized care are also informed by cultural and social class norms regarding work. These norms are experienced in the context of employment history and opportunities that are, in turn, informed by race ethnicity and immigrant status. In the case of the Mexicanas with whom I spoke, the decision to serve low-income families was interwoven with their racial ethnic and cultural identity and their immigrant status, all of which shape the economic and social circumstances of these providers as well as the families they serve. As a result, the provision of licensed, state-subsidized care through affiliation with a local community service agency becomes one of the most viable and desirable employment options available for these women.

Because geography and social networks serve as a primary basis for the organization of family child care, this care as a practice reinforces existing social class boundaries as well as racial ethnic and cultural boundaries between communities. This has direct economic implications for family child care providers. All providers work within the constraints of the markets and families they serve. Regardless of its location in low- or middle-income communities, family child care is low-wage work. As a result, providers in low-income communities face particularly powerful constraints in their attempt to support themselves and their families through family child care work. Serving state-subsidized children is a means by which providers in low-income communities, often communities of color, effectively address these constraints. Offering state-subsidized family child care enables them to deal with the reality of the geographic and social networks that structure their family child care work, address parents' limited ability to pay for care, and counteract the direct consequences this has for providers—reducing their income. But providers are caught between a rock and a hard place. Despite their creative use of accessing the state as a stable source of income for themselves and of affordable care for members of their community, the state itself contributes to the care penalty providers bear. In spite of its recognition of the public value of child care and its willingness to subsidize the cost of care, the state pays family child care providers at only the fifty-fifth percentile (a rate less than the already low market rates charged by 45 percent of the providers in a given region). Consequently, the state exacerbates the low wages already experienced by providers and contributes to the care penalty they pay as a result of the lack of public resources devoted to the work of caring. Thus, providing state-subsidized family child care becomes a creative means whereby providers ensure a stable and reliable, albeit very limited, income for themselves and their families.

6

"THAT'S WHERE I SAW THE NEED"
Family Child Care As Community Care Work

In chapter 5, we saw the ways in which geography and social networks facilitate the provision of family child care in community-based markets in which providers and family members often share a common social class as well as racial ethnic and cultural identity. But to limit our analysis of the organization of family child care to a structural analysis of geography and social networks would be a huge mistake. Community is relational and political as well as locational, and in my interviews I learned that cultural values of care and community are primary factors influencing women's decisions to provide family child care. Rooted in this cultural context, the African American providers I interviewed experienced their family child care work as community care work. Drawing on the experience of these providers, I define *community care work* as a conscious cultural and political act: a commitment to collective survival and community advancement through the provision of family child care work. A commitment to community care work was demonstrated time and again in my interviews with African American providers and was most often motivated by a synthesis of providers' political responsibility, spiritual call to serve the community, and commitment to both racial safety and cultural pride. For African American women in low-income communities, the choice to provide family child care was an active decision to aid in the collective development of their communities.

FAMILY CHILD CARE, KINWORK, AND THE COLLECTIVE GOOD

My understanding of family child care as community care work first began to emerge clearly in my interview with Cora Jenkins, an African American woman who has been providing family child care for more than nineteen years. My conversation with Cora proved particularly instructive because I began to see more fully the ways in which social class, gender, and race ethnicity are principles of social organization that incorporate both material relations and cultural meaning (Glenn 1999). More specifically, I became increasingly appreciative of the ways in which family child care providers who are members of historically subordinate groups contest dominant ideologies and construct alternative meanings regarding their child care work. Together, social structures and cultural meaning derived through group identity play a primary role in the family child care provided by the African American women with whom I spoke.

I drove to Cora Jenkins's home along the surface streets of south Seattle, passing convenience stores, neighborhood groceries, bus stops, and some light industry bordering the arterial. As I drove further south, white faces on the street gradually became less evident until the face of everyone on the street was black or Asian. I turned off the major arterial and wound my way through a lower-income neighborhood filled with ranch-style homes built in the 1950s. I identified Cora's house by the sandwich sign in the yard announcing "Our Place Child Care." Parking the car, I walked toward the door of the daylight basement and knocked. Cora opened the door and welcomed me. She was poised and confident, an African American woman in her early forties, I surmised.

Cora invited me in, and we settled on the couch in the finished basement, the site established for family child care in her home. Pictures of her four children, her husband, and herself hung in one corner of the room. Toys of various kinds were stacked up in other corners. A two-year-old child lay napping on a mat on the floor. Cora offered me a cup of coffee, and we launched into the interview in which she spoke clearly and confidently of her experience as a professional family child care provider. When I asked how she got started in the field, she spoke, as have other providers, of the need to support her family through paid work (see chapter 4). Nevertheless, her motivation was not solely monetary: "I had always worked with children all my life in one capacity or another. So I knew that was something I could do and live with what I was doing. Being at home but meeting someone else's need. And working with kids: it not only fulfills a need for me, but for those individual children."

I was immediately struck by the ways in which Cora used the language of care rather than the market to describe her motivation for entering family child care work. In her choice of language— "fulfills a need," "meeting someone else's need"—Cora identifies many of the elements of care recognized by scholars. Care is relational. It involves attending to the needs of others, responsibility for others. Care incorporates reciprocity (Cancian and Oliker 2000, Gordon 1996, Tarlow 1996). Through this work, Cora acts on her own need to provide care and to meet the needs of others for care. In her story we see the values and forces that convinced her to provide family child care in her community. I highlight these forces not because of their uniqueness to Cora but because other African American providers often raised them as well. In the course of my interviews I found them to be central to the organization and provision of the family child care offered by the African American women I interviewed.

Cora serves families in her community because "that's where I saw the need." As we learned in chapter 5, the provision of family child care is organized through social networks and geographic location. As a result, cultural identity, racial ethnic identity, and financial resources in community and neighborhood markets directly affect the clientele served by family child care providers. Cora is aware of the economic circumstances of families in her community: to be employed, parents need someone to care for their children. The market for care is evident. But her entry into family child care was not determined solely by economics and geography. As she and I talked, she spoke of the poverty in her community and her commitment to serving families in need.

> And so people who are trying to get off the system [public assistance] need quality day care, but at the same time it's not a whole lot of day cares that will accept state kids. All of the chil-

dren here come through [state-subsidized] programs. Because
that's where I saw the need. I felt that, especially living in the
area we live in, there were a lot of people out there who needed
the assistance of the state welfare department to provide care for
their children while they attempted to go back to school or go
to work. There were very few day cares who would take state-
subsidized children. So that's the part I play, in providing a service, is to take mostly state kids and special-needs children.

Cora's conscious service to families in her community is also
evident in the way in which she sets her rates, which ensures that
low-income families without the financial resources to pay for care
will qualify for government-subsidized child care.[1]

My rates are set by—it's kind of a midpoint. My rates are the
city's maximum rate. That way I know that, whether I take city
[subsidized] kids or private[-pay] kids, I'll be meeting the needs
of some people who need day care without [them having to pay]
the extra cost. . . . The other thing is I kind of assess the type of
people that I serve. And I don't want my rate to be so high that,
for a child coming from two parents, [the rate] would surpass a
mortgage payment. You know what I'm saying? Who can pay
child care costs if it's [like] adding another mortgage payment?
And most of the parents I serve are single parents anyway. Because there's more single parents than there are married couples,
and so you have to look at that. If you're living in an area where
there's a lot of doctors and lawyers—well, that's fine. But what
about the others?

In determining what she charges for child care, Cora ensures
that low-income working families will have access to care through
government-funded programs. But different government programs
subsidize care at different rates. The programs funded by the city of
Seattle pay providers at a higher rate than do programs funded by
the state of Washington. Nonetheless, Cora continues to serve children subsidized by the state, and does so at a literal cost to herself
and her own family. Clearly, her motivation for providing family
child care is not solely economic. Nor is she the only provider who
chooses to serve state-subsidized families, even though she can
earn more by serving city-subsidized and private-pay families. Jennie Davis, an African American provider for three years, reports
that, while the city pays $817 a month for infant care, the state
pays $650 a month—more than 25 percent below city rates. Sondra
Ames also reports that she can earn more from city-subsidized and

private-pay clients than from state-subsidized children. But "people are so desperate. [I earn] a little less, but it's not that much." In Sondra's case, like Jennie's, "a little less" means a 25 percent reduction in income each month. But because they value service and community, Sondra and other African American providers in lower-income communities are often willing to make such sacrifices.

Clearly, among the women I interviewed, the decision to provide family child care to families in need is not motivated solely by economic considerations. In particular, African American providers' commitment to serving such families is located within the cultural meaning and construction of social networks as a means of sustaining the community. Kinscripts is a conceptual framework for understanding family and kin networks and the role they play in sustaining families (Stack and Burton 1993). Kinwork plays a central role in sustaining families culturally as well as economically and is defined as "the collective labor expected of family-centered networks across households and within them. [Kinwork] defines the work that families need to accomplish to endure over time. . . . Kinwork regenerates families, maintains lifetime continuities, sustains intergenerational responsibilities, and reinforces shared values" (160).

Kinwork occurs not just within households but across households as well. Extended kin networks are consciously constructed ties and obligations that emerge from economic, social, physical, and psychological family needs (161) and are well documented among not only black families in slavery but also in contemporary black families (Dill 1998, Stack 1970). Extended kinship incorporates social ties and obligations, and extended kin often play a central role in childrearing and other domestic, social, and economic activities. When kinship networks become a vehicle for survival among historically subordinated groups, the formation and activation of kin networks becomes a political act—an act of resistance (DiLeonardo 1987) that contributes to the survival of not only individual families but also the communities that comprise them.

The centrality of kinwork and extended kin networks within the community emerged in my conversations with African American family child care providers. Patricia James is an African American provider who has worked in the field for eight years. She spoke of the ways in which other members of the community supported her when she was in need. Now as a member of the community, she continues that extended kinship network by helping other families through her provision of government-subsidized child care. "I saw all these kids and women walking up and down where I lived at. Catching the bus. Packing their babies. I was only a block away from the bus stop. They're trying to go to school, or they're trying to go to work. And it's hard when you're just by yourself. I was a single mother for a couple years. . . . I had people. They helped me. And that's why I don't mind taking DSHS children."

Patricia Hill Collins (1992) coined the now well recognized phrase "other mothers" to describe the extended kinship networks of women in many African American communities. She argues that other mothers within kin networks are culturally constructed as a means of addressing both racial and gender oppression within historically subordinated communities.

> In African-American communities, fluid and changing boundaries often distinguish biological mothers from other women who care for children. Biological mothers, or bloodmothers, are expected to care for their children. But African and African-American communities have also recognized that vesting one person with full responsibility for mothering a child may not be wise or possible. As a result, other mothers—women who assist bloodmothers by sharing mothering responsibilities—traditionally have been central to the institution of Black motherhood. The centrality of women in African-American extended families reflects both a continuation of West African cultural values and functional adaptations to race and gender oppression (219).

Through my conversations with providers I gained an appreciation for the ways in which the provision of family child care as a form of other mothering is a cultural and political act.

PROVIDING FAMILY CHILD CARE AS A POLITICAL ACT

I have come to call the conscious commitment to community betterment and survival through the provision of family child care *community care work*. By performing community care work, providers consciously contribute to the economic and cultural survival and viability of the entire community as well as to the individual children and families who comprise it.

Among the African American women I interviewed, community care work is motivated by a synthesis of spiritual, economic, cultural, and political forces. The provision of care begins with a conscious recognition of the practices and structures that shape their own lives and the lives of others, including structures that purport to challenge poverty within communities but in fact perpetuate it. Cora Jenkins spoke of her choice to enter family child care work as one motivated by a desire to aid low-income families in gaining employment and thereby leaving public assistance. When understood in the context of Cora's analysis of the underlying purpose of the state's welfare system, her provision of family child care as a means of "helping people get off the system" is clearly a political act.

> The state I don't believe intends for people to get completely off of welfare. Because if they did, you'd have no use for the state. I think the state system, meaning the welfare system, breeds that kind of limit on people's lives. It breeds poverty. They give you nowhere near enough to raise kids. But then the other part of the government limits how much money they have [available to pay] for these people to go to school. Or how much funding they have in the child care areas for these people to go to work and be subsidized in child care. So what happens is, if you have to go to work making $5 an hour, after the taxes are done and you have to pay for child care, you don't have money to pay rent. So you're back on welfare. . . . I just feel there's certain parts of government [that] breed poverty within itself in order to keep that government going. . . . I believe that for the people who run the state government system, in order for them to hold those positions, they have to have so many people in need of that program. And if they don't allow those people [on assistance] to come up, I call it being at the bottom of the barrel. . . . they never completely see out of the barrel. They're always in that confinement. And I think that [people in government] do that in order to keep their system going.
>
> I think more of the people who make decisions about the lives of people in poverty should have to live in poverty to see it. Because you can not touch poverty or feel it by standing on the outside. You have to have lived in poverty to understand the mentality of those particular people. No one's willing to do that.

While those making public policy and implementing government poverty programs may remain on the outside, unwilling to touch poverty, the African American women I interviewed cared for community members with whom they shared a common identity and heritage. As women and mothers, members of a historically subordinate racial ethnic group, and residents of lower-income communities, the providers identified with the families they served. When Euro-American providers who served low-income families talked about their humanistic motivation to care for lower-income families, they distinguished themselves from families in need: "I feel badly that those kids don't have equal opportunity." In contrast, African American providers did not distance themselves from or distinguish between the families they served and themselves. Jennie Davis spoke of her empathy for low-income, single mothers as one of the motivations for her provision of care to government-subsidized families in need: "Again, I'm in that mode of working with the low income because they're the ones that's always getting overlooked. They're always getting overlooked. They just have it very hard. And I can relate to that because I've been there. And I guess I can just relate to the parents and what they're going through."

A sense of responsibility for the welfare of the people for whom they care is common among paid care workers (Himmelweit 1999). While the African American women I interviewed experienced this sensitivity, they also took it to another level. Their motivation was empathetic: a common history, experience, and identity, including their own participation in extended kinship networks. The provision of family child care in their own communities was a political and cultural act that challenged structures perpetuating poverty and thereby facilitated the economic and cultural survival of the communities and their members.

CALLED TO SERVE

One of the most apparent differences in the meaning of family child care work among providers is the spiritual and community significance unique to urban, African American providers. Of the African American women I interviewed, all but one spoke explicitly of being called to the work by God and of the importance of serving families in need. Thus, for them the act of providing community care work is often spiritually as well as politically motivated. While all of the women I interviewed saw their work as socially valuable, for African American women, service to the community was rooted in a spiritual motivation and call. When I asked Cora Jenkins about her motivation to provide care to families in need, she responded without equivocation: "God. God was my motivating factor. Because I've known all my life that that's where God wanted me. There are people who are to provide care for children. There are people who will be mothers, doctors, teachers. Mine was the little small part that nobody wanted to do. And that was to provide care for kids."

When Sondra Ames recounted how she came to be a family child care provider, she spoke of her spiritual identity and commitment as a Christian: "See, I'm very—I'm a Christian. . . . We believe in prompting from the Holy Spirit through God." For five years after her early retirement, she anticipated her entry into family child care work—she "just believed through [her] relationship with God" that she would do the work. Like most of the African American providers I interviewed, nearly all of the children Sondra serves are government-subsidized from low-income families. When I asked Sondra why she primarily serves families in need, she reflected, "Well, I don't know. Really. Expect that I think that I have a calling for special people that always have special problems. . . . Most of [my families] are DSHS. And you know, I just can't say, 'No. I'm not going to take you.' I believe that everybody deserves quality child care." Here, Sondra synthesizes her belief that all families deserve affordable, quality child care with her spiritual call to serve.

Sharon Fleming, an African American provider of licensed family child care, described her work as "doing something for God. You know, helping the people out there. Because so many people out there need help." Patricia James believes that God has given her a skill: "[Family child care] is *me*. . . . When you're doing something that's you, it doesn't seem like a job. It just seems like something you do that's a part of your life. It's like eating. You know, it's something that's you. It fits me. I'm a very religious person, and I think that it's something's that's given to you. It's like you're a good basketball player, and God gave you that skill to be that thing."

African American providers also report a specific commitment to serving families in their own communities; and because of the racial and economic segregation of neighborhoods and communities, the families these women serve are low-income families who qualify for government-subsidized child care. So specifically, the call is to serve a community in need—a community for which child care is often unaffordable but nonetheless essential if parents are to gain and maintain economic self-sufficiency through stable employment. Their call to serve reflects aspects of the "ethic of care" first articulated by Carol Gilligan (1982). Gilligan identifies women's moral thinking as based in an ethic of care that values relationship and interdependence and is rooted in empathy and compassion. She contrasts this with the male ethic of justice, which embraces the values of liberal individualism: rights, autonomy, and self-reliance.

Although Gilligan first explicated the link between gender, individualism, and autonomy in ethical decision making and action, other scholars have incorporated race ethnicity as an additional force operating to construct an ethic of care. Collins (1993) spoke of the importance of an ethic of care in African American communities: "The convergence of Afrocentric and feminist values in the ethic of caring seems particular acute. . . . Black women have long had the support of the Black church, an institution with deep roots in the African past and a philosophy that accepts and encourages expressiveness and an ethic of caring" (101). While scholars rightly question the universal gender- or race-based ethic of care implied in Collins's statement (King 1992, Pollit 1992, Thorne 1992), they do not refute the existence of an ethic of care. Instead, they acknowledge it as rooted and emerging within a social and cultural context. Increasingly, researchers argue, the development of an ethic of care among individuals and social groups is shaped by the historical, political, and economic conditions and cultural ideologies within social groups (Kerber 1993, Puka 1993, Nicholson 1993). Thus, while cautious of its use, many scholars affirm the existence of an ethic of care and specifically the ways in which social and cultural contexts and experiences may serve as the basis for such an ethic. Philosopher Joan Tronto (1993), for example, encourages us to consider that an ethic of care may be created by the social conditions of subordination—and both gender and racial ethnic identity are two such historical conditions in our own society.

The expansion of Gilligan's concept of an ethic of care embraced by individuals to an ethic of community care that is embraced by a social group is readily apparent in the historical role played by extended social networks in African American communities. Individual autonomy and competition are insufficient to sustain the community. In African American culture, individual identity operates in tandem with group membership and responsibility. Karen Brodkin Sacks (1989) explains, "This is very different from the opposition between group and individual in dominant white American cultural constructs. . . . Afro-American women—and the Afro-American feminism that derives from their experiences as everyday black women—are central to culture and community-building by virtue of their places in families and churches" (540).

Identifying the social construction of an ethic of care enables us to understand more about the call to community care work voiced by many of the African American providers I interviewed. That call is rooted in a history in which black women play a central role in church and community. "Black women have a sense of their own importance in their churches and communities that is perhaps unmatched in the sense of self-importance felt by women in other racial-ethnic communities in the United States. . . . These women, through their public participation on so many levels, claim a prominent place in the community's history" (Gilkes 2000, 7, 19). Among the women I interviewed, the spiritual call to serve the community and its members—the call to care for others—constituted a social identity in which their contributions to their families and communities played a central and important role. This family-, community-, and church-based identity affirms child care work as socially valued and valuable—an alternative to the low status and stigma frequently associated with gender- and race-segregated care work. While family child care work, with its attendant low wages, sex segregation, and nonexistent employment benefits, can certainly be viewed as low-status work, providers drawn by God to the field do not perceive their work in this way. They have been called to the work by the Holy Spirit, called to serve children with special needs, called to contribute labor essential to the advancement of their communities.

RACIAL SAFETY, CULTURAL PRIDE, AND FAMILY CHILD CARE WORK

As we have learned, community-based markets increase the likelihood of similarities between providers and the families they serve. In addition, however, mothers frequently seek out child care providers who share their cultural values and practices and race ethnicity (Blau 1991, Uttal 1996b, Wrigley 1995). Similarly, provider concerns about their own racial and cultural safety and their conscious commitment to racial ethnic pride and identity shaped their decisions to care for families who shared, understood, and appreciated their own cultural and racial ethnic heritage.

These concerns and commitments were voiced by provider Patricia James when she spoke with me about cultural and racial ethnic differences between providers and the families for whom they care—and the need for providers to protect themselves from racial prejudice and discrimination.

> You know, we don't have no advocate for us. And I think that is something that is *very* needed in this profession because people can say anything. Valerie [a friend of Patricia's] has a cousin [who is a family child care provider]. . . . Someone said she was mistreating kids when this one lady got mad because the provider had hired a Hispanic person. And she's prejudiced against Hispanic people, and she didn't want the Hispanic person to be in the child care, so she alleged a falsehood: that the provider was abusing kids. There's no one to stand up for the child care providers.

Kim Phan, a Vietnamese provider, spoke directly to the ways in which cultural difference and native language influenced her decision to provide care solely for other Vietnamese immigrant families: "I babysit for American children, but just part time and just about two months [out of a total of five years of caregiving]. I wanted to babysit for American children also, but I felt that my English—they would not understand—and the culture difference. And that's why I was afraid. Many people asked me, but I refused because at that time I can't speak English. My English was really bad."

I asked, "So Euro-American families asked you if you would provide child care and you said no?"

"Yeah," she answered. "Because I think it's a difficult culture. And I don't know what they expect from me. . . . I don't understand what they expect from me. Like if something happened to the children, I was afraid. . . . It's too difficult for you to explain to them. I think that's difficult for me, and I am afraid that something would happen."

These findings about how providers respond to cross-cultural child care arrangements are similar to what Lynet Uttal (1996a, 1997) discovered in her analysis of race, class, and gender dynamics between child care providers and the mothers they serve. Coining the terms *racial safety and cultural maintenance,* Uttal (1996a) found that

> Awareness of racism in U.S. society was a common topic when mothers of color talked about their child care arrangements. Because of their own experiences with racism, they were concerned about how their children would be treated when the child care providers were White. . . . Racist encounters ranged from outright hostile relations with child care staff and other parents at the daycare to incompetent interactions with well-intentioned White child care providers who lack experience with caring for children of color and negotiating cross-cultural interactions. (46, 51)

In contrast to Anglo-American mothers, mothers of color were highly aware of the racial composition of their child care arrangements, especially when cross-racial arrangements increased the concern that "White children would receive preferential treatment and children of color might be maltreated" (Uttal 1997, 264). As one strategy to protect their children from racism, mothers of color sought child care within their own racial ethnic communities. Although Uttal identified racial safety as a factor considered by mothers when selecting a provider, my research reveals that providers also make decisions based on a desire to ensure their own racial safety. A provider's membership in a subordinate racial ethnic group, her own knowledge of the dominant culture, parents' attitudes and behaviors regarding race ethnicity, as well as parents' own racial ethnic and cultural heritage are primary factors that can make a work environment more or less safe for providers of color. And these are factors that providers consider in determining the families for whom they will provide care.

In addition to racial safety, African American providers spoke of a commitment to building racial identity and pride as a motivation for caring for children who share their racial ethnic identity. They spoke specifically of the roles their own parents played in both modeling and encouraging racial pride and a commitment to the black community. Sondra Ames explained how her commitment to generating children's confidence and pride grows from her own experiences as a child and from her relationship with her father.

> I'm determined with everything in me that black people will be confident. My father installed confidence in me. He always told us that we were as good as the next person. My mother hated white people. And here was my father always trying to undo all this damage that my mother was doing. But his side won out for me. And I lacked confidence as a child. I mean, there was insecurity inside, hidden. You know, my dad tried to build it up, but we were very poor. I went through an all-white school. And I was very poor. I had some pride [instilled by my father], but I was still embarrassed about a lot of my circumstances. So what I try to teach children is the confidence. No matter what you have, it's *who* you are. I always tell them that they're just *smart*. And that they're *special* . To build confidence. Because if you're *confident*, you'll go out there, and you'll be willing to make some mistakes to get what you want. So that's the goal.

Patricia James spoke of her mother's work in the 1960s as a community organizer in the housing project in which they lived, reflecting on the ways her mother's activism and encouragement influenced her to enter family child care work.

> [My mother] was a community organizer for Henley Park Housing project. She would get together in there and organize block parties, and at the time the Black Panthers were very prominent. She got involved with all that. . . . One of the things I said to my mother before she died was "I'm going to go ahead and get my own [family child care] business." She thought that was just *perfect*. She said, "It's about time you did something with that money I spent on your education."

Justine Reeves spoke of her mother as a role model for her own commitment to the community where she grew up.

> My mother was a strong black woman. Came from the south up to the north. Find a different and better life. Because in the south then, it wasn't, you know—she had to deal with the prejudice. And up here, up north, at the time there was a lot more

freedom for blacks. And we just learned how to survive. She
taught us survival. My mother—I'm *so* proud of her. She raised
the five children on $35 a day and transportation money. We al-
ways had a place to stay. . . . We stayed in one place. I grew up in
one place which actually is about four blocks from where we're
at right now.

Thus, although community-based markets segregated by race
ethnicity and social class increase the likelihood that providers will
care for children who share their own racial ethnic identity and economic status, providers also make conscious choices to serve families who share their own racial ethnic heritage. By doing so they
gain a degree of racial safety, act on their feelings of racial ethnic
pride, and contribute to the cultural survival of their communities.

FAMILY CHILD CARE AS COMMUNITY CARE WORK

To better understand community care work, we return to the feminist concept of standpoint first introduced in chapter 1. With its
explicit recognition of power and hierarchy, standpoint moves beyond the individualistic social analysis common in both the historical and contemporary United States. Our previous discussions
of liberal individualism as a political ideology remind us that this
market-based and -embracing ideology valorizes the autonomous
(masculine) individual who makes choices that will best advance
his individual position within the competitive marketplace. Con-
trasting analyses of community draw heavily on philosophical traditions of Plato, Aristotle, and Rousseau and on the social contract;
community is the extent to which we are willing to forego a part of
our individual betterment to gain a larger benefit through collective identity and action (Heller and Rook 1997, Patrick and Wickizer 1995). The community care work of family child care providers
who act as other mothers offers us a way of understanding the relationship between the individual and society that goes beyond
the depictions of liberal individualism. Rather than autonomous
individuals seeking to better themselves by amassing as much
material wealth as possible, the African American providers I interviewed developed relationships of reciprocity within their communities. Providing government-subsidized care to low-income
families enabled them to support themselves and their families

while engaging in spiritual, political, and cultural work that contributed to the development of the community.

Standpoint theory helps us to understand the community-based nature and significance of child care among these providers.

> The notion of standpoint refers to groups having shared histories based on their shared location in relations of power. . . . It is common location within hierarchical power relations that creates groups. . . Race, gender, social class, ethnicity, age, and sexuality are not descriptive categories of identity applied to individuals. Instead, these elements of social structure emerge as fundamental devices that foster inequality resulting in groups. (Collins 1997, 375)

Shared group identity is a primary force in creating what we have come to recognize as communities organized by race ethnicity and social class. As we have seen, these communities are key to the organization and provision of family child care. Group identity within community plays a central role in urban, African American providers' motivation to enter family child care as a form of community care work. Among these women, community is not limited to locality—a sense of geographic place. Rather, it is also experienced through social interaction—as relational communities characterized by social support, shared values, perceptions, beliefs, and knowledge. Communities are also infused with and informed by a common social identity (such as racial ethnic identity) and a common history or oppression (Heller 1989, MacQueen et al. 2001, Patrick and Wickizer 1995). In addition, community is often experienced as joint action—what some scholars of community have come to define as political and social responsibility. As Keller (1988) explains, political and social motivations play a central role in the formation of community. "Community must include . . . a collective framework, participation in a common enterprise, a sense of social solidarity that transcends individuals and private networks; and most especially a sense of mutual obligation and responsibility for survival" (169).

When the women I spoke with referred to "the community," they often opened their arms in a large, arcing sweep to indicate the neighborhood—one in which members share a common racial ethnic identity, social and economic status, history of social and economic oppression, and cultural and religious beliefs. In identifying their community, these African American providers synthesized the geographic, social, and political context of their lives and that of their neighbors—the community in which they lived, worked, and were called to serve. They understood their provision of family child care to be work that would contribute to the advancement of community members and therefore of the community as a whole—a community built on a shared cultural identity and social history. Thus, their decision to provide family child care was motivated by an explicit synthesis of personal identification and political activism.

Justine Reeves grew up about four blocks from where she and her husband bought their current home. "Me and my husband just kind of bought back into the community. That was the kind of vision—that we just wanted to buy back into our community." I asked her to explain what that meant.

> My meaning is that I'm putting back into my community. Just being an asset to this community. Meaning that we're property owners in this community. I also work in my community, and I'm proud of working in my community. The children that I care for—community is just a little bit wider. My parents know what I do. They know me. They know what I can do with their child. So that's saying that this woman in this community—she's an asset. She's good. She knows what she's doing.

Scholarship on black women's social history documents their ongoing importance as intergenerational resources sustaining African American families and communities. Black women's community activism, differing from black men's, is informed by women's own gendered and racial ethnic experiences, including mothering and other mothering (Gilkes 1980, McDonald 1997). Thus, the role of women is not limited to performing direct care for immediate family members. The work of social motherhood—the work of other mothering—is a political necessity as well as a self-help ideology (Boris 1993). Other mothering encompasses community activism to address the needs of children and the community—what Naples (1992, 1998b) in her analysis of antipoverty program workers has come to call "activist mothering."

> Activist mothering not only involves nurturing work for those outside one's kinship group, but also encompasses a broad definition of actual mothering practices. The community workers [I

interviewed] defined "good mothering" to comprise all actions, including social activism, that addressed the needs of their children and their community—variously defined as their racial-ethnic group, low-income people, or members of a particular neighborhood. (Naples 1998b, 113)

The similarities between activist mothering and the community care work undertaken by family child care providers are clear. The women I interviewed engaged in family child care work in part to support themselves and their families. But their particular location in the social world (shaped by gender, racial ethnic identity, cultural identity, and social class) gave rise to additional motivations. Through their provision of community care work, they helped address and alter the economic and racial ethnic discrimination faced by themselves and other members of their community. They consciously responded to a spiritual call to contribute to the community's racial ethnic identity and pride as well as its economic betterment and survival.

After nineteen years in family child care, Cora Jenkins spoke of her plans to leave family child care but to continue to draw on her value of community as well as her work experience in developing a new community-based child care program.

> I'm getting ready to leave family child care. I'm going to be directing programs that are being developed at this time. And the programs will be the same as [in my family child care]. The same guidelines. The same assessments. All of that will just go into a center atmosphere. . . . [This] is a new community program that has been developed that will serve young men and women from age thirteen to twenty-five years. The program will be teaching not only parenting skills, but there's an educational area for completing GEDs and going on to college. So I'm working on developing child care centers, and then [will be] directing those four centers.

"Are you excited?" I asked.

> Oh yeah! I really am. Because it's something I've often wanted to do. I've wanted to utilize the skills I had from family day care but offer it to a larger population of people. And what I'm doing now [in family child care], I could only serve a handful at a time. But the need is greater than a handful. So . . . I see it as a challenge. And I like a challenge. I see it as being fruitful. And I figure I've been at this stage for nineteen years. And that's how I

look at life. You do certain things for a period of time. And you must grow with time. And this is just another step. That's how I see it.

So while she plans to leave family child care, Cora's commitment to serving children and families within her community takes a new form. As Cora says, "You must grow with time," but doing so involves holding on to core values of community and care. Although structural forces of race ethnicity and social class organize the provision of family child care, women such as Cora also make active choices to serve the community through the provision of family child care, thereby consciously challenging structures that contribute to racial ethnic and social class subordination. Community, then, is created and maintained by both internal and external forces. While it is built and sustained through external structures of economic oppression and racism, it is also sustained through conscious strategies "developed to combat white racism and to strengthen black social, economic, and political institutions for group survival and advancement" (Blackwell 1985, xi). The decision to provide family child care is one such strategy among African American women in lower-income neighborhoods.

This commitment to community care work both calls into question and moves beyond liberal individualist ideology, which has little, if any, room for values of care, relational commitment, and collective good. By advancing values of care and community, the African American women I interviewed ascribe an alternative meaning—and a higher social and public value—to women's historically devalued child care work. Through advocacy of the value of public responsibility for children and families, they begin to reframe the cultural and political debate and identify child care as a social and public good.

7

"I HAD TO EDUCATE THE WORLD THAT THIS IS MY WORK"

Redefining and Revaluing Family Child Care Work

Over the past twenty years, as mothers of young children have increasingly entered the paid labor force, child care has assumed a prominent place in the public eye. At both state and national levels, policymakers debate the costs and benefits of child care as a service for parents, focusing on their need—in particular, that of mothers—to participate in paid labor. But rarely, if ever, do policymakers consider the workers who provide paid child care when other mothers enter employment. Why do women enter paid child care work despite its notoriously low wages and lack of status? Why do some women (often mothers) provide paid care in their own homes so that other mothers can engage in paid work outside the home? What role does women's family child care work play in sustaining families and communities? To this point, the public debates regarding child care have been woefully ignorant of the work of family child care: of family child care as a large and stable source of paid care, of why women enter this work, and of the public value of this work. My aim in telling providers' stories is to make both the women and their work increasingly visible and, in doing so, influence both public knowledge and the public debate regarding the value of family child care work and its centrality in sustaining the social and economic viability of families and communities.

THE PUBLIC NEED FOR CARE VERSUS
THE PUBLIC VALUE ASCRIBED TO IT

The stories of providers who share gender identity but differ in racial ethnic identity, cultural identity, country of origin, and social class enable us to understand the multiple social forces and personal responsibilities that draw women into family child care work as well as the ways in which the work not only reproduces but also challenges existing ideologies and social relationships regarding the family, the market, work, and care. Gloria Zuñiga is one of the providers whom we have come to know in this book. She is a married mother of two young children whose paid employment is providing family child care. Her experiences and analysis of child care offer us insights into the social, economic, and public value of family child care from the multiple social locations that she inhabits. As a working mother, Gloria understands that accessible, quality child care is essential to both her paid employment and her peace of mind. As a paid provider, she understands that quality child care is available only through trained providers and that these providers deserve public recognition and respect. And as a citizen, she understands the centrality of child care to the successful functioning of both families and the economy.

> [Family child care] is very, very important. What I didn't like when we were in Texas is that there weren't enough day care homes over there. You always had problems finding care for the children. Sometimes you couldn't find care; and if you couldn't, then you just left the children with anyone. You should give a lot of credit to this type of work. We are trained to do this. And it's very much needed. If you don't have someone to take care of your children, how are you going to work?

The work of Gloria and other family child care providers is central to parents and to the businesses who seek to employ them. Fully one-quarter of children under age five who are in paid child care are cared for by family child care providers (U.S. Department of Commerce, Bureau of the Census 2002). Despite the prominence of family child care as a source of care, providers nationwide report that their work is marginalized and devalued (Haack 1998). The providers I interviewed were no exception. Consistently, the women spoke with genuine passion about how undervalued and underrespected their work is: lack of credibility, no professional recognition, no respect, stereotyped as babysitters. These manifestations of the devaluation of family child care workers arose consistently in my discussions with providers and are rooted in the social structure of families and the cultural meaning and value ascribed to women's care work within families, as discussed in the preceding chapters.

In chapter 1, I spoke of ideologies as systems of belief that directly shape social relationships and social structures. An ideology is a belief system that produces and organizes social relations. In this book, I have explored the family as a social location, an ideology, and a practice; the ways in which the ideology of the family is gendered and racialized; and in turn, how it informs the organization and ideology of the market economy and women's paid employment within it. Through the stories of family child care providers, I've elucidated the social processes that we participate in every day and how these processes contribute to ideologies of gender, race, and family and their material outcomes. I've demonstrated the dynamic relationship between institutions, ideologies, and individual actors. The lives and work of providers serve as a window onto our understanding of the social processes through which providers create, maintain, and transform the social structures and cultural meanings of community, work, and care.

In developing our understanding of these processes it is essential to remember the centrality of gender and race in the dominant ideology of the family and to remember that gender and race (which are themselves ideologies) are formed of both cultural meaning and material relations (Glenn 1999). Gender and race are not essential, universal characteristics and arrangements. They are "both an outcome and a rationale for various social arrangements" (including the family) and "serve as a means of justifying [two] of the most fundamental divisions of society" (West and Fenstermacher 1995, 9). Ideologies of gender and race are systems of belief that are linked with social consequences. Gender and race are, then, a social rationale as well as a material outcome. We see this outcome in the lack of public value accorded to the care work of women of color and white women, whether they provide care in the family as unpaid work or in the market as paid labor.

Consistently, the providers with whom I spoke talked of the lack of respect and status they and their work receive. Cora Jenkins is an African American provider with an associate's degree in administrative management who spoke to me about this issue. "I don't think people realize that [family child care] is a profession that has requirements and meets a need for people who hold other types of jobs. They still look at child care providers as babysitters. But I don't sit babies. I provide care for children. Anybody can babysit and sit a kid in front of a TV. But family child care workers are providing more than that. You should get paid for that."

Martha Buxton, a Euro-American provider and former schoolteacher, talked about the low wages of family child care providers, linking public perceptions of caregiving with unskilled and therefore low-waged labor.

"Why do you think family child care work is low paid?" I asked.

Martha responded, "Probably because it was once babysitting, I suppose. And people used to pay babysitters a cheap wage. And maybe this thought that 'Oh, It's just a babysitting job' has continued. . . . And they figure people that are educated who can't get any other kind of job ordinarily do child care. Or will do child care."

Justine Reeves, an African American provider, worked as head teacher in a child care center before entering family child care two years ago. She also spoke about the lack of respect and public value accorded to providers and their work.

> Child care providers need to be recognized as professionals. We've been put back on the back shelf for too long. People look down on us. We're not respected. We're not treated with dignity. And we're *definitely* not being paid well at all for the work that we do. . . . We need to be paid better wages. And until we're recognized, those wages are not going to come. So we have to be out there and be recognized and be respected. You know, we are the workers that nobody ever sees. So we're the workers that people think don't do anything. That's the attitude. That we don't do anything, but nobody ever sees.

Joan Tronto (1996) critiques the ideology that separates private care from public work and politics and thereby contributes to the situation described by Justine—one in which "nobody ever sees" or values the work of child care. In traditional political theory, care is viewed as either below or above, but never within, the polity, which is the sphere of public discourse and public value. Tronto argues that, within political theory, the private realm (encompassing the emotional, the subjective, the relational) has historically been constructed in opposition to the public realm (encompassing the abstract, the objective, the rational). Thus, care is below the public realm and has limited, if any, public value. In contrast, care is sometimes constructed as being above the public sphere of the market and politics. In this case, care, a relational process requiring reciprocity and at times putting the needs of others before one's own, is seen as attaining a higher moral value than that ascribed to the public realm of political and economic life in which autonomy and self-maximization motivate one's actions. In this construction, care is a religious, spiritual, or moral activity and, as such, care is viewed as above the realm of the rational, the objective, and hence the public. In either case, care is cast outside the parameters of the public sphere, so those who engage in the work of care are at best revered and at worst entirely invisible; but in either case, they exist outside of the public realm.

Lack of social and professional recognition, low wages, and economic insecurity are inherent in the work of family child care and will remain so as long as our political theory and practice continue to mask the importance of care work in our lives. Deborah Stone (1991) is one of the first theorists to explore the bifurcated ideologies of the family and the market and the way in which these ideologies (rooted in liberal individualism) contribute to the invisibility and devaluing of care work. "At the heart of liberal political philosophy is the autonomous man. Liberal polities are built on the premise that their individual members are capable of caring, providing, and deciding for themselves. . . . This is by now a standard feminist critique of Western political theory: it has no place for dependence and the caring work that goes with it" (547, 548).

In a more recent analysis, Eva Kittay (1999) notes that what appears as autonomy under the ideology of liberal individualism is really purchased at a price. "The purchase price of independence is a wife, a mother, a nursemaid, a nanny—a dependency worker" (183). Paradoxically, the dependency worker enables others to become independent by attending to their dependencies. The liberal individualist ideal on which public life in the contemporary United States is founded—that of a society comprised of an association of autonomous equals—masks the centrality of dependency in all of our lives. It masks the needs of the seemingly autonomous man, the existence of dependents, and the existence of those who care for dependents. This obscuring and devaluing of care and care work lead to what Kittay calls the "dialectic of dependency." Due to gendered and racialized ideologies and practices that associate women with care, when women enter the paid work force they often do so vis-à-vis the role of paid care workers. But when women enter the market economy as paid care workers, thereby gaining a promise of some measure of independence through paid work, the care worker herself, as a result of the cultural devaluation of care, becomes vulnerable. The lack of public value and social status ascribed to her work translate into low wages and economic vulnerability. By caring for others she herself is at risk and becomes vulnerable to poverty and secondary social status.

This dialectic of dependency is evident in the lives and work of family child care providers. In our conversations, their concerns about the lack of respect and value accorded to their work were consistently accompanied by real anxieties about poor compensation. As full-time, year-round workers, they reported a mean net income of $15,280 and an average work week of sixty to sixty-five hours. At an hourly wage of between $4.45 and $4.82, their earnings fell well below the $5.15 federal minimum wage and the $6.50 minimum wage in effect in Washington State at the time of my interviews. Just as two-thirds of child care workers nationwide earn below poverty-level wages (Whitebook and Phillips 1999), fully two-thirds of the women I spoke with earned wages below the poverty threshold. The lack of public value and the subsequent poverty-level wages ascribed to child care work are further reflected in government policies regarding child care. The vast majority of women of color I interviewed were de facto state employees. Through their provision of state-subsidized child care, a large portion, if not all, of their income came from government sources. Nonetheless, a number earned wages so low that they or their children qualified for government-subsidized health care for low-income families. Ironically, one even qualified for government-subsidized child care—the very care she provided to families to facilitate their economic self-sufficiency.

The providers voiced genuine concern about their low wages and lack of benefits. When I asked Patricia James, an African American provider of licensed care, what she disliked about family child care work, she explained, "You're not making an income, even though you may be running your whole household on your family child care earnings. . . . We don't get enough respect on that issue [of wages]." Patricia was also frustrated because the state pays lower rates for family child care than for center-based care. (For example, although Washington pays family child care providers in Seattle $660 a month for state-subsidized infant care, it pays child care centers in Seattle $832 a month for the same care, a rate more than 25 percent higher). On the public-private continuum, women's care work that is most removed from the public sphere seems to have the least public value and receives the least economic reward.

> And the state giving different rates for family child care versus center child care. That, to me, doesn't make sense. You're doing the same job. In fact, you're providing *better* service in the home because you have a *limited* number of children that you supervise. Therefore, you're able to give more *quality* care. I think it [the wage ratio] should be reversed. If not reversed, equalize them. Pay them both the same amount of money for doing the same job.

Although the state subsidizes child care costs so that low-income mothers may receive education and job training and become more self-sufficient, current government policies regarding payment for subsidized family child care incorporate and perpetuate the historical devaluation of women's care work. The state structures its compensation system (by contracting out work) so that family child care providers do not qualify for the benefits historically associated with paid work in the market economy: worker's compensation, Social Security, or retirement benefits. While providing child care services essential to the functioning of the welfare state, state policies deny providers their full recognition as bona fide workers and the full benefits historically identified with paid labor. As a result, the low-waged work of women providers enables other low-income women to prepare for and enter the paid work force. The cycle feeds on itself.

Despite her full-time, year-round work as a licensed family child care provider, Jennie Davis earns so little money providing state-subsidized child care to low-income families that she and her daughter constitute a low-income family and, as a result, qualify for government-subsidized health care. An African American family child care provider for three years, Jennie spoke of the importance of providers' ability to earn a living wage sufficient to purchase health insurance, housing, and food.

> [Child care providers] are not getting paid a livable wage. You've got the turnover because of that. And I feel that if the state was that concerned, they would do something to help. Because the workers, they have to live, too. And you can't do a good job if you're not financially being taken care of. It all boils down to finances. Productivity comes with the workers being reasonably happy and being able to take care of their own families. And to be able to afford medical insurance and housing and food and all that.

Across the board, family child care providers earn so little that they are unable to invest in medical insurance or retirement savings. This situation, which was clear among the providers I interviewed, is also evident among providers nationwide (Galinsky et al. 1994, Modigliani 1993). Kay Schilling, a Euro-American licensed provider for eleven years, has neither health insurance or retirement savings.

> If I were to leave this field, it would be to get a job that has benefits. Medical insurance gives you peace of mind—to make sure that you and your family can stay healthy. Because the lack of health care, it's really scary. Lack of retirement benefits. Like I say, I've been doing this for eleven years; and if I had been working with a company for eleven years, I would have a pretty good retirement. And we haven't been able to save for our retirement. So it's a question of that sense of security. When you're in family child care, you don't have that sense of security. Financial security.

Like Kay, Gloria Zuñiga has no retirement savings; but she reported that family child care is her permanent employment. She will stay in the field until she cannot work any longer. "I like the job very much," explained Gloria. "I like what I'm doing. But I'm concerned about when I get older. Then what? When I can no longer do child care. I don't have a pension. I don't have any type of benefits. When I get older how is that going to affect me in the long run. What do I have to look forward to? To keep doing child care, one of my biggest concerns is when I get old and when I cannot work anymore. What's going to happen then?"

Gloria's question is a valid one: what's going to happen to her and her family in the future? Despite her full-time, year-round employment, her low wages, lack of health insurance, and lack of retirement savings leave her and her family in a precarious economic position. Gloria is confronted with a paradox. In choosing family child care employment, she lays claim to work that offers meaning and social value. Yet labor markets for care work are organized and infused with ideologies of gender and race ethnicity. As a result, the work that Gloria finds meaningful and believes to be of social import compromises her economic security and that of her family.

Gloria is the rule, not the exception. The "intersectionality" (Zinn and Dill 1996) of Gloria's experience as a woman, a woman of color, and an immigrant woman contributes to her economic vulnerability and, as result, to her family's. Glenn (2000) explicates the social forces that contribute to the provision of care work by women such as Gloria and how the devaluation of care leads to further social and economic degradation among those who provide care.

> To the extent that caring is devalued, invisible, underpaid, and penalized, it is relegated to those who lack economic, political, and social power and status. And to the extent that those who engage in caring are drawn disproportionately from among disadvantaged groups (women, people of color, and immigrants), their activity—that of caring—is further degraded. In short, the devaluing of caring contributes to the marginalization, exploitation, and dependency of care givers. (84)

While policymakers and the public increasingly recognize the importance of child care for employed parents, particularly for middle-class, white mothers, the actual work of care and the women who provide care continue to be devalued. Child care providers are themselves most often mothers and are disproportionately members of historically subordinate and marginalized groups, which contributes to the further devaluation of their work. The location of family child care work in the social structure of the family and the attendant cultural devaluation ascribed to the care work of women within families and households also contributes to the devaluation, low status, and economic vulnerability of family child care providers. As Romero (2002) observes, "The family is the archetypical ideological apparatus. Its goal is reproduction in a physical sense but, more importantly, the family oversees the reproduction of the basic ideological forms—class, race, age, and gender ideologies, social expectations, folkways, mores, norms and the like" (30).

As a social structure and an ideology, however, the family is not static. Although powerful and tenacious, its social organization and dominant ideology are not fixed. Located within a larger set of social values and practices, the family is subject to change as cultural values, economic conditions, and political processes change. Like all social structures and ideologies, the family is continually negotiated, reconstituted, and redefined. As such, the social organization and cultural meaning of family child care, located within the structural and ideological context of the family, is also dynamic. Although family child care may be perceived as maintaining and reproducing the gendered and racialized ideologies and practices of the family, it can also challenge these same ideologies and practices—and it does.

REDEFINING SOCIAL STRUCTURES AND THEIR CULTURAL MEANING THROUGH FAMILY CHILD CARE WORK

How do women, through the provision of family child care, challenge the social structure as well as the gendered and racialized meaning of family? Although institutions and ideologies are powerful forces that influence the place of individuals and groups within the social world, this process is dynamic. While our daily lives are embedded in social structures and processes, we also act on a daily basis in ways that not only contribute to but challenge these structures and processes. Through their daily lives and work within families, family child care providers not only contribute to the dominant ideology of family. They also challenge and redefine the gendered and racialized ideology of the family and the devaluation of women's care work that is inherent in this ideology. When we seek to understand the social organization of family child care from the perspective of the women who perform this work, we come to understand work, care, and the cultural meaning of both in new ways. While dominant ideologies contribute to the belief that family child care is something other than real work, providers are redefining the meaning of families and the paid care work they perform within families. In my interviews, I listened to and for the providers' interpretations of their own lives—their work, their families, and their communities. In doing so, I came to appreciate that, while family child care work may reflect and recreate dominant ideologies and structures, it challenges them as well.

In our conversations, providers contest the belief that child care is not work and that it is not skilled. Their provision of child care for pay within their own homes disputes the historical ideologies that distinguish care in families from work in the market economy. Providing care for pay challenges the belief that child care is an activity motivated by women's natural love for children. The process of challenging the historical ideology identifying women's child care, including that of paid care, as something other than real work is an ongoing one for family child care providers—and is one in which they actively engage. Janice Newman, a Euro-American provider for twelve years, explained.

> I had to educate my spouse. I really did. He was saying things like "Oh. Well, I really need my coaching clothes washed. Do you suppose you could do that today?" You know, because I was at home [doing family child care]. And I had to educate the world that this is my work. Not just my spouse, but the world. Anybody that knew me. This is what I do for a living. You'll find that other people . . . think that you have nothing else to do. You're at *home*. "Oh, well, you're home, so could you provide three dozen cupcakes for the party at school?"
>
> "I'm working."
>
> "Yes, but you're home." They just in general—unless people have visited and seen what I do—they don't understand that I'm working. . . . And it's taken my friends and the family [a long time]. My mother-in-law, after twelve years, probably for the last two years has quit asking when I'm going to get a job and go back to work. And I think that's real typical with providers. Having to convince [people] what they're doing is credible and that it is a job. And it's a hard job. And it's long hours.

Consistently the providers with whom I spoke represented their family child care work as not only real work but important work requiring training, skill, and responsibility. In defining their work as skilled labor, providers redefine the market ideology that has contributed to the historical devaluation of women's care work. By harnessing the power of market ideology, they give new cultural meaning and value to women's care work and encourage others to do so as well. Kay Schilling spoke of the skills and responsibilities involved in the daily work of family child care.

> We're not babysitters. We're professional business people. We take our jobs very seriously. I would have to call us passionate about it. We truly care about the children and families. . . . We're trained to provide well-balanced, nourishing meals for the children, and we provide that for them. We're trained to perform CPR and first aid. A lot of us work a ten- to eleven-hour day, and in the evenings we go on to take classes to get better at what we're doing for the children. So we're not babysitters. We work really *hard* at what we do, and we try to do a very good job.

Like Kay, Justine Reeves related that licensed family child care providers are required to engage in ongoing training, just like other professionals. By using the ideology of the market and the recognized place and value of professionals within it, Justine demonstrates that ideologies are not fixed. They are, in fact, dynamic and can be called into question and redefined.

> [Family child care providers] do have our continuing education. If there's a class through the community college that interests me, I jump in it. So I've been going to school since 1990. I was certified [as a child development associate] in 1996. And I've been going to classes ever since then. I think that's important to us as child care workers. So I'm just trying to set up an image or role model. This is what we have to do also. Doctors have to continue with their training and reading and so on. And that's what we as child care workers have to do. And that, again, shows our professionalism.

Given providers' identification of family child care as skilled work, I asked them what they thought would be a fair wage. Allie McGinnis, an unlicensed Euro-American provider and former public schoolteacher, responded:

> About $60 an hour [laughter]. Isn't that what some lawyers make? I *know* this work is harder than being a lawyer. That is

just so convoluted for me. Because the people who really need good child care *can't afford it.* So I'll just say what I think they should be paid, and then how to get there is a different story. But I really think $20 to $25 an hour in terms of the skills you need to do *good, responsible* child care. You have to be someone who knows about child development. And have a lot of skills and access to ways of finding out if you don't know. I really do think that. I know a lot of state workers, and that's what they make. And I think child care work is equally as demanding.

By redefining family child care as demanding work requiring training and responsibility, providers draw on available rhetoric, on the dominant ideology of the market, as a means of claiming the need for public recognition of their work and of themselves as skilled workers. In so doing, they offer further evidence of the dynamic relationship between material conditions and cultural meaning. The historical provision of child care by women of color and white women in families and households contributes to its identification with the gendered and racialized ideology of the family and subsequently to the devaluation of the work. But when the work becomes paid (that is, when the social and material relations of the work itself change), it has the potential to be ascribed with new cultural meaning. In social movement parlance, a political opportunity arises (McAdam 1982). As they begin to apply public ideals of the social and economic value of skilled labor to their family child care work, providers draw on a strategy long used by disenfranchised groups in making political and public claims (Omi and Winant 1994).

Providers challenge social structures and ideologies (and the dynamic relationship between the two) in other ways as well. Paula Shelton, a Mexicana and coordinator of a community-based Seasonal Farmworker Child Care Program, identified a number of ways in which family child care employment contests historical ideologies and structural practices in her community. Her analysis reveals, yet again, the dynamic relationship between ideologies, social relations, and social structures. When home-based child care becomes paid work, changes in material conditions contribute to changes in ideologies: by providing occupational mobility and economic stability for providers, enabling women to engage in meaningful and rewarding paid work, challenging gender ideologies of dependence, and giving women collective experiences with other women workers.

> The people who are doing [family] child care—they would normally be working out in the orchards or doing that type of work. They're now in their homes taking care of children, doing a job that they really do enjoy. They're buying their own homes. A lot of our new child care providers are buying their own homes. Gloria just bought hers. Isabel bought hers. Segunda bought hers. A lot of them have bought homes. It's helped them to become independent. Just being independent—they always have been under the wings of their husbands. You know, you've got to understand the Mexican culture. . . . I think family child care and family child care training has made them independent. I think it's made them proud that "This is my business. This is *mine.*" There's something they can call their own, and they can be proud of, you know, instead of going to work in the orchard and the employer pays the husband for both of them. And they don't get any of the money. . . . So it's teaching them independence. It's giving them a lot of training. And just being together—I see it when we have the provider training meetings. They *enjoy* getting together. And all the women, just women, no guys. No men. Just the women.

For many of the providers I interviewed, family child care is a means by which to secure permanent employment and a stable income. By providing licensed child care to state-subsidized families, economically vulnerable workers are able to access year-round, full-time employment in communities in which their employment options are limited by the gendered- and racial ethnic–segregation of jobs as well as their immigrant status. Additionally, by becoming licensed family child care providers and affiliating with a local community service agency staffed by employees who share one's native language and cultural and racial ethnic identity, immigrant women are able to use resources within an English-speaking community that would otherwise be less accessible to both themselves and members of their community. By offering state-subsidized child care, women not only increase their own economic stability. They enable community members to do so as well by offering other immigrant families the affordable child care needed by parents who are finding and maintaining paid employment. As a result, the actions of providers challenge social class and racial ethnic structures as these women help their own families as well as families in their communities move toward economic self sufficiency.

Family child care is a means of professional mobility for a number of the providers I interviewed, thereby enabling them to challenge structures that maintain their subordinate social class status. Native-born providers with more formal education and native English skills and who live in urban rather than rural communities envision and experience family child care as an important step in occupational advancement. Having greater access to larger labor markets, these providers either plan to or have successfully used family child care work as a springboard into other, better-paid early childhood or social service employment.

Additionally, providers consistently told me that they found their family child care work personally and professionally rewarding. Meaningful employment has made a significant change in the lives of these women. Family child care enables them to have more control over their work environment than they had in their previous jobs. Furthermore, the women reported experiencing the rewards of creativity and flexibility in their work as well as engaging in work that they believe to be socially valuable—a contribution to their communities and the larger society. In so doing, providers go beyond market ideology as a means of laying claim to the public value of their work. While they adhere to conventional market ideology in framing their work as a skilled profession, they simultaneously challenge liberal individualist ideals that celebrate autonomy and self-interest at the expense of the collective good. In claiming the value of their work, providers often draw on a religious ideal that contests the historical market devaluation of care as a private activity and instead affirms care as socially valued public work. Providers draw on values of racial ethnic identity and cultural pride that contribute to collective survival and advancement. And they claim the political value of community care work as a means of challenging structures and ideologies of gender, race ethnicity, and social class that seek to perpetuate their social subordination.

The spiritual call to serve the community through the provision of family child care serves as an important source of racial ethnic and cultural identity as well as cultural survival for African American providers. In our conversations, these providers spoke of the call to serve as a primary motivation for entering the work.

While concerned about the low wages and benefits and the lack of status accorded to family child care in the larger society, the providers themselves did not view their work as low-status. Instead, they were called by the Holy Spirit to serve families in need and to contribute to the cultural and economic survival of their communities.

Motivated by both a call to serve and by racial safety and cultural pride, African American women act on a conscious commitment to collective survival and advancement by providing family child care as community care work. This vision of collective responsibility for both children and the community challenges the individualism inherent in both liberal political philosophy and the dominant ideology of the family. By reconstituting family child care as community care work, providers contest the autonomous, self-sufficient individual as both an ideal and a reality, as well as the belief and practice that children and child care are the responsibilities of individual women whose work has limited meaning and value outside of the sphere of the immediate family.

FAMILY CHILD CARE AS WORK OF PUBLIC VALUE

Although family child care work reflects certain ideologies identifying women with families and nurturance, the work also enables women to redefine social structures of family, work, and care as well as the cultural meanings historically ascribed to them. By claiming the public value of family child care, providers challenge the historical devaluation of those in need of care and those who provide it. Allie McGinnis spoke of her concern about the lack of priority given to children in need of care and the social value and importance of children to our collective future: "I think that children are not respected in this society. Their needs are met last, and I don't get it. Other than being a resource—I mean [they are] the people who are going to be the next teachers, the next leaders, the next mothers, the next fathers. . . . Intellectually, I know that there are all these prejudices and decades-long traditions in our culture that make [that lack of concern for children] what it is. But, I can't reconcile it with how I feel about what children need and deserve."

Research confirms Allie's assessment that public investment in what children need and deserve is essential. The social and public benefits of good child care, including lower crime, higher employment rates, lower poverty rates, greater economic productivity, and a better work force, are well documented (Folbre 2001, 1994; Shonkoff and Phillips 2000). Caring labor generates public benefits that accrue even to those who do not pay for them—those who, in the parlance of economists, are recognized as "free riders" (England and Folbre 1999).

Although all citizens benefit from good child care, the costs of caring are largely borne by private individuals—not only parents but also child care providers, who pay double the costs of caring. First, providers pay through the poverty-level wages they derive from child care employment, wages that subsidize the true cost of care and result in the economic vulnerability of providers and their families. Second, many providers are parents themselves and must pay for care for their own children from the low wages they derive from caring for the children of others.

When public recognition of the costs and benefits of child care does emerge, it is most often motivated by the desire to improve the quality of care for children rather than by an interest in providing greater compensation and professional recognition for providers. Nonetheless, the two goals are closely linked. Multiple studies document that the presence of well-educated, well-compensated, and consistent child care providers are significant predictors of quality care for children (Phillips et al. 2000, Ripple 2000, Whitebook et al. 2001). Clearly, the needs of families, providers, and society are linked. Children deserve quality care. Parents require affordable, accessible child care. Providers require better-paying jobs in order to provide stable, skilled care. And the public at large reaps the benefits of the social and economic contributions of the future generation. These mutual interests and the ensuing need to move beyond privatizing the costs of care are reflected in a jingle sung by child care advocates in the Worthy Wage Campaign:

> Parents can't afford to pay,
> Teachers and providers can't afford to stay,
> Help us find a better way.

What is the better way? Given the inability of many parents to pay for care, providers' subsidy of the true costs of care, and the benefits to the public that accrue from quality care, advocates and policymakers increasingly recognize that the child care crisis will not be resolved by market forces alone, nor should it be. Markets are designed for profit; and while quality child care results in long-term economic and social benefits, it is not an immediately profitable venture (England and Folbre 2002). The growing care gap between the public need for care and the public resources allotted to it has motivated a number of states to institute or expand publicly funded initiatives to increase the compensation, training, and stability of the child care work force (Whitebook and Eichberg 2002). Suzanne Helburn and Barbara Bergman (2002) estimate that incentives to increase subsidies for child care and better compensation for providers nationwide would cost $46.4 billion a year (209–21). The cost may appear high, but it is essential to remember two facts. First, a lack of public understanding of the true social and economic costs of care exists because of our historical ideology and practice that frame care work as an unpaid and altruistic activity carried out by women in families. This historical invisibility leads to a widespread perception that care costs nothing when, in reality, women have paid (and continue to pay) the true social and economic costs of care by foregoing paid work to provide unpaid care, engaging in low-paid child care employment, and foregoing future earnings as a result of unpaid and low-waged care work. Second, funds are available to pay for quality child care. For example, federal spending on transportation totaled $47 billion in 2000, and the Department of Defense budget totaled $278 billion that same year (Nelson 2001). The question is clearly one of political priorities and will.

As care and the value of care become increasingly visible, so does disparity between the public need for providers and the social value by which their pay is set. This is a dilemma not only in family child care work but in other forms of care work as well: nannies, home health care assistants, elder care workers. In each case, the social and economic devaluation of care and care workers are linked to ideologies that devalue care provided by women. As a result, social recognition and support of the true public value of care will require a considerable shift in attitudes about the value of women and their care work, a transformation already articulated by the women who do the daily work of family child care. As provider Cora Jenkins observed, "Although this is a day care home, this is still public service work."

Family child care is work in transition: child care is now being drawn into the market economy. Because its social location bridges the structures and ideologies of both the family and the market, family child care work enables women to redefine the social structures of the family and the market and the cultural meanings historically ascribed to both. Providers see the opportunity to bring their redefinition of the social and economic value of women's child care work into the public arena and are beginning to do so. Provider Justine Reeves reflected on the struggle for public recognition among family child care providers: "Recognition is starting to come in this new millennium. Home providers have really gotten the scraps of the bowl. I think that's because they have not been able to use their voices. So with studies like this, our voices are coming out. And once they come out . . . then [family child care providers] will get more vocal. . . . And with the power of our voice, nothing can't be done."

Julia Deavers, a Euro-American family child care provider for four years, spoke about the lack of public value accorded to family child care work. She is conscious of the skills necessary to successfully undertake her work, the public import of her work, and its cultural and economic devaluation. She also appreciates the fact that the devaluation of her work is grounded in a political and economic system that does not clearly recognize the needs of children and others who require care, nor of those who care for them.

> I know how hard I work. And I know how many areas of life I have to cover. I have to have some sort of medical training and be alert to that sort of thing. I have to be a janitor. I have to be a psychologist. I have to be a cook. I have to be a server. I have to know the educational needs [of the children]. You know, I have to know *so much*. And I have to be a mother. I have these kids how many more hours than their *own* parents? I have to know *so much* in order to have a healthy child come out at the end of it. I just know that I'm worth a lot. And I know that I'm totally under paid. I know child care providers with the *exact* same education as teachers, they start in the field at $6,000 less a year. So I know it's not fair. So they should at *least* be making the same amount as teachers. But I know teachers are underpaid too. So

all I know is that our focus on children, across the board, in this country is totally wrong.

Julia offers a perceptive social analysis in which she calls into question the devaluation of women's care for children. Rooted in liberal individualism, the ideologies and practices that organize child care in the contemporary United States valorize the ideals of autonomy and self-interest and conceal the importance of care work in all our lives. Obscuring and devaluing care work leads to the assignment of care to members of historically subordinate social groups: women of color, white women, immigrant women. As mothers of young children enter the paid work force and the need for alternative sources of child care grows, the social organization of child care work and the women who do it become increasingly visible. So do the gendered and racialized ideologies that identify women as natural caregivers and thereby devalue care work, assigning it to the private sphere as something other than real work worthy of recognition, respect, and a living wage.

The competing demands for women as mothers and as participants in the paid labor force reveals the work of child care as a fundamental component of economic and social life, as well as the false duality that distinguishes care from work and the family from the market. This awareness calls us to question, as does Julia, the ideologies and practices that have historically devalued and ignored the care work of women and that subsequently contribute to the devaluation of family child care work. Centering our analysis of women and child care within the daily lives of providers makes visible the gendered and racialized processes that draw women into the work. Their experiences and the processes that shape the organization and provision of their work call for a reexamination and expansion of our understanding of family, work, and care and of the dynamic relationship between the three. Such recognition requires that the wages, working conditions, and status of family child care providers be improved to reflect the true social and economic value of their work.

Notes

CHAPTER 1

1. In this book I use a variety of terms to describe the race ethnicity of family child care providers (for example, African American, black, white, Euro-American, Hispanic, Latina, and Mexicana). The terms reflect the sources from which they were derived (that is, interview transcripts, other research studies, and census data).
2. I use the term *race ethnicity* to emphasize the historical and cultural experiences that shape group identity rather than the term *race*, which defines groups on the basis of purported biological characteristics. While race is a fundamental organizing principle of social relationships, it is the social definition and construction of race that have historically shaped the cultural identities and experiences of groups.
3. The federal government uses a variety of terms to describe child care providers. *Preschool teachers* are defined as presuming primary classroom responsibility for instructing children up to age five "in activities designed to promote social, physical, and intellectual growth." *Teacher aides and assistants* work under the supervision of a preschool teacher, and *child care workers* are defined as assuming less responsibility for child development and more responsibility for the custodial care of children (U.S. Department of Labor, Bureau of Labor Statistics 2000).

CHAPTER 2

1. Portions of this chapter appeared in Mary Tuominen, 2000, "The Conflicts of Caring: Gender, Race Ethnicity, and Individualism in Family Child Care Work," in *Care Work: Gender, Labor, and the Welfare State,* ed. Madonna Harrington Meyer (New York: Routledge), 112–35.
2. In my research I did not evaluate the actual quality of care provided by the women I interviewed. The most comprehensive evaluation of the quality of family child care to date found predictors of quality to include sensitivity, responsiveness, and commitment to taking care of children and found the quality of family child care to be "just slightly less than the average" of quality scores received by child care centers (Galinsky et al. 1994). Nevertheless, findings regarding the quality of child care, especially in different cultural and racial ethnic contexts, are highly varied; and techniques of quality assessment are highly controversial. While some researchers find little difference in actual care when comparing diverse families (Kontos 1992), others find lower-quality care among low-income children and children of color (Galinsky et al. 1994). All of these findings need

to be viewed in the context of emerging research on cultural differences in educational and communication styles that appear strongly biased toward white, middle-class standards of child care and early childhood education (Bromer 2001, Cancian 2002).

CHAPTER 3

1. Kim is the only provider I interviewed who referred to her work as "babysitting." The other providers I interviewed were adamant in their disgust at the use of the word to describe work they viewed as skilled labor of important social value.
2. Annual net income in 1999 dollars is calculated as gross income less business expenses (such as food, cooking and cleaning supplies, toys, business taxes, and liability insurance). Annual net income gives a more accurate measure of family child care wages because expenses reduce the gross income of providers by an estimated 20 to 30 percent (Fosburg 1981).
   Consistent with other researchers' findings regarding providers' wages (Fosburg 1981, Galinsky et al. 1994, Hofferth and Kisker 1992b), the unlicensed providers I interviewed earned considerably lower wages than did licensed care workers. Among the women I spoke with, unlicensed providers earned 74 percent less than the wages earned by licensed providers (an annual median income of $4,673 as compared to $17,522).
3. When gross income is adjusted for experience, the net annual family child care providers in Washington State ranges from $14,000 to $16,000. While family child care earnings of the women participating in this study are within the norm for Washington State, their earnings of these women (and of family child care providers in Washington State) are about 28 percent higher than that reported by the Center for the Child Care Workforce (2000). When comparing the results of family child care wage studies nationally, however, we see that geographic location is a primary factor influencing wage levels (Kontos 1992). As a result, wage comparisons across regions and nationwide are misleading. Those within regions are more accurate. The wages of providers in this study are consistent with those reported by family child care providers within Washington State and within the various geographic regions of the state (Miller and Schrager 2000).

CHAPTER 4

1. The federally funded Comprehensive Education and Training Act (CETA) provided entry-level jobs for urban youth and unemployed adults from 1973 to 1979.

CHAPTER 5

1. As discussed in chapter 3, Kim is the only provider who used the term "babysit" to discuss her child care work.
2. As of January 2002, the rate was increased to payment at the fifty-eighth percentile. All state-subsidy rates presented in this chapter are presented at the fifty-fifth percentile (the rate in effect at the time of the interviews) and are converted to 1999 dollars. All provider rates presented in this chapter are presented as 1999 dollars.
3. *DSHS kids* or *state kids* are terms used to describe children who receive state-subsidized care administered through the state's Department of Social and Health Services. *Private-pay kids* are children whose parents pay directly for child care using their own resources.

CHAPTER 6

1. At the time of these interviews, the city of Seattle funded a subsidized child care program for working-poor families and parents in job-training programs. The subsidy amount depended on the amount of family income and ranged from 25 percent to 90 percent of a family's child care costs. Families with incomes of up to 76 percent of the poverty level could qualify for city-subsidized care. While still having incomes substantially lower than the poverty level, families qualifying for city-subsidized care could have more financial resources than those qualifying for state-subsidized care. Thus, while both city and state (DSHS) programs fund families in poverty, city programs fund families who have somewhat higher incomes than families who qualify for state-subsidized child care.

Bibliography

Abel, Emily, and Margaret Nelson, eds. 1990. *Circles of Care: Work and Identity in Women's Lives*. Albany: State University of New York Press.

Abramovitz, Mimi. 1989. *Regulating the Lives of Women: Social Welfare Policy from Colonial Times to the Present*. Boston: South End.

Amott, Teresa, and Julie Matthaei. 1991. *Race, Gender, and Work: A Multicultural Economic History of Women in the United States*. Boston: South End.

Auerbach, Judith, and Barry Woodill. 1992. "Historical Perspectives on Familial and Extrafamilial Child Care: Toward a History of Family Day Care." In *Family Day Care: Current Research for Informed Public Policy*, ed. Donald Peters and Alan Pence, 9–27. New York: Teachers College Press.

Auerbach, Stevanne. 1975. "What Parents Want from Day Care." In *Child Care: A Comprehensive Guide*, ed. Stevanne Auerbach and James Rivaldo, 137–55. New York: Human Sciences Press.

Barrett, Michele, and Mary McIntosh. 2000. "The 'Family Wage': Some Problems for Sociologists and Feminists." In *Inside the Household from Labour to Care*, ed. Susan Himmelweit, 1–24. New York: St. Martin's.

Bellm, Dan, Alice Burton, Renu Shukla, and Marcy Whitebook. 1997. *Making Work Pay in the Child Care Industry: Promising Practices for Improved Compensation*. Washington, D.C.: National Center for the Early Childhood Work Force.

Blackwell, James E. 1985. *The Black Community: Diversity and Unity*, 2d ed. New York: Harper and Row.

Blau, David M. 1991. "The Quality of Child Care: An Economic Perspective." In *The Economics of Child Care*, ed. David M. Blau, 145–74. New York: Russell Sage Foundation.

Boris, Eileen. 1993. "The Power of Motherhood: Black and White Activist Women Redefine the 'Political.'" In *Mothers of a New World: Maternalist Politics and the Origins of Welfare States*, ed. Seth Koven and Sonya Michel, 213–45. New York: Routledge.

Brewer, Rose M. 1988. "Black Women in Poverty: Some Comments on Female-Headed Families." *Signs* 57, no. 2: 331–39.

Bromer, Juliet. 2001. "Helpers, Mothers, and Preachers: The Multiple Roles and Discourses of Family Child Care Providers in an African-American Community." *Early Childhood Research Quarterly* 16, no. 3: 313–27.

Cancian, Francesca. 2002. "Developing Non-Oppressive Standards of 'Good' Care." In

Child Care and Inequality: Rethinking Care Work for Children and Youth, ed. Francesca Cancian, Demie Kurz, Andrew London, Rebecca Reviere, and Mary Tuominen. New York: Routledge.

Cancian, Francesca, and Stacey Oliker. 2000. *Caring and Gender*. Thousand Oaks, Calif.: Pine Forge.

Center for the Child Care Workforce. 1997. *Worthy Work, Unlivable Wages: The National Child Care Staffing Study, 1988–1997*. Washington, D.C.: Center for the Child Care Workforce.

———. 1998. *Current Data on Child Care Salaries and Benefits in the United States*. Washington, D.C.: Center for the Childcare Workforce, March.

———. 1999. *Current Data on Child Care Salaries and Benefits in the United States*. Washington, D.C.: Center for the Childcare Workforce, March.

———. 2000. *Current Data on Child Care Salaries and Benefits in the United States*. Washington, D.C.: Center for the Child Care Workforce, March.

Children's Foundation. 2001. *The 2001 Family Child Care Licensing Study*. Washington, D.C.: Children's Foundation.

Cobble, Dorothy Sue. 1993. " Remaking Unions for the New Majority." In *Women and Unions : Forging a Partnership*, ed. Dorothy Sue Cobble, 3–23. Ithaca, N.Y.: ILR Press.

———. 1996. "The Prospects For Unionism in a Service Society." In *Working in the Service Society*, ed. Cameron Lynne Macdonald and Carmen Sirianni, 333–58. Philadelphia: Temple University Press.

Collins, Patricia Hill. 1986. "Learning from the Outsider Within: The Sociological Significance of Black Feminist Thought." *Social Problems* 33 (October–December): 14–32.

———. 1987. "The Meaning of Motherhood in Black Culture and Black Mother/Daughter Relationships." *Sage* 4, no. 2: 3–10.

———. 1990. *Black Feminist Thoughts: Knowledge, Consciousness, and the Politics of Empowerment*. New York: Routledge.

———. 1992. "Black Women and Motherhood." In *Rethinking the Family: Some Feminist Questions*, ed. Barrie Thorne and Marilyn Yalom, 215–45. Boston: Northeastern University Press.

———. 1993. "Toward an Afrocentric Feminist Epistemology." In *Feminist Frameworks: Alternative Theoretical Accounts of the Relations between Women and Men*, ed. Alison M. Jaggar and Paula S. Rothenberg, 333–58. New York: McGraw-Hill.

———. 1997. "Comment on Hekman's Truth and Method: Feminist Standpoint Theory Revisited: Where's the Power?" *Signs* 22, no. 4: 375–79.

Coverman, Shelley. 1989. "Women's Work Is Never Done: The Division of Domestic Labor." In *Women: A Feminist Perspective*, ed. Jo Freeman, 356–70. Mountain View, Calif.: Mayfield.

Crittenden, Ann. 2001. *The Price of Motherhood: Why the Most Important Job in the World Is Still the Least Valued*. New York: Metropolitan Books.

Daniels, Arlene Kaplan. 1987. "Invisible Work." *Social Problems* 34, no. 5: 403–15.

DeVault, Marjorie. 1991. *Feeding the Family: The Social Organization of Caring As Gendered Work*. Chicago: University of Chicago Press.

———. 1999. *Liberating Method: Feminism and Social Research*. Philadelphia: Temple University Press.

DeVault, Marjorie, and Liza McCoy. 2002. "Institutional Ethnography: Using Interviews to Investigate Ruling Relations." In *Handbook of Interview Research: Context and Method*, ed. Jaber F. Gubrium and James A. Hostein, 751–76. Thousand Oaks, Calif.: Sage.

Diamond, Tim. 1992. *Making Gray Gold: Narratives of Nursing Home Care*. Chicago: University of Chicago Press.

DiLeonardo, Micaela. 1987. "The Female World of Cards and Holidays: Women, Families, and the Work of Kinship." *Signs* 12, no. 3: 440–53.

Dill, Bonnie Thornton. 1988. "Making Your Job Good Yourself: Domestic Service and the Construction of Personal Dignity." In *Women and the Politics of Empowerment*, ed. Ann Bookman and Sandra Morgen, 33–52. Philadelphia: Temple University Press.

———. 1994. *Across the Boundaries of Race and Class: An Exploration of Work and Family among Black Female Domestic Servants*. New York: Garland.

———. 1998. "Fictive Kin, Paper Sons, and Compadrazgo: Women of Color and the Struggle for Family Survival." In *Families in the U.S.: Kinship and Domestic Politics*, ed. Karen V. Hansen and Anita Ilta Garey, 431–48. Philadelphia: Temple University Press.

Dill, Bonnie Thornton, and Maxine Baca Zinn. 1990. "Race and Gender: Re-Visioning Social Relations." Research paper no. 11. Memphis, Tenn.: Memphis State University, Center for Research on Women.

Eisenstein, Zillah. 1981. *The Radical Future of Liberal Feminism*. Boston: Northeastern University Press.

England, Paula. 1984. "Socioeconomic Explanations of Job Segregation." In *Comparable Worth and Wage Discrimination: Technical Possibilities and Political Realities*, ed. Helen Remick, 26–46. Philadelphia: Temple University Press.

———. 1992. *Comparable Worth: Theories and Evidence*. Hawthorne, N.Y.: Aldine De Gruyter.

England, Paula, and Nancy Folbre. 1999. "The Cost of Caring." *Annals of the American Academy of Political and Social Science* 561 (January): 39–51.

———. 2002. "Care, Inequality, and Policy." In *Child Care and Inequality: Rethinking Care Work for Children and Youth*, ed. Francesca Cancian, Demie Kurz, Andrew London, Rebecca Reviere, and Mary Tuominen, 133–44. New York: Routledge.

Ferree, Myra Marx. 1991. "The Gender Division of Labor in Two-Earner Marriages: Dimensions of Variability and Change." *Journal of Family Issues* 12, no. 2: 158–80.

Fisher, Berenice, and Joan Tronto. 1990. "Toward a Feminist Theory of Caring." In *Circles of Care: Work and Identity in Women's Lives*, ed. Emily Abel and Margaret Nelson, 35–62. Albany: State University of New York Press.

Fitz Gibbon, Heather. 1998. "From Baby-sitters to Child Care Providers: The Development of a Feminist Consciousness in Family Day Care Workers." In *Working Families: The Transformation of the American Home*, ed. Rosanna Hertz and Nancy L. Marshall, 270–90. Berkeley: University of California Press.

———. 2002. "Child Care across Sectors: A Comparison of the Work of Child Care in Three Settings." In *Child Care and Inequality: Rethinking Care Work for Children and Youth*, ed. Francesca Cancian, Demie Kurz, Andrew London, Rebecca Reviere, and Mary Tuominen, 145–58. New York: Routledge.

Folbre, Nancy. 1994. "Children As Public Goods." *American Economic Review* 84, no. 2: 86–90.

———. 1995. "'Holding Hands at Midnight': The Paradox of Caring Labor." *Feminist Economics* 1, no. 1: 73–92.

———. 2001. *The Invisible Heart: Economics and Family Values*. New York: New Press.

Fosburg, Steven. 1981. *Family Day Care in the United States: Summary of Findings* (U.S. Department of Health and Human Services). Vol. 1. Washington, D.C.: U.S. Government Printing Office.

Galinsky, Ellen, Carollee Howes, Susan Kontos, and Marybeth Shinn. 1994. *The Study of Children in Family Child Care and Relative Care*. New York: Families and Work Institute.

Garey, Anita. 1999. *Weaving Work and Motherhood*. Philadelphia: Temple University Press.

Gerson, Kathleen. 1987. "How Women Choose between Employment and Family: A Developmental Perspective." In *Families and Work*, ed. Naomi Gerstel and Harriet Gross, 270–88. Philadelphia: Temple University Press.

———. 2002. "Moral Dilemmas, Moral Strategies, and the Transformation of Gender: Lessons from Two Generations of Work and Family Change." *Gender and Society* 16, no. 1: 8–28.

Giddings, Paula. 1984. *When and Where I Enter: The Impact of Black Women on Race and Sex in American*. New York: Morrow.

Gilkes, Cheryl Townsend. 1980. "Holding Back the Ocean with a Broom: Black Women and Community Work." In *The Black Woman*, ed. LaFrances Rodgers-Rose, 212–32. Beverly Hills, Calif.: Sage.

———. 2001. *If It Wasn't for the Women: Black Women's Experience and Womanist Culture in Church and Community*. Maryknoll, N.Y.: Orbis.

Gilligan, Carol. 1993 [1982]. *In a Different Voice: Psychological Theory and Women's Development*. Cambridge, Mass.: Harvard University Press.

Glenn, Evelyn Nakano. 1986. *Issei, Nisei, War Bride: Three Generations of Japanese American Women in Domestic Service*. Philadelphia: Temple University Press.

———. 1992. "From Servitude to Service Work: Historical Continuities in the Racial Division of Paid Reproductive Labor." *Signs* 18 (autumn): 1–43.

———. 1994. "Social Constructions of Motherhood: A Thematic Overview." In *Mothering: Ideology, Experience, and Agency*, ed. Evelyn Nakano Glenn, Grace Chang, and Linda Rennie Forcey, 1–29. New York: Routledge.

———. 1999. "The Social Construction and Institutionalization of Gender and Race: An

Integrative Framework." In *Revisioning Gender*, ed. Myra Marx Ferree, Judith Lorber, and Beth B. Hess, 4–27. Thousand Oaks, Calif.: Sage.

———. 2000. "Creating a Caring Society." *Contemporary Sociology* 29, no. 1: 84–94.

Gordon, Linda. 1990a. "The New Feminist Scholarship on the Welfare State." In *Women, the State and Welfare*, ed. Linda Gordon, 9–35. Madison: University of Wisconsin Press.

———, ed. 1990b. *Women, the State and Welfare*. Madison: University of Wisconsin Press.

Gordon, Suzanne. 1996. "Feminism and Caring." In *Caregiving: Readings in Knowledge, Practice, Ethics, and Politics*, ed. Suzanne Gordon, Patricia Benner, and Nel Noddings, 256–77. Philadelphia: University of Pennsylvania Press.

Gordon, Suzanne, Patricia Benner, and Nel Noddings. 1996. *Caregiving: Readings in Knowledge, Practice, Ethics, and Politics*. Philadelphia: University of Pennsylvania Press.

Gutierrez, Lorraine M., and Edith A. Lewis. 1992. "A Feminist Perspective on Organizing with Women of Color." In *Community Organizing in a Diverse Society*, ed. Felix G. Rivera and John L. Erlich, 113–32. Boston: Allyn and Bacon.

Haack, Peggy. 1998. "Family Child Care Peer-to-Peer Exchange: December 10–12, 1998." Executive summary. New York: Ms. Foundation for Women.

Haraway, Donna. 1988. "Situated Knowledges: The Science Question in Feminism and the Privilege of Partial Perspective." *Feminist Studies* 14 (fall): 575–600.

Harding, Sandra. 1993. *The "Racial" Economy of Science: Toward a Democratic Future*. Bloomington: Indiana University Press.

———. 1998. *Is Science Multicultural? Postcolonialisms, Feminisms, and Epistemologies*. Indianapolis: Indiana University Press.

Harrington, Mona. 2001. *Care and Equality: Inventing a New Family Politics*. New York: Routledge.

Hartmann, Heidi. 1987. "Changes in Women's Economic and Family Roles in the Post–World War II United States." In *Women, Households, and the Economy*, ed. Lourdes Beneria and Catherine Stimpson, 33–64. New Brunswick, N.J.: Rutgers University Press.

Hartsock, Nancy C. M. 1987. "The Feminist Standpoint: Developing the Ground for a Specifically Feminist Historical Materialism." In *Feminism and Methodology: Social Science Issues*, ed. Sandra Harding, 157–80. Bloomington: Indiana University Press.

Hays, Sharon. 1996. *The Cultural Constructions of Motherhood*. New Haven, Conn.: Yale University Press.

Helburn, Suzanne. 1995. *Cost, Quality and Child Outcomes in Child Care Centers, Technical Report*. Denver: University of Colorado, Department of Economics, Center for Research in Economic and Social Policy.

Helburn, Suzanne, and Barbara Bergmann. 2002. *America's Childcare Problem: The Way Out*. New York: Palgrave.

Heller, Kenneth. 1989. "The Return to Community." *American Journal of Community Psychology* 17, no. 1: 1–15.

Heller, Kenneth, and Karen S. Rook. 1997. "Distinguishing the Theoretical Functions of Social Ties: Implications for Support Interventions." In *Handbook of Personal Relationships*, 2d ed., ed. Steve Duck, 649–70. New York: Wiley.

Hertz, Rosanna. 1997. "A Typology of Approaches to Child Care: The Centerpiece of Organizing Family Life for Dual-Earner Couples." *Journal of Family Issues* 18 (July): 355–85.

Heymann, S. Jody, and Alison Earle. 1998. "The Work-Family Balance: What Hurdles Are Parents Leaving Welfare Likely to Confront?" *Journal of Policy Analysis and Management* 17, no. 2: 313–21.

Himmelweit, Susan. 1999. "Caring Labor." *Annals of the American Academy of Political and Social Science* 561 (January): 27–38.

———, ed. 2000. *Inside the Household: From Labour to Care*. New York: St. Martin's.

Hochschild, Arlie. 1983. *The Managed Heart: Commercialization of Human Feeling*. Berkeley: University of California Press.

Hofferth, Sandra. 1999. "Child Care, Maternal Employment, and Public Policy." In *Annals of the American Academy of Political and Social Science* 563: 20–38.

Hofferth, Sandra, and Nancy Collins. 2000. "Child Care and Employment Turnover." *Population Research and Policy Review* 19, no. 4: 357–95.

Hofferth, Sandra, and Ellen Eliason Kisker. 1991. *Family Day Care in the United States, 1990*. Washington, D.C.: Urban Institute.

Hondagneu-Sotelo, Pierette. 2001. *Domestica: Immigrant Workers Cleaning and Caring in the Shadows of Affluence*. Berkeley: University of California Press.

hooks, bell. 1984. *Feminist Theory: From Margin to Center*. Boston: South End.

Howe, Carollee. 1997. "Children's Experiences in Center-Based Child Care As a Function of Teacher Background and Adult:Child Ratios." *Merrill-Palmer Quarterly* 43, no. 3: 404–42.

Huber, Joan, and William Form. 1977. *Income and Ideology*. New York: Free Press.

Hurd, Richard W. 1993. "Organizing and Representing Clerical Workers: The Harvard Model." In *Women and Unions : Forging a Partnership*, ed. Dorothy Sue Cobble, 316–36. Ithaca, N.Y.: ILR Press.

Jones, Jacqueline. 1986. *Labor of Love, Labor of Sorrow: Black Women and the Family, from Slavery to Present*. New York: Random House.

Kahn, Alfred J., and Sheila B. Kamerman. 1987. *Child Care: Facing the Hard Choices*. Dover, Mass.: Auburn House.

Kappner, Augusta Souza. 1984. "Factors Affecting the Visibility of Family Day Care Providers in New York City." Ph.D. diss., School of Social Work, Columbia University.

Kasarda, John, D. 1996. "Family Policy for School Age Children: The Case of Parental Evening Work." Working paper. Cambridge, Mass.: Harvard University, John F. Kennedy School of Government, Malcolm Weiner Center for Social Policy.

Keller, S. 1988. "The American Dream of Community: An Unfinished Agenda." *Sociological Forum* 3, no. 2: 167–83.

Kerber, Linda. 1993. "Some Cautionary Words for Historians." In *An Ethic of Care: Feminist and Interdisciplinary Perspectives*, ed. Mary Jeanne Larrabee, 102–7. New York: Routledge.

Kessler-Harris, Alice. 1982. *Out of Work: A History of Wage-Earning Women in the United States*. New York: Oxford University Press.

King, Deborah K. 1992. "Review Symposium: Patricia Hill Collins, Black Feminist Thought: Knowledge, Consciousness, and the Politics of Empowerment." *Gender and Society* 6, no. 3: 512–15.

Kittay, Eva Feder. 1995. "Taking Dependency Seriously: The Family and Medical Leave Act Considered in Light of the Social Organization of Dependency Work and Gender Equality." *Hypatia* 10, no. 1: 8–29.

———. 1999. *Love's Labor*. New York: Routledge.

Kontos, Susan. 1992. *Family Day Care: Out of the Shadows and into the Limelight*. Washington, D.C.: National Association for the Education of Young Children.

Kontos, Susan, Carollee Howes, Marybeth Shinn, and Ellen Galinsky. 1995. *Quality in Family Child Care and Relative Care*. New York: Teachers College Press.

Lofland, John, and Lyn H. Lofland. 1995. *Analyzing Social Settings: A Guide to Qualitative Observations and Analysis*, 3d ed. Cincinnati: Wadsworth.

Macdonald, Cameron. 1996. "Shadow Mothers: Nannies, Au Pairs, and Invisible Work." In *Working in the Service Society*, ed. Cameron Macdonald and Carmen Sirianni, 244–63. Philadelphia: Temple University Press.

Macdonald, Cameron, and Carmen Sirianni. 1996. "The Service Society and the Changing Experience of Work." In *Working in the Service Society*, ed. Cameron Macdonald and Carmen Sirianni, 1–26. Philadelphia: Temple University Press.

Macpherson, Crawford B. 1990. *The Life and Times of Liberal Democracy*. New York: Oxford University Press.

MacQueen, Kathleen M., Eleanor McLellan, David Metzger, Susan Kegels, Ronald Strauss, Roseanne Scotti, Lynn Blanchard, and Robert Trotter. 2001. "What Is Community? An Evidence-Based Definition for Participatory Public Health." *American Journal of Public Health* 91, no. 12: 1929–39.

Marger, Martin. 1999. *Social Inequality: Patterns and Processes*. Mountain View, Calif.: Mayfield.

Martens, Margaret Hosmer, and Swasti Mitter, eds. 1994. *Women in Trade Unions: Organizing the Unorganized*. Geneva, Switzerland: International Labour Office.

Mason, Jennifer. 1996. *Qualitative Researching*. Thousand Oaks, Calif.: Sage.

Matthaei, Julie. 1982. *An Economic History of Women in America: Women's Work, the Sexual Division of Labor, and the Development of Capitalism*. New York: Schocken.

Mazur, Rosaleen. 1981. "The Relationship Between the Life Cycle Status of Caregivers and Caregivers' Affiliation with Strategies for Regulating, Training and Support of Family Day Care in New York City." Ph.D. diss., Teachers College, Columbia University.

McAdam, Doug. 1982. *Political Process and the Development of Black Insurgency, 1930–1970*. Chicago: University of Chicago Press.

McDonald, Katrina Bell. 1997. "Black Activist Mothering: A Historical Intersection of Race, Gender, and Class." *Gender and Society* 11, no. 6: 773–95.

Meyers, Marcia K. 2001. "Child Care in the Wake of Welfare Reform: The Impact of Government Subsidies on the Economic Well-Being of Single-Mother Families." *Social Service Review* 75, no. 1: 29–59.

Michel, Sonja. 1999. *Children's Interests/Mother's Rights: The Shaping of America's Child Care Policy.* New Haven, Conn.: Yale University Press.

Mies, Maria. 1986. *Patriarchy and Accumulation on a World Scale.* Atlantic Highlands, N.J.: Zed.

Miller, Marna Geyer, and James S. Hu. 1999. *DSHS Subsidized Child Care: A Briefing Paper.* Olympia: Washington State Department of Social and Health Services.

Miller, Marna Geyer, and Laura Schrager. 2000. *Licensed Child Care in Washington State: 1998.* Olympia: Washington State Department of Social and Health Services.

Mink, Gwendolyn. 1995. *The Wages of Motherhood: Inequality in the Welfare State, 1917–1942.* Ithaca, N.Y.: Cornell University Press.

Modigliani, Kathy. 1993. *Child Care As an Occupation in a Culture of Indifference.* Boston: Wheelock College.

Naples, Nancy. 1992. "Activist Mothering: Cross-Generational Continuity in the Community Work of Women from Low-Income Urban Neighborhoods." *Gender and Society* 6, no. 3: 441–63.

———. 1998a. "Bringing Everyday Life to Policy Analysis: The Case of White Rural Women Negotiating College and Welfare." *Journal of Poverty* 2: 23–53.

———. 1998b. *Grassroots Warriors: Activist Mothering, Community Work, and the War on Poverty.* New York: Routledge.

National Black Child Development Institute. 1993. *Paths to African American Leadership Positions in Early Childhood Education: Constraints and Opportunities.* Washington, D.C.: National Black Child Development Institute.

Nelson, Barbara J. 1990. "The Origins of the Two-Channel Welfare State: Workmen's Compensation and Mothers' Aid." In *Women, the State, and Welfare*, ed. Linda Gordon, 123–51. Madison: University of Wisconsin Press.

Nelson, Julie A. 1999. "Of Markets and Martyrs: Is It OK to Pay Well for Care?" *Feminist Economics* 5, no. 3: 43–59.

———. 2001. Why Are Early Education and Care Wages So Low? A Critical Guide to Common Explanations. New York: Foundation for Child Development.

Nelson, Margaret. 1988a. "Negotiating Care: Relationships between Family Daycare Providers and Mothers." *Feminist Studies* 15, no. 1: 7–33.

———. 1988b. "Providing Family Day Care: An Analysis of Home-Based Work." *Social Problems* 35, no. 1: 7–33.

———. 1990. *Negotiated Care: The Experience of Family Day Care Providers.* Philadelphia: Temple University Press.

———. 1994. "Family Day Care Providers: Dilemmas of Daily Practice." In *Mothering: Ideology, Experience, and Agency*, ed. Evelyn Nakano Glenn, Grace Chang, and Linda Rennie Forcey, 181–209. New York: Routledge.

Ng, Roxana. 1995. "Multiculturalism As Ideology: A Textual Analysis." In *Knowledge, Experience, and Ruling Relations: Studies in the Social Organization of Knowledge*, ed. Marie Campbell and Ann Manicom, 35–48. Toronto: University of Toronto Press.

Nicholson, Linda J. 1993. "Women, Morality, and History." In *An Ethic of Care: Feminist and Interdisciplinary Perspectives*, ed. Mary Jeanne Larrabee, 87–101. New York: Routledge.

Omi, Michael, and Howard Winant. 1994. *Racial Formation in the United States: From the 1960s to the 1990s.* Rev. ed. New York: Routledge.

Palmer, Phyllis. 1989. *Domesticity and Dirt: Housewives and Domestic Servants in the United States, 1920–1945.* Philadelphia: Temple University Press.

Parrenas, Rhacel Salazar. 2001. *Servants of Globalization : Women, Migration and Domestic Work.* Stanford, Calif.: Stanford University Press.

Pateman, Carole. 1988a. "The Patriarchal Welfare State." In *Democracy and the Welfare State*, ed. Amy Gutman, 231–60. Princeton, N.J.: Princeton University Press.

———. 1988b. *The Sexual Contract.* Stanford, Calif.: Stanford University Press.

Patrick, Donald L., and Thomas M. Wickizer. 1995. "Community and Health." In *Society and Health*, ed. Benjamin C. Amick III, Sol Levine, Alvin R. Tarlov, and Diana Chapman Walsh, 46–92. New York: Oxford University Press.

Peisner-Feinberg, E., M. Culkin, C. Howes, S. Kagan. 1999. "Cost, Quality and Outcomes Study." Executive summary. *http://www.fpg.unc.edu/~NCEDL/PAGES/cq.htm*.

Peters, Donald, and Alan Pence. 1992. *Family Day Care: Current Research for Informed Public Policy*. New York: Columbia University, Teachers College.

Phillips, Deborah, Debra Mekos, Sandra Scarr, Kathleen McCartney, and Martha Abbott-Shim. 2000. "Within and Beyond the Classroom Door: Assessing Quality in Child Care Centers." *Early Childhood Research Quarterly* 15, no. 4: 475–96.

Phillipsen, Leslie, Margaret Burchinal, Carollee Howes, and Debby Cryer. 1997. "The Prediction of Process Quality from Structural Features of Child Care." *Early Childhood Research Quarterly* 12, no. 3: 281–304.

Pollitt, Katha. 1992. "Marooned on Gilligan's Island: Are Women Morally Superior to Men?" *Nation*, December, pp. 799–807.

Puka, Bill. 1993. "The Liberation of Caring: A Different Voice for Gilligan's 'Different Voice.'" In *An Ethic of Care: Feminist and Interdisciplinary Perspectives*, ed. Mary Jeanne Larrabee, 215-239. New York: Routledge.

Rapp, Rayna. 1992. "Family and Class in Contemporary America: Notes toward an Understanding of Ideology." In *Rethinking the Family: Some Feminist Questions*, rev. ed., ed. Barrie Thorne, 49–70. Boston: Northeastern University Press.

Remick, Helen, ed. 1984. *Comparable Worth and Wage Discrimination: Technical Possibilities and Political Realities*. Philadelphia: Temple University Press.

Ripple, Carol. 2000. *Economics of Caring Labor: Improving Compensation in the Early Childhood Workforce*. New York: Foundation for Child Development.

Rollins, Judith. 1985. *Between Women: Domestics and Their Employers*. Philadelphia: Temple University Press.

Romero, Mary. 1999. "Immigration, the Servant Problem, and the Legacy of the Domestic Labor Debate: 'Where Can You Find Good Help These Days?'" *University of Miami Law Review* 53, no. 4: 1045–64.

———. 2002 [1992]. *Maid in the U.S.A.* New York: Routledge.

Rothman, Barbara Katz. 1989. *Recreating Motherhood: Ideology and Technology in a Patriarchal Society*. New York: Norton.

Rubenstein, Carin. 1998. "Superdad Needs a Reality Check." *New York Times*, April 19, p. A23.

Rutman, Deborah. 1996. "Child Care As Women's Work: Workers' Experiences of Powerfulness and Powerlessness." *Gender and Society* 10, no. 5: 629–49.

Sacks, Karen Brodkin. 1989. "Toward a Unified Theory of Class, Race and Gender." *American Ethnologist* 16, no. 3: 534–50.

Saraceno, Chiara. 1984. "Shifts in Public and Private Boundaries: Women As Mothers and Service Workers in Italian Daycare." *Feminist Studies* 10, no. 1: 7–30.

Sassoon, Anne Showstack. 1987. "Women's New Social Role: Contradictions of the Welfare State." In *Women and the State: Shifting Boundaries of Public and Private*, 158–90. London: Hutchinson.

Scharlach, Andrew E., and Blanche Grosswald. 1997. "The Family and Medical Leave Act of 1993." *Social Service Review* 71 (September): 335–59.

Segura, Denise. 1986. "Chicanos and Mexicana Immigrant Women in the Labor Market: A Study of Occupational Mobility and Stratification." Ph.D. diss., University of California, Berkeley.

———. 1994. "Working at Motherhood: Chicana and Mexican Immigrant Mothers and Employment." In *Mothering: Ideology, Experience, and Agency*, ed. Evelyn Nakano Glenn, Grace Chang, and Linda Rennie Forcey, 211–33. New York: Routledge.

Shonkoff, Jack P., and Deborah A. Phillips. 2000. *From Neurons to Neighborhoods: The Science of Early Childhood Development*. Washington, D.C.: National Academy Press.

Smith, Dorothy. 1987. *The Everyday World As Problematic: A Feminist Sociology*. Boston: Northeastern University Press.

———. 1989. "Feminist Reflections on Political Economy." *Studies in Political Economy* 30 (autumn): 37–59.

———. 1999. *Writing the Social: Critique, Theory, and Investigations*. Toronto: University of Toronto Press.

Smith, George W. 1990. "Political Activist As Ethnographer." *Social Problems* 37, no. 4: 629–48.

Stack, Carol. 1970. *All Our Kin*. New York: Harper and Row.

Stack, Carol B., and Linda M. Burton. 1993. "Kinscripts." *Journal of Comparative Family Studies* 24, no. 2: 157–70.

Steinem, Gloria. 1983. *Outrageous Acts and Everyday Rebellions*. New York: New American Library.

Stone, Deborah. 1991. "Caring Work in a Liberal Polity." *Journal of Health Politics, Policy and Law* 16, no. 9: 547–52.

———. 1998. "Care As We Give It, Work As We Know It." Paper prepared for meeting on children's studies, Harvard University, Cambridge, Mass., December 1.

———. 2000. "Caring by the Book." In *Care Work: Gender, Labor, and the Welfare State*, ed. Madonna Harrington Meyer, 89-111. New York: Routledge.

Tarlow, Barbara. 1996. "Caring: A Negotiated Process That Varies." In *Caregiving: Readings in Knowledge, Practice, Ethics, and Politics*, ed. Suzanne Gordon, Patricia Benner, and Nel Noddings, 56–82. Philadelphia: University of Pennsylvania Press.

Thorne, Barrie, ed., 1992a. *Rethinking the Family: Some Feminist Questions*. Boston: Northeastern University Press.

———. 1992b. "Review Symposium: Patricia Hill Collins, Black Feminist Thought: Knowledge, Consciousness, and the Politics of Empowerment." *Gender and Society* 6, no. 3: 515–17.

Tom, Allison. 1992. "The Messy Work of Child Care: Addressing Feminists' Neglect of Child Care Workers." *Atlantis* 18, nos. 1 and 2: 70–81.

Treiman, David, and Heidi Hartmann. 1981. *Women, Work and Wages: Equal Pay for Jobs of Equal Value*. Washington, D.C.: National Academy Press.

Tronto, Joan. 1993. "Beyond Gender Difference to a Theory of Care." In *An Ethic of Care: Feminist and Interdisciplinary Perspectives*, ed. Mary Jeanne Larrabee, 240–57. New York: Routledge.

———. 1996. "Care As a Political Concept." In *Revisioning the Political: Feminist Reconstructions of Traditional Concepts in Western Political Theory*, ed. Nancy J. Hirshmann and Christine DeStefano, 139–56. Boulder, Colo.: Westview.

Tuominen, Mary. 1991. "Caring for Profit: The Social, Economic and Political Significance of For-Profit Child Care." *Social Service Review* 65, no. 3: 450–67.

———. 1992. "Gender, Class, and Motherhood: The Legacy of Federal Child Care Policy." *Affilia* 7, no. 4: 8–25.

———. 1994. "The Hidden Organization of Labor: Gender, Race/Ethnicity and Child-Care Work in the Formal and Informal Economy." *Sociological Perspectives* 37, no. 2: 229–245.

———. 1997. "Exploitation or Opportunity? The Contradictions of Child-Care Policy in the Contemporary United States." *Women and Politics* 18, no. 2: 53–80.

Ungerson, Clare. 2000. "Cash in Care." In *Care Work: Gender, Labor, and the Welfare State*, ed. Madonna Harrington Meyer, 68–88. New York: Routledge.

U.S. Department of Commerce, Bureau of the Census. 1982. *Trends in Child Care Arrangements of Working Mothers*. Current Population Reports, series P-23, no. 30. Washington, D.C.: Government Printing Office, June.

———. 1987. *Who's Minding the Kids? Child Care Arrangements: Winter 1984–1985*, Current Population Reports, Household Economic Studies, series P-70, no. 30. Washington, D.C.: Government Printing Office.

———. 1990a. Unpublished tabulation from *1990 Census of Population and Housing, Language Spoken at Home*. Washington, D.C.

———. 1990b. Unpublished tabulations from *1990 Census of Population and Housing, Educational Attainment*, summary tape file 3A. Washington, D.C.

———. 1990c. *Census of Population and Housing*, summary tape file 3A. Washington, D.C.

———. 2000. Unpublished calculations derived from *Detailed Occupation by Race, Hispanic Origin and Sex*. http://tier2.census.gov/cgi-win/eeo/eeodata.exe.

———. 2002. *Who's Minding the Kids? Child Care Arrangements: Spring 1997*. Current Population Reports, Household Economic Studies, series P-70, no. 86. Washington, D.C.: Government Printing Office, July.

U.S. Department of Health, Education, and Welfare, Children's Bureau; and U.S. Department of Labor, Women's Bureau. 1968. *Child Care Arrangements of Working Mothers in the United States*, no. 461-1968. Washington, D.C.: Government Printing Office.

U.S. Department of Labor, Bureau of Labor Statistics. 1998. "Employment Status of the

Civilian Population by Race, Sex, Age, and Hispanic Origin." In "The Employment Situation News Release," tab. A-2. www/bls/gov.release/empsit.t02.htm.

———. 1999a. *Employment and Earnings, January 1999.* Washington, D.C.: Government Printing Office.

———. 1999b. *Highlights of Women's Earnings in 1998, April 1999.* Report 928. Washington, D.C.: Government Printing Office.

———. 2002. "Employment Characteristics of Families in 2001," March 29. ftp://146.142.4.23/pub/news.release/famee.txt.

U.S. Department of Labor, Women's Bureau. 1997. *Facts on Working Women,* no. 98-01, November. www.dol.gov/dol/wb/public/wb_pubs/childc.htm.

———. 1999. *Facts on Working Women, April 1999. http://www.dol.gov/dol/wb/public/wb_pubs/fact98.htm.*

———. 2000. *Facts on Working Women, March 2000. www.dol.gov/dol/wb/public/wb-pubs/fact98.htm.*

Uttal, Lynet. 1996a. "Custodial Care, Surrogate Care, and Coordinate Care: Employed Mothers and the Meaning of Child Care." *Gender and Society* 10 (June): 291–311.

———. 1996b. "Racial Safety and Cultural Maintenance: The Childcare Concerns of Employed Mothers of Color." *Ethnic Studies Review* 19, no. 1: 43–59.

———. 1997. "'Trust Your Instincts': Racial Ethnic and Class-Based Preferences in Employed Mothers' Childcare Choices." *Qualitative Sociology* 20, no. 2: 253–74.

Uttal, Lynet, and Mary Tuominen. 1999. "Tenuous Relationships: Exploitation, Emotion and Racial Ethnic Significance in Paid Childcare Work." *Gender and Society* 13, no. 6: 758–80.

Vogel, Lise. 1993. *Mothers on the Job: Maternity Policy in the U.S. Workplace.* New Brunswick, N.J.: Rutgers University Press.

Waerness, Kari. 1996. "The Rationality of Caring." In *Caregiving: Readings in Knowledge, Practice, Ethics, and Politics,* ed. Suzanne Gordon, Patricia Benner, and Nel Noddings, 231–55. Philadelphia: University of Pennsylvania Press.

Walker, James. 1992. "New Evidence on the Supply of Child Care: A Statistical Portrait of Family Providers and an Analysis of Their Fees." *Journal of Human Resources* 27, no. 1: 40–69.

Washington State Department of Social and Health Services. n.d. *Child Care Options in Washington State: A Quick Reference Guide.* Olympia, Wash.

———. 1992. *DSHS Child Care Subsidies.* Olympia, Wash.

Washington State Office of Financial Management, Forecasting Division. 1992. *Poverty in Washington State and Its Counties: Results from the 1990 Census.* Olympia, Wash., May.

Washington, Valora, and Ura Jean Oyemade. 1987. *Project Head Start: Past, Present, and Future Trends in the Context of Family Needs.* New York: Garland.

Weaver, Michael Afaa. 2002. *These Hands I Know: African American Writers on Family.* Louisville, Ky.: Sarabande.

West, Candace, and Sarah Fenstermaker. 1995. "Doing Difference." *Gender and Society* 9, no. 1: 8–37.

West, Candace, and Don H. Zimmerman. 1987. "Doing Gender." *Gender and Society* 1, no. 2: 125–51.

Whitebook, Marcy, and Abby Eichberg. 2002. "Finding the Better Way: Assessing Child Care Compensation Initiatives." *Young Children* 57, no. 3: 66–72.

Whitebook, Marcy, Carollee Howes, and Deborah Phillips. 1998. *Worthy Work, Unlivable Wages: The National Staffing Study, 1988–1997.* Washington, D.C.: Center for the Child Care Workforce.

Whitebook, Marcy, and Deborah Phillips. 1999. *Child Care Employment: Implications for Women's Self Sufficiency and for Child Development.* New York: Foundation for Child Development.

Whitebook, Marcy, Deborah Phillips, and Carollee Howes. 1993. *National Child Care Staffing Study Revisited: Four Years in the Life of Center-Based Child Care.* Washington, D.C.: National Center for the Early Childhood Workforce.

Whitebook, Marcy, Laura Sakai, Emily Gerber, and Carollee Howes. 2001. *Then and Now: Changes in Child Care Staffing, 1994–2000,* Washington, D.C.: Center for the Child Care Workforce.

Williams, Wendy. 1992. "The Equality Crisis: Some Reflections on Culture, Courts, and Feminism." *Women's Rights Law Reporter* 7, no. 3: 175–200.

Wright, Eric Olin, Karen Shire, Shu-Ling Hwand, Maureen Dolan, and Janeen Baxter. 1992. "The Non-Effects of Class on the Gender Division of Labor in the Home: A Comparative Study of Sweden and the U.S." *Gender and Society* 6, no. 2: 252–82.

Wrigley, Julia. 1995. *Other People's Children: An Intimate Account of Dilemmas Facing Middle-Class Parents and the Women They Hire to Raise Their Children*. New York: Basic Books.

Zavella, Patricia. 1987. *Women's Work and Chicano Families: Cannery Workers of the Santa Clara Valley*. Ithaca, N.Y.: Cornell University Press.

Zinn, Maxine Baca, and Bonnie Thornton Dill. 1996. "Theorizing Difference from Multiracial Feminism." *Feminist Studies* 22, no. 2: 321–31.

Index

Note: An *f* denotes a figure; a *t* denotes a table.

About the Author

Mary Tuominen is associate professor of sociology/anthropology at Denison University. She previously served as a policy analyst with the Washington State Legislature and as the Governor's Budget Assistant for Children and Family Services. These positions, combined with her previous work as a community organizer, have influenced her research interests, which include the politics and economics of women's care work, social welfare policy, and women's grassroots political activism. Tuominen is co-editor of *Child Care and Inequality: Rethinking Carework for Children and Youth.* Her most recent publications include "Tenuous Relationships: Exploitation, Emotion, and Racial Ethnic Significance in Paid Childcare Work" (with Lynet Uttal) and "'Where Teachers Can Make a Livable Wage': Organizing to Address Gender and Racial Inequalities in the Child Care Workforce."